New Christian's Handbook

New Christian's Handbook

Everything Believers Need To Know

MAX ANDERS

THOMAS NELSON
Since 1798

NASHVILLE   DALLAS   MEXICO CITY   RIO DE JANEIRO

Published in Nashville, Tennessee, by Thomas Nelson. Thomas Nelson is a registered trademark of Thomas Nelson, Inc.

Thomas Nelson, Inc. titles may be purchased in bulk for educational, business, fund-raising, or sales promotional use. For information, please email SpecialMarkets@ThomasNelson.com.

ISBN: 978-1-4185-4593-2

The library of congress has catalogued the earlier printing as follows:

Anders, Max E., 1947–
    New Christian's handbook / by Max Anders.
       p.   cm.
    ISBN: 978-0-7852-0707-8
    1. Theology, Doctrinal—Popular works. 2. Christianity—Miscellanea.
I. Title.
BT77.A465   1999
238—dc21

99-11283
CIP

Printed in the United States of America

11 12 13 14 — 5 4 3 2

I dedicate this book to our children
Katherine Tatyana Anders
and
Christopher Kirill Anders

CONTENTS

Title	Chapter	Page

1. Discipline is necessary for freedom
2. Meditation renews the mind
3. Prayer links us with God
4. Fasting heightens spiritual sensitivity
5. Simplicity frees us from bondage
6. Solitude frees us from distractions
7. Submission creates trust
8. Repentance restores integrity
9. Worship deepens relationship with God
10. Generosity detaches us from the world

Part 1

▼▼▼▼▼▼▼▼▼▼▼▼▼▼▼▼▼

What Do We Believe?

▲▲▲▲▲▲▲▲▲▲▲▲▲▲▲▲▲▲

Who Is God?

Well Said

*A man can no more diminish God's glory
by refusing to worship him than a
lunatic can put out the sun by scribbling
the word "darkness" on the
walls of his cell.*

—C. S. Lewis

What Do We Mean When We Say, "God"?

A young woman fell in love, and according to tradition, brought her husband-to-be home to meet her family. After dinner, her father invited the fiancé into his study for a man-to-man chat. "So, what are your plans?" he opened.

"I'm a theology scholar," the husband-to-be replied.

"That's very fine," the father returned, "but how will you provide a nice home for my daughter?"

"I will study, and the Lord will provide," he explained.

"How will you raise children and send them to college, and how will you prepare for your retirement?"

"The Lord will provide" came the answer again.

The young man left the study and the mother asked her husband, "How did it go?"

"Well, he has no money or employment plans," the father said. "But on the other hand, he thinks I'm the Lord."

We may chuckle, but many people's understanding of God is nearly as far-fetched. Fifty years ago, if we had asked a large number of people who God was, we would have gotten a pretty uniform answer. Today we wouldn't. Each person feels free to decide for himself or herself who God is.

A book entitled *What Do We Mean When We Say God?* is a compilation of answers received when thousands of people were

Snapshot

God Is Still Alive and Well

As the 21st century opens, though other religions are proliferating, Americans still believe in the God of the Bible.

90 percent believe in God

90 percent pray to God

88 percent believe God loves them

78 percent say they have given a lot or a fair amount of thought to their relationship with God over the past two years.

George Gallup, Jr., *The People's Religion* (New York: Macmillan, 1989), 45.

In a Nutshell

Ways God Is Like Us

God is holy

God is loving

God is just

God is merciful

God is good

asked that question. The answers varied widely. One person wrote, "My opinion of God is that everyone sees God in their own way. I see God as being black . . . a white person might see God as being white. I have no objection . . . we just see Him differently."[1] Another wrote, "I know Santa Claus is not real, but if he was, God would have the exact personality of him."[2]

However, if there is a God, then no matter what *we* mean when we say "God," it has no real value unless God says the same thing. If there is a God, then He is who He is, regardless of what we think. We cannot invent a definition of God and expect it to be true. Therefore, one of the great challenges in life is to find out who God is. It is from the Bible that Christians get their understanding of who God is (see chapter 25, "Why Believe in God?"). He is more than Santa Claus, more than a kindly grandfather, more than the conjurings of our imaginations.

God Is the Creator of the Universe and Ruler over It

"God is an infinite, eternal spirit, the self-existent creator of the universe and the sovereign over it." While this definition is not complete, it is a good beginning. The God we are talking about is the creator of the universe, the original being, the sovereign ruler of all that is, the sole judge of all that is true and false, right and wrong, good and bad. No one created Him (Acts 17:23-25). He has always been there and will continue eternally unchanged (Heb. 13:8). James I. Packer writes, "God does not have it in him to go out of existence."[3]

God has two different kinds of characteristics: those which He shares with humanity (sometimes called His moral attributes or His communicable attributes), and those which He does not share with humanity (sometimes called His natural attributes or His incommunicable attributes).

God Is Like Us in Some Ways

Think about It

If you don't know who God is . . .

- You may have a lack of peace because you do not trust God's character or power to always act in your benefit.

- You may have a lack of self-esteem, feeling that God does not love you enough to go to the trouble to answer your prayers.

- You may not love God as much as you could, because you do not believe that He is who He says He is.

God is holy. Technically, "holiness" means "set apart" from sin to righteousness. Not only has God never sinned but in fact He is incapable of sin because His character—His very nature—is what defines sin. Anything that is like God is not sin. Anything that is not like God is sin. It is not that He has the ability to live up to some high standard; rather, He *is* the standard (Isa. 6:3).

God is loving. Three words in the original Greek language of the New Testament are all translated into English as the one word "love." *Eros* is physical, sensual love. *Philos* is emotional love, such as one might have for a parent or close friend. *Agape* (pronounced uh-GOP-ay) is the exercise of one's will for the good of another. When the Bible says that God is love, it is saying that God is *agape*. He has committed His will to the good of humanity (1 John 4:8).

God is just. Today it is considered impolite to stick our nose into anyone else's business. Therefore, we hear little of God's justice. Nevertheless, justice is one of God's characteristics (Rev. 15:3). Justice applies consequences to a person's actions according to a fixed standard, without regard to favoritism or any other intervening thing.

God has said that "all have sinned and fall short of the glory of God" (Rom. 3:23), and that the "wages of sin is death" (Rom. 6:23). Therefore, God's justice requires that all die.

God is merciful. Mercy is God's characteristic that causes Him to provide a way of escape when we deserve judgment (Titus 3:5-7). We deserve to die, but God sent Jesus to earth to die for us. Therefore, since God has provided a way of escape from judgment that satisfies Him, when we accept that way of escape, God would be unjust not to save us. God's justice and His mercy combine to provide humanity a safe haven from the consequences of our sin.

God is good. God is not a celestial scientist fooling around with human toys for His own enjoyment, regardless of the negative impact on those toys. "Goodness" must mean "goodness" from His children's point of view, not just God's. Otherwise, He could hatch all kinds of sadistic schemes against His hapless children, plunging them into misery purely for His own enjoyment. Such is not the case. He intends to do good for His children (Deut. 8:16; Mark 10:18).

This does not mean that life will always be easy and pleasurable. God's goodness means that, in the end, all will be well, even though some things between now and then may be difficult.

These characteristics are not all the ones that God shares with humankind. But they are among the most important ones.

 **Insight:**

God is enough like us to understand our problems and enough above us to be able to solve them.

God Is Unlike Us in Some Ways

God is eternal—with no beginning and no end. God never had a beginning, and He will never have an end (Ps. 90:2). It is much easier to think of humans, who have a beginning but no end. That is not so difficult. But to imagine that someone never had a beginning, that He has always existed, takes us beyond our ability to grasp. Nevertheless, that is true of God. It is a reassuring thought to me. It makes me feel safe. The universe can make sense to me. He always has been, and He always will be, and I am safe, loved, and significant. Nothing could be better.

God is immutable—*unchanging*. God has never and will never change. Webster defines *immutability* simply as "unchanging." God cannot change because His very nature is unchanging. Therefore, He can never be wiser, more holy, more just, more merciful, more truthful—nor less. Nor do His plans and purposes change. He is the same yesterday, today, and forever (Heb. 13:8). The apostle James wrote that He is "the Father of lights, with whom there is no variation or shadow of

Ways God Is Not Like Us

God is eternal

God is immutable

God is omnipresent

God is omniscient

God is omnipotent

turning" (Jas. 1:17). Speaking for God, Malachi wrote, "I am the LORD, I do not change" (Mal. 3:6).

God is omnipresent—everywhere simultaneously. The next three characteristics of God form a well-known triad, each one beginning with the prefix "omni," which means "unlimited." The first one is "omnipresence," meaning that God is present everywhere simultaneously (Ps. 139:7-10). That is good news for the child of God. There is nowhere we can be that God is not there with us.

God is omniscient—all-knowing. Psalm 139:4 reads, "There is not a word on my tongue, but behold, O LORD, You know it altogether." When we say God knows everything, we mean that He know all things, both actual and possible. As an example of a possible thing Jesus knew, in Matthew 11:21 He said, "If the mighty works which were done in you had been done in Tyre and Sidon, they would have repented long ago in sackcloth and ashes."

There is no hoodwinking God. There is no wool to be pulled over His eyes. Jeremiah wrote, "I, the LORD, search the heart, I test the mind, even to give every man according to his ways, according to the fruit of his doings" (Jer. 17:10).

God is omnipotent—all-powerful. The final characteristic of God we want to look at is His omnipotence. Omnipotence means that God can do anything He chooses. Job 42:2 reads, "I know that You can do everything, and that no purpose of Yours can be with-held from You." He put the stars in place. He spoke the world into existence. He breathed life into a lump of clay and created the first man.

Conclusion

Sometimes we may be tempted to question God's character because He does not treat us better. I read one time of a missionary couple who had spent their entire lives on the mission field working tirelessly to improve the quality of life and to spread the gospel. When they retired, they sailed home on the same passenger ship carrying Teddy Roosevelt home from one of his famous safaris. As the ship docked in New York harbor, there was a band playing, crowds cheering, confetti flying, and banners waving, just for the president.

It's not fair, thought the missionary. *The president goes hunting for a few weeks, and when he comes home, he receives a hero's welcome. We spend our entire lives in an underdeveloped country, and when we come home, there isn't even anyone at the dock to meet us.* And then in a flash of insight given by the Holy Spirit, he realized, *Ah, yes. But the difference is, I am not home yet.*

Let Me Ask You

1. Have you ever thought about God's never having a beginning? What do you think about it now?

2. Which of God's moral attributes (those He shares with humanity) seem most wonderful to you? Why? Which of God's natural attributes (those He does not share with humanity) seem most wonderful to you? Why?

3. Have you had problems in your spiritual life because you did not know or believe one of these attributes? How can you solve those problems?

You may be treated poorly in this life. You may not get the reward that is due you. That doesn't mean God has failed. It only means that you are not home yet.

Insight:

You'll get your party when you get home!

Instant Recall

1. God is the c_____ of the universe and ruler over it.

2. God shares His m_____ attributes with humanity.

3. God does not share His n_____ attributes with humanity.

Action Line

Read: My book *What You Need to Know about God* for more helpful information about this subject. To learn even more about this, read *My God* by Michael Green and *Knowing God* by James I. Packer.

Memorize: 1 Timothy 1:17.

Pray: Dear Lord, I am so grateful for who You are—that You are perfect in character and so great in ability. Thank You that You chose to let me know who You are. Help me trust You to rule my life with wisdom, love, and power. Amen.

What Is the Trinity?

CHAPTER 2

Chapter at a Glance

- God is one.

- God is three.

- The Father initiates, provides, and protects.

Well Said

God does not live in isolation—not in the solitude of a single person, but three persons in one essence.

—Louis Everly

Believing the Impossible

In Lewis Carroll's *Alice through the Looking Glass* (a companion volume to *Alice in Wonderland*), Alice is asked to believe something that is impossible. Alice replies, "One can't believe impossible things!" The White Queen fires back that of course one can believe impossible things if one tries hard enough. She, herself, has made it a habit of believing six impossible things each day before breakfast.

Jefferson Chokes on the Trinity

Thomas Jefferson, American founding father, struggled mightily with the idea of the Trinity. He once wrote:

When we shall have done away with the incomprehensible jargon of the Trinitarian arithmetic, that three are one, and one is three; when we shall have knocked down the artificial scaffolding, reared to mask from view the very simple structure of Jesus; when, in short, we shall have unlearned everything which has been taught since his day, and got back to the pure and simple doctrines he inculcated, we shall then be truly and worthily his disciples.

Quoted in Alister E. McGrath, *Understanding the Trinity* (Grand Rapids: Academie, 1988), 110.

The doctrine of the Trinity seems impossible to believe. Overly simplified, it says that God is one and yet three. A person could be excused for stumbling over the mathematics of it. Surely, if something is one it cannot be three, or vice versa!

Nevertheless, the doctrine of the Trinity has stood for centuries and is stoutly defended as one of the fundamentals of the faith. But where did the doctrine come from? The word "Trinity" never occurs in the Bible, but we come to the conclusion of the Trinity simply by endeavoring to be faithful to Scripture. The Bible says there is only one God. Yet the New Testament calls not only the Father God, but also Jesus and the Holy Spirit God. The doctrine of the Trinity is simply an effort to put these statements together.

No one started out saying, "I think we need an incomprehensible doctrine." Rather, any reader can see that the Bible teaches, with reasonable clarity, both truths: God is three and God is one. So we must either hold to the doctrine of the Trinity or begin whacking things out of our Bibles (which Jefferson did, cutting out what he didn't like, pasting together everything he did, creating the "Jeffersonian" Bible). But if we are not prepared to begin whacking things out of our Bible, how do we understand the Trinity?

God Is One

The Old Testament emphasizes that there is only one true God, and He alone is to be worshiped. "You shall have no other gods before Me," God declared in the Ten Commandments (Ex. 20:3). Forty years later, by the inspiration of God, Moses declared, "Hear, O Israel! The LORD our God, the LORD is one! And you shall love the LORD your God with all your heart, with all your soul, and with all your strength" (Deut. 6:4-5).

The concept of one God is reinforced in the New Testament. "There is no other God but one" (1 Cor. 8:4). "[There is] one God and Father of all, who is over all, and through all, and in you all" (Eph. 4:6). "You believe that there is one God. You do well" (James 2:19).

These Old and New Testament passages state clearly that there is only one true God.

God Is Three

On the other hand, the New Testament also recognizes Jesus as God. When He appeared to His disciples after His crucifixion and resurrection and revealed to Thomas the scars in His hands and side, Thomas replied, "My Lord and my God!" (John 20:28). Earlier in that same Gospel (John 8:58) we learn that Jesus claimed deity for Himself. Also, in Titus 2:13, Jesus is called "our great God and Savior Jesus Christ." Throughout the New Testament, Jesus is presented as God.

Concerning the Holy Spirit, in Acts 5:3-4 the Spirit is equated with God. Also, the Holy Spirit has some of the same attributes as God, such as omniscience (1 Cor. 2:10) and omnipresence (Ps. 139:7). Moreover, He participated in the creation of the world (Gen. 1:2), along with the Father and the Son (Col. 1:15-16).

Think about It

If you don't have an accurate picture of God . . .

- You may not think highly enough of Jesus and the Holy Spirit, not believing that they are equal to God the Father.

- You may not understand that you can have similar rich relationships with other people as you imitate the Godhead.

- You may not realize how much God loves you and how much He has done in providing salvation for you.

Fact File

What the Trinity Is and What It Isn't

"The basic assertion of the doctrine of the Trinity is that the unity of the one God is complex. The three personal 'subsistences' (as they are called) are coequal and coeternal centers of self-awareness, each being 'I' in relation to two who are 'you' and each partaking of the full divine essence (the 'stuff' of deity, if we may dare to call it that) along with the other two. They are not three roles played by one person (that is *modalism*), nor are they three gods in a cluster (that is *tritheism*); the one God (*'he'*) is also, and equally, 'they' and 'they' are always together and always cooperating, with the Father initiating, the Son complying, and the Spirit executing the will of both, which is his will also."

James I. Packer, *Concise Theology* (Wheaton, Ill.: Tyndale, 1993), 42.

Add to all this the fact that, in 2 Corinthians 13:14, the Father, Son, and Holy Spirit are linked together in a benediction. Furthermore, in Matthew 28:19 the three are linked together in the Great Commission. These and more evidences link the Father, Son, and Holy Spirit as co-equal, coeternal members of the Trinity.

The doctrine of the Trinity is a vital doctrine. You cannot remain true to the teachings of the Scripture and hold to another position. Admittedly, it is a mystery, and our finite minds will never be able fully to comprehend an infinite mind. But it is not a muddle to God, and in the day when we will understand all things, it will become clear to us as well.

The Father Initiates, Provides, and Protects

The first person in the Trinity is God the Father. The apostle John recorded these words of Jesus: "Do not labor for the food which perishes, but for the food which endures to everlasting life, which the Son of Man will give you, because God the Father has set His seal on Him" (John 6:27). Peter supported this when he mentioned "God the Father" in 1 Peter 1:2.

Each person in the Trinity has a distinct role to play. The role of the Father is to initiate relationships and plans, playing the lead role in the Trinity, as well as to provide and to protect His own.

First, in John 6:38 we see God's authoritative role of initiating: "For I have come down from heaven, not to do My own will, but the will of Him who sent Me." Creation was the Father's idea, and He set it in motion. It was He who initiated a plan for intimate fellowship with His created beings.

Second, in Matthew 7:7, 11 we read, "Ask, and it will be given to you; seek, and you will find; knock, and it will be opened to you. . . . If you, then, being evil, know how to give good gifts to your children, how much more will your Father who is in heaven give good things to those who ask Him!" In this we see a second role of God the Father: provider.

Finally, in John 10:27-29 we read, "My sheep hear My voice, and I know them, and they follow Me. And I give them eternal life, and they shall never perish; neither shall anyone snatch them out of My hand. My Father, who has given them to Me, is greater than all; and no one is able to snatch them out of My Father's hand." In this passage we see a third characteristic of the role of God the Father in the Trinity, which is that of protector.

The roles of the Son and Holy Spirit integrate with the role of the Father, whose plan is being worked out in history.

Think about It

I need to understand that God is both three and yet one. Like riding a bicycle, I can fall off on either side. I can emphasize His threeness to the detriment of His oneness, or His oneness to the detriment of His threeness. Both are errors, and falling off on either side will skin our doctrinal knees equally.

Conclusion

Fathering is no easy task. I heard of one father who got a letter from his daughter in college. It read:

"Dear Dad, I have decided to drop out of college. I am failing everything anyway, and have come to realize that

Fact File

God Is the Father of All

The role of God the Father in creation and redemption has been to plan and direct and send the Son and Holy Spirit. This is not surprising, for it shows that the Father and the Son relate to one another as a father and son relate to one another in a human family: the father directs and has authority over the son, and the son obeys and is responsive to the directions of the father. The Holy Spirit is obedient to the directives of both the Father and the Son.

Wayne A. Grudem, *Systematic Theology* (Grand Rapids: Zondervan, 1994), 249.

college is irrelevant. What does a degree mean, anyway? I mean, it's just a piece of paper! I have met a wonderful man, Gordo, who is a drummer in a rock 'n' roll band. We are going to get married and live in a commune in Oregon. We'll let you know when we get settled. We'd love to have you and Mom come and visit us and gain greater cosmic consciousness. Love, Susan.

"P.S. None of the above is true, but I did get a D in chemistry and I do need $100.00."

Ah, yes, fathering is a great challenge, and if done well, a rare art form.(Great mothering is just as much a challenge and as rare an art form, of course, but "fathering" happens to be the subject of this chapter.)

Our heavenly Father is the perfect father. He is our great leader. He is our great protector. He is our great provider. God is more loving, more caring, more wise, more knowledgeable, more zealous to provide for and protect, and more capable of fathering than any earthly father could be (Heb. 12:9-10).

Instant Recall

1. There are two important truths that we must balance regarding the Trinity:

a. God is t_____
   yet one.
b. God is o_____
   yet three.
2. The role of God the
   Father is to
   i_____ rela-
   tionships and plans, to
   p_____ for
   His own, and to
   p_____ His
   own.

Action Line

Read: My book *What You Need to Know about God* has much more helpful information on this subject. To learn even more about this, read *Understanding the Trinity* by Alister McGrath.

Memorize: 2 Corinthians 13:14.

Pray: Dear Lord, thank You for creating me in Your image. Thank You that I can have the same type of relationships with others that You have within the Trinity, though imperfectly, of course. And thank You that I can look forward to an eternity of perfect relationships with other people and with You. How wonderful that is, and how grateful I am! Amen.

Let Me Ask You

1. What was your understanding of the Trinity before you read this chapter? Has your understanding of the Trinity changed?

2. What seems to you to be the most important "so what?" regarding the truth of the Trinity?

3. What do you like most about the roles of God the Father in the Trinity? What do you think is the more important truth about God the Father's roles?

What Has God Done?

Well Said

At first laying down, as fact fundamental, That nothing with God can be accidental.

—Henry Wadsworth Longfellow

Barking at Boots

Late one night when my wife and I were in bed, we were awakened when our dog, Sugar Bear, barked for half an hour, seemingly into the woods in front of our house. I went outside. "Sugar Bear, what's wrong?" I wheedled. She came over to be near me, but kept up a constant din. As I walked closer to the driveway, her barking took on a shrill, near hysterical pitch. I knelt down at some boots I had left in the driveway after a long day of working in the yard.

She was directly behind me now, trying to wake the dead. I picked up the boots and held them toward her to let her see them, and I said, "Is this what you are barking at?" As if shot out of a cannon, she turned and sprinted away wildly, yelping and crying as if she were being stung by a thousand bees. I shook my head in utter disbelief. She had been barking at boots! I took the boots inside and went back to a silent night of sleep.

The boots took Sugar Bear beyond her understanding, and she didn't trust what she

Fact File

Creation out of Nothing

When theologians use the phrase *ex nihilo* to describe how God created the universe, they are drawing on two Latin words:

ex = out of
$nihilo$ = nothing

didn't understand. The same is often true of us. We don't understand God, so we don't trust Him. But as we get to know Him better, we can learn to trust Him more fully. Our first step can be to look at what He has done.

God Has Created Everything Out of Nothing

Creation is an astounding event, well beyond our ability to comprehend. Genesis 1:1 says, in simple and dramatic understatement, "In the beginning, God created the heavens and the earth." There is no attempt to explain fully, because any explanation would be futile. We wouldn't be able to understand it. We would end up barking at God's boots.

What we do know is that God created *ex nihilo,* or out of nothing. He didn't take a great ball of mud and make something clever out of it; rather, there *was* no ball of mud. He spoke, and the earth, which did not exist before, now existed.

Not only did God create the obvious things, such as stars, planets, and humans, but he also created space and time. Everything in space and time has a beginning, but God does not.

There are several things we can know about God as a result of looking at creation. First, He is a God of unimaginable power and intelligence. The size and scope of the universe is so great that we cannot even grasp it.

Second, God is capable of marvelous order and precision. From the macro level of the stars and galaxies to the micro level of molecules, we see amazing evidences of design.

Third, God is inclined toward wonderful beauty. From the beauty of an inverted reflection of a spider web seen in a dewdrop to the spectacle of the Grand Canyon to the drama of the Milky Way on a clear night, the beauty that God has created gives us some insight into the character and nature of this supreme being whom we worship.

The power that holds everything together, from the level of galaxies to that of molecules, makes us realize how utterly dependent we are on the grace and benevolence of God for our very existence.

God Is All-Powerful and Has Authority over All Creation

The universe is not only dependent upon God for its creation; it is dependent upon Him for its continual existence. The universe can neither exist nor operate on its own power. R.C. Sproul has written:

> The central point of the doctrine of providence is the stress on God's government of the universe. He rules His creation with absolute sovereignty and authority. He governs everything that comes to pass, from the greatest to the least. Nothing ever happens beyond the scope of His sovereign providential government. He makes the rain to fall and the sun to shine. He raises up kingdoms and brings them down. He numbers the hairs on our head and the days of our lives.[1]

God Has Decided Beforehand Everything that Will Happen

This sovereignty of God over the physical world is affirmed throughout Scripture (see, for example, Pss. 47; 93; 97). But God's will does not extend merely to the ordering of stars and planets; it also extends to angels and humans. Theologians speak of the "decrees of God." The Westminster Shorter Catechism provides a classic definition: "The decrees of God are his eternal purpose, according to the counsel of his will, whereby, for his own glory, he hath foreordained whatsoever comes to pass" (Q.7).

This immediately brings up questions concerning why there is evil, where the evil came from, and why God does not do something about the evil. And these are valid questions. However, we deal with those issues in another chapter (28). For now, we are simply making the points that God has planned ahead of time everything that will happen, that He has created the universe and humanity with His purpose in mind, and that He oversees the entire creation with absolute power.

God Performs Miracles When He Wants To

Many people choke on miracles, like a picnicker choking on a chicken bone. When they read of Noah riding out a catastrophic flood in an ark, or of God's talking to Moses out of a burning

 Snapshot

We Believe in Miracles

Most people take the Bible at face value when it comes to miracles. Three out of four people believe that "all the miracles described in the Bible actually took place."

bush, or of Jonah being swallowed by a great fish, they roll their eyes, heave a sigh, and dismiss God as impossible and Christians as gullible. When they come to the death, burial, and resurrection of Jesus, it is the last straw. They throw up their hands—and throw out the Bible. It is simply too much to ask anyone to believe, they think.

This response has never made any sense to me, even in the days before I became a Christian. My perspective was this: what good is a God who can't do the miraculous? The very definition of God is that He is above and beyond the human, that His powers transcend the ordinary. If God created the universe, the stars, the earth and all that is in it, why would He have trouble flooding the world or talking out of a burning bush or keeping a prophet alive in a fish for a few days?

▼▼▼▼▼▼▼▼

The problems facing humanity are so enormous that if God cannot or will not do miracles, we are all in deep, deep trouble.

▲▲▲▲▲▲▲▲

The problems facing humanity (not the least of which is death) are so enormous that if God cannot or will not do miracles, we are all in deep, deep trouble. The good news is that the Bible certainly presents a picture of a God who is capable of performing miracles.

The term "miracle" can refer to one of two things. First, it can refer to a common, natural event that happens at exactly the right time to produce a miraculous result (see 1 Kings 17:1 for an example). Or, second, it can refer to an act of God that transcends the laws of nature.

The second is the usual meaning of the word. When Jesus raised Lazarus from the dead (John 11:43-44), there was no natural explanation for it. We call it a miracle.

The primary purpose of miracles was to validate a spiritual truth. Hebrews 2:3-4 speaks of signs and wonders given by God to demonstrate that the new message of salvation was a true message from God. When Jesus fed five thousand people with only five loaves of bread and two fish, the miracle supported the fact of who Jesus was: the bread of life. Certainly, some miracles were motivated out of compassion for the suffering of individuals, but even those miracles brought glory to God.

Conclusion

When we talk about the works of God, what we know exceeds what we understand. How can God be eternal? How can He have created everything out of nothing? How can God have decreed everything that will happen and yet leave all humans a free will, the ability to chose? In many of these cases, we don't know. The work of an infinite being (God) transcends the ability of a finite being (you or me) to fully comprehend. But the fact that we do not fully understand God does not prohibit us from believing what we do understand about Him. Just because we do not understand creation does not keep us from believing that God created.

Instant Recall

1. God has c_____ everything out of nothing.

2. God is all-powerful and has a _____ over all creation.

3. God has d_____ beforehand everything that will happen.

4. God performs m_____ when He wants to.

Think about It

If you don't believe in what God has done . . .

- Regarding creation, you are left to explain the world in terms of evolution, which is scientifically proving more and more unbelievable.

- Regarding God's sovereignty, you are left to believe that life deals you random blows and that there is no meaning to life.

- Regarding God's decrees, you are left to believe that history is an accident and is headed nowhere.

- Regarding miracles, you are left to believe that God does not intervene in the affairs of people or history.

Action Line

Read: My book *What You Need to Know about God* has much more helpful information about this subject.

Memorize: Psalm 73:25-26.

Pray: Dear Lord, thank You for helping me know that You have created everything and You are sovereign over it. Thank You that You are guiding all history, as well as my life, toward a predetermined—and good—end. Help me to trust in You at all times and to take courage and comfort in Your plan and Your power. Amen.

Let Me Ask You

1. Do you believe that God created everything out of nothing? How would you explain this to someone who thinks the world evolved?

2. If God is sovereign over His creation, why do you think He does not fix more of the problems than He does?

3. Does it trouble you that much that happens in the world seems to occur by chance? How do you understand that, given that God has decreed all that happens?

4. From the Bible it appears that most of the miracles in history have occurred during three different periods of time: at the time of the Hebrews' Exodus from Egypt, during the time of the prophets Elijah and Elisha, and at the time of Christ and the apostles. Why do you think God does not perform more miracles today like those in other times?

Who Is Jesus?

Chapter at a Glance

- Jesus is the Son of God.

- Jesus is both perfect deity and perfect humanity.

- Jesus emptied Himself.

- Jesus was miraculously conceived and born of a virgin.

- Jesus lived a sinless life.

CHAPTER 4

Well Said

If Shakespeare were to enter the room, we would all rise. But if Jesus were to enter the room, we would all kneel.

—Charles Lamb

A Black-Haired, Brown-Eyed Jew

The Gospels tell us nothing about Jesus' physical features. The writers were apparently little interested in His size, the color of His eyes and hair, and even His age and strength. And even if they did tell us these things, it wouldn't give us any answers to our fundamental questions about who Jesus is.

The picture we see of Jesus in the Gospels is quite different from the image that many people have of Him. He is often thought of as an unassertive figure pleading fruitlessly with humanity to be better. Or else He is thought of as a stained-glass super-saint, cold and lifeless. Neither image is correct.

Jesus Is the Son of God

When we say "Jesus," we mean that He is the Son of God, the second member of the Trinity, who existed before the creation of the world, participated in creation, and became a human (Jesus of Nazareth), having been given birth by a virgin, coming to earth to do the will of God the Father. He lived without sin, died for our sins, was bodily resurrected, ascended into heaven, and will come again someday to judge sin and establish permanent righteousness on earth. That is Jesus.

We have already seen in the second chapter that there is only one God but that in the unity of the Godhead there are three eternal and co-equal Persons, the same in substance but distinct in personhood.

As the second member of the Trinity, Jesus was subject to the Father because, while all members of the Godhead are equal, they have distinct

Fact File

How a Palestinian Jew Looked

In his book *Who Is This Jesus?* Michael Green addressed the question of how Jesus looked:

There is a great deal [about Jesus] we would love to know that we simply are not told. We do not even know what He looked like. He was a Palestinian Jew, and as such the color of His skin would be olive, His eyes brown, and His nose hooked. Palestinian Jews had black hair and usually wore it long and carefully groomed. They valued a full beard, and it appears on many of the coins of the day. His mother tongue was Aramaic, a dialect of Hebrew, which He would have spoken with a northern accent common to Galilee where He was brought up. But He could speak Greek and probably some Latin and was thoroughly at home in the Hebrew Scriptures. He wore a sleeveless undergarment with a girdle, the customary cloak and sandals, and carried a staff on journeys. That is all we know about His appearance or can guess with confidence.

Michael Green, *Who Is This Jesus?* (Nashville: Thomas Nelson, 1992), 8–9.

roles. In the eternal relationships within the Trinity, God the Father has always been in loving authority and Jesus has always been in loving submission.

Jesus Is Both Perfect Deity and Perfect Humanity

As the second member of the Trinity, as eternal God, Jesus existed before He was born as Jesus of Nazareth. We see the angel of the Lord in the Old Testament, who was probably the second member of the Trinity before He came to earth to be born as a human (Josh. 5:13-15).

When He was born as a human, He did not give up any of His divinity. As complete God, He took on complete humanity.

People have tended to fall into one of two imbalances regarding Jesus: to conclude that He was really God and not really human, or to conclude that He was really human and not really God. Historic Christian teaching, however, has always held that He was fully God and fully human at the same time, without becoming some kind of third thing.

Shortly after Jesus died, some people claimed that Jesus did not have a truly human body, that He only *seemed* to be human. That was rejected at the Council of Chalcedon (A.D. 451), where early church leaders affirmed that Jesus was truly divine and truly human. Another error is that Jesus did not have two natures, human and divine, but that the two were mixed together, resulting in either a deified human or a humanized deity. This error was also rejected by the early church. Jesus was a unique being, the only God-man ever to have existed.

Jesus Emptied Himself

When theologians sit around in walnut-paneled rooms and talk about the combining of divinity with humanity, they use the word *kenosis* to describe what happened.

It comes from Philippians 2:5-8. Read this powerful passage with reverence, for in it is reflected one of the most towering "callings" of humanity.

Let this mind be in you which was also in Christ Jesus, who, being in the form of God, did not consider it robbery to be equal with God, but made Himself of no reputation [emptied Himself], taking the form of a bondservant, and coming in the likeness of men. And being found in appearance as a man, He humbled Himself and became obedient to the point of death, even the death of the cross.

Christ's Self-Emptying

The theological word *kenosis* comes straight from a Greek word meaning "to empty." The apostle Paul wrote of Christ "emptying" Himself by voluntarily cgiving up the privileges of deity.

We might wonder at the words meaning "emptied Himself." How-ever, when we think about it, the passage itself describes what the words mean.

1. He came as a servant. Jesus did not come as a pompous tyrant but rather as a humble servant (Mark 10:45). So the first thing it means for Him to have "emptied" Himself is that He came to earth as a servant, even though as God He had every right to come as a sovereign.

2. He became human. He did not come only as God; He did not come as the angel of the Lord; He did not come as some unique celestial being. Rather, He became a man, born of a woman, with a fully human body.

3. He humbled Himself. He played the role God the Father had chosen for Him.

Jesus, then, gave up nothing of His deity. He just took on humanity. The New King James Version translates *kenosis* as "made Himself of no reputation," and the New International Version translates it as "made himself nothing." These are less literal translations, but in this case, probably more accurate and helpful.

However, we must admit that some of His divine attributes did not seem to be in operation during His time on earth. How, then, can we describe what the kenosis is?

1. The kenosis involves the veiling of Christ's preincarnate glory. During the Transfiguration (Matt. 17:1-13) and during His appearance to the apostle John as recorded in Revelation 1, we see a bedazzling Jesus. While neither of these pictures may be accurate representations of Jesus' glory prior to His Incarnation, we can imagine that such glory was impressive indeed. If He had looked that way on earth, it would have made a normal life impossible.

2. The kenosis involves the voluntary nonuse of some of His divine attributes some of the time (Matt. 24:36). Nonuse does not mean subtraction. Just because He didn't use them doesn't mean He did not have them or could not have used them if He had chosen.

That is what kenosis means. Jesus voluntarily veiled His divine glory, and He did not use some of His attributes some of the time. Instead, He took on human form, humbled Himself to the plan of God the Father, and died on the cross for our sins.

Jesus Was Miraculously Conceived and Born of a Virgin

When Jesus took on humanity, He did so in a very special way. His birth was a result of a miraculous conception. In the womb of

Snapshot

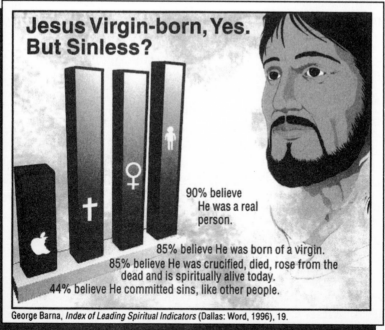

Jesus Virgin-born, Yes. But Sinless?

90% believe He was a real person.

85% believe He was born of a virgin.
85% believe He was crucified, died, rose from the dead and is spiritually alive today.
44% believe He committed sins, like other people.

George Barna, *Index of Leading Spiritual Indicators* (Dallas: Word, 1996), 19.

Think about It

- If Jesus was not the second member of the Trinity, then He is not God and cannot be your Savior.

- If Jesus was not fully human as well as fully divine, then He could not have died for your sins and cannot be your Savior.

- If you do not believe that Jesus was born of a virgin and was sinless, then you do not believe the Scriptures. You are without a reliable guide for life or death.

the virgin Mary, Jesus of Nazareth was supernaturally conceived by the power of the Holy Spirit, without a human father. Luke 1:35 records the message of the angel Gabriel to Mary, telling her what was to happen to her: "The Holy Spirit will come upon you, and the power of the Highest will overshadow you; therefore, also, that Holy One who is to be born will be called the Son of God." The Bible tells us that Joseph, even though married to Mary, did not have relations with her until after Jesus was born. Jesus, then, was born of a virgin.

Jesus Lived a Sinless Life

Jesus' miraculous conception tells us that, though Jesus was human, He was not exactly like us. We are corrupted by original sin and are therefore incapable of not sinning. He was not corrupted by original sin, and though He was tempted by sin, He lived a sinless life.

The fact that Jesus was sinless provides a good example for us all to follow, and while that is important, the significance of His sinlessness goes way beyond that. He had to be sinless or else His death on our behalf would have been worthless. Since the wages of sin is death (Rom. 6:23), meaning eternal spiritual and physical death, if Jesus had sinned, He would Himself have suffered eternal spiritual and physical death. His death on the cross, then, could have done nothing for us. But because He was sinless, He did not deserve to die; and because He was God, His death could count for ours.

Conclusion

Jesus was certainly a remarkable person. He was born in obscurity, lived a simple, almost primitive life. He gained no worldly positions or credentials. He lived for three years as an itinerant preacher, was crucified on false charges, died a pauper, and was buried in a borrowed tomb. Yet two thousand years later it can safely be said that no person has ever made a fraction of the impact on earth that He did. In fact, no institution or nation has. He is the single most important person, and his life, death, and resurrection are the most important events in the history of the world. Although in an unexpected way, He made the kind of impact one would expect God to make if He came to earth.

Let Me Ask You

1. How has your understanding of the Trinity changed since reading this chapter?

2. What seems the most important thing to you concerning the fully deity and full humanity of Jesus?

3. Are you comfortable believing the miraculous conception and virgin birth of Jesus? Why or why not?

Instant Recall

1. Jesus is the S_____ of God.

2. Jesus is both perfect d_____ and perfect h_____.

3. Jesus e_____ Himself.

4. Jesus was miraculously c_____ and born of a v_____.

5. Jesus lived a s_____ life.

Action Line

Read: My book *What You Need to Know about Jesus* has much more helpful information about this subject. If you want to learn even more about this, read *Who Is This Jesus?* by Michael Green.

Memorize: Colossians 2:9.

Pray: Dear Lord, thank You for coming to earth to be my example and my Savior. I can never repay You for all You have done for me. The best I can do is trust You and give my life to You. Thank You for saving me from my sins and giving me the hope of heaven. Amen.

What Did Jesus Teach?

CHAPTER 5

Chapter at a Glance

- Jesus taught that humanity needs to be saved.

- Jesus taught that righteousness is internal, not external.

- Jesus taught that love is life's priority.

Well Said

We are all born for love. It is the principle of existence, and its only end.

—Benjamin Disraeli

'To the Right!'

A young couple, both blind, were walking arm in arm across a busy intersection, with cars whizzing by in every direction. Each tapped the pavement with a white cane as they attempted to cross the street. To the horror of all who witnessed it, the blind couple began veering into the middle of the intersection. Oblivious to the danger, they were walking directly into the path of oncoming cars.

Then every car in every direction came to a simultaneous stop. A driver stuck his head out of his car and yelled, "To your right! To your right!" Other people joined in, shouting, "To your right!"

Without missing a step, the couple turned back to the right and got back on course, tapping with their canes and listening to the shouts from the fellow players in this drama. They made it to the other side of the road without incident, still arm in arm.[1]

That story makes me think of Jesus. He came to earth because He loved us. Not only were we lost, but indeed we were marching off a cliff to certain death. In that situation He did not teach with the excitement of a new teacher, come to impart knowledge He loved to students. He taught with the urgency of all those drivers trying to keep the blind couple from getting killed. He did not say, "Now, class, turn to your reading lesson for today. There you will find a story you will greatly enjoy." Rather, he shouted to humanity, "To your right! To your right!"

Jesus Taught that Humanity Needs to Be Saved

Humanity is separated from God because of sin, and unless one believes in Jesus (which means committing your life to Him—John 1:1, 12), he or she will be separated from God forever (Rom. 3:23; 6:23). Jesus came to reconcile us to God (John 3:1-21). That is the first and most important thing Jesus taught when He began His ministry. "What profit is it to a man if he gains the whole world, and loses his own soul?" Jesus asked (Matt. 16:26). The obvious answer is "nothing."

What did Jesus teach about our greatest need? That humanity is lost and needs to be saved.

Jesus Taught that Righteousness Is Internal, Not External

The ship of Judaism (those who held to the Jewish faith) was encrusted with so many barnacles of tradition, hypocrisy, injustice, and apathy that, from Jesus' perspective, it was no longer afloat. "You teach as law the traditions of men and in doing so, violate the Law!" He charged.

Eight Woes: In a classic exchange in Matthew 23:13-36, Jesus was addressing a large multitude of people that included scribes and Pharisees (religious leaders), and He aimed eight "woes" directly at them, by name. His whole point, in denouncing these men, was that they kept the traditions of men but did not keep the Law of God.

"Woe to you, scribes and Pharisees, hypocrites!" because . . .

1. You miss heaven and keep others from it.
2. You take advantage of disadvantaged people.
3. You make converts, then pervert them.
4. You split hairs to your own advantage.
5. You keep the Law in little things but not in big.
6. You are okay on the outside but not on the inside.
7. You look good but are full of hypocrisy.
8. You honor past prophets but kill current ones.

In this scathing rebuke, Jesus called them hypocrites, blind guides, whitewashed tombs, serpents, a brood of vipers, and murderers. But for the most part it fell on deaf ears.

The whole point of Jesus' best-known major address, the Sermon on the Mount in chapters 5—7 of the Gospel of Matthew, is that true righteousness is internal, not external. If it were external, the Pharisees would have had heaven wrapped up, because on the outside (religiously speaking) they were as pretty as a teacup. Inside, they were full of mold and rot. "Unless your righteousness surpasses the righteousness of the scribes and Pharisees, you will by no means enter the kingdom of heaven," Jesus said (5:20).

Eight Blessings: In stark contrast to the eight woes He pronounced on the scribes and Pharisees, Jesus offered eight beatitudes (blessings) to those who are inwardly righteous:

1. To the spiritual needy—the kingdom of heaven is theirs.
2. To the sad—God will comfort them.
3. To the humble—the earth will belong to them.
4. To those who want to do right—God will satisfy them.
5. To those who give mercy—mercy will be given to them.
6. To those who are pure in heart—they will be with God.

7. To those who work for peace—God will call them His children.
8. To those who suffer—the kingdom of heaven is theirs.

It really is absurd to live as though we could pull the wool over God's eyes. Do we think we can hoodwink someone who knows all things both actual and possible? What a collapse of logical thought it is to live one way on the outside, be another way on the inside, and think that God would be pleased. No, God is not vulnerable to spiritual sleight of hand. True righteousness is internal, not external.

▼▼▼▼▼▼▼▼

Our task is to determine what it means to love God.

Jesus Taught that Love Is Life's Priority

▲▲▲▲▲▲▲▲▲   Jesus was speaking to a group of religious leaders when one of them, an expert in the religious law, asked Him what the greatest commandment was. He asked this question to try to trip Him up on an answer somehow. Jesus replied, " *You shall love the LORD your God with all your heart, with all your soul, and with all your mind.'* This is the first and great commandment" (Matt. 22:37-38). Our task, then, is to determine what it means to love God.

What does it mean to love God?

*   Does it mean to have great swells of emotion race up and down your spine like a finger ripping up and down the piano keyboard?
*   Does it mean to live with goose pimples on the back of your neck?
*   Does it mean to be filled at all times with warm thoughts of God?

The apostle John recorded Jesus' answer to the question in John 14:21, "He who has My commandments and keeps them, it is he who loves Me." He wrote also, in 1 John 5:3, "This is the love of God, that we keep His commandments." To love God is to keep His commandments. Not with gritted teeth. Not with clenched fist. But with a trusting heart.

If we love God, we do as He asks us. Emotions may run up and down our spine, or they may not; it doesn't matter. What matters is that we have obeyed Him. If we keep His commandments, the Lord promises joy: "These things I have spoken to you, that My joy may remain in you, and that your joy may be full" (John 15.11).

We may fear that if we obey God fully, He will send us to deepest, darkest Africa. But the only people I know whom God has sent to deepest, darkest Africa are people who would rather be there than anywhere else in the world. We find our greatest fulfillment in the center of God's will.

Do you want to love God? If so, then obey Him. That is the way we demonstrate our love for Him. We all love Him imperfectly, but we do better by understanding that love is obedience, rather than thinking that love is an emotion.

Jesus also taught that we should love our fellow man. After identifying love of God as the first and great commandment, Jesus added, "And the second is like it: *'You shall love your neighbor*

Snapshot

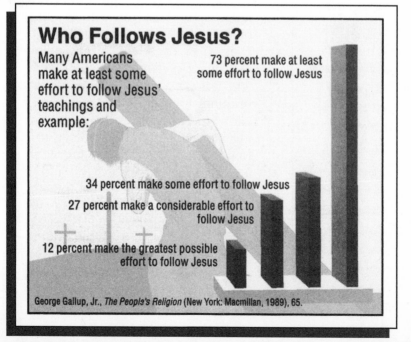

Who Follows Jesus?

Many Americans make at least some effort to follow Jesus' teachings and example:

73 percent make at least some effort to follow Jesus

34 percent make some effort to follow Jesus

27 percent make a considerable effort to follow Jesus

12 percent make the greatest possible effort to follow Jesus

George Gallup, Jr., *The People's Religion* (New York: Macmillan, 1989), 65.

as yourself.' On these two commandments hang all the Law and the Prophets" (Matt. 22:39-40).

In response to a question as to what it means to love one's neighbor (since to love God means to keep His commandments), Jesus told the parable of the Good Samaritan (Luke 10:25-37). A man who was robbed and beaten was ignored by supposedly righteous men, but a common citizen (a Samaritan) helped him. Jesus said the Samaritan was the one who loved his neighbor. The second greatest command is to love your neighbor as yourself.

Conclusion

Michael Green, in his excellent volume *Who Is This Jesus?* wrote:

It is not religious ritual, however worthy, that brings you into the kingdom of God but a lovely filial (son or daughter) relationship with Him. God does not want endless servants: He wants sons and daughters. It is not a question of doing lots of things for God: it is a question of allowing Him to become your loving heavenly Father and being true to that relationship. It will inevitably lead to a life of love to God and to your fellows. It is hardly surprising, in the light of all this, that the Christian word for "love," *agape*, (uh-gop'-ay) was practically introduced into the language by Jesus. It did exist beforehand—just. But until He came, nobody had seen what it really meant. Yet, if God so *loved* the world that He gave His only Son for us, why, that shed an entirely new light on love. It meant total self-giving for the totally unworthy. That is what God the Father did. That is what Jesus embodied. That is what He called on His disciples to do.[2]

What Jesus taught was that we all need to be saved from our sin, and we do that not through good works but through faith in Jesus. A life of righteousness is not a matter of keeping external religious rituals but an internal commitment to love God and others.

Instant Recall

Jesus taught three major things:

1. Humanity needs to be s_____.

2. Righteousness is i_____, not merely e_____.

3. L_____ is life's priority.

Let Me Ask You

1. What would you tell someone now who wanted to know how to get to heaven?

2. If righteousness is internal, do we have to go to church, read our Bible, and pray? Why or why not?

3. Has your understanding of loving God and others changed as a result of reading this chapter? If so, how?

Action Line

Read: My book *What You Need to Know about Jesus* has much more helpful information about this subject. If you want to learn even more about it, read *Loving God* by Charles Colson.

Memorize: Matthew 22:37-39.

Pray: Dear Lord, thank You for making it possible for me to be saved from my sin. Thank You that though You want me to be a good person, I am acceptable to You because of what Christ has done for me, not because of what I can do for You. Amen.

What Did Jesus Do?

- Jesus performed miracles.

- Jesus confronted religious leaders.

- Jesus preached to many and discipled a few.

- Jesus provided an example for our lives.

- Jesus accomplished salvation for all who believe.

- Jesus prays for us today.

Well Said

[Jesus] became what we are that He might make us what He is.

—Athanasius

Matching Words and Deeds

Winston Churchill, prime minister of England during World War II, had a gruff exterior. He was often abrupt and caustic. His capacity to insult was legendary. Shortly before World War II, Lady Astor became agitated over Churchill's stand on women's rights, and said, "Winston, if I were married to you, I'd put poison in your coffee." Churchill responded, "And if you were my wife, I'd drink it."

Yet inside this gruff exterior beat a heart that could be tender. In the summer of 1941 Sergeant James Allen Ward was awarded the Victoria Cross for climbing out onto the wing of his Wellington bomber, thirteen thousand feet above the ground, to extinguish a fire in the starboard engine, secured only by a rope around his waist. Churchill summoned the shy New Zealander to 10 Downing Street. Ward, struck dumb with awe in Churchill's presence, was unable to answer the prime minister's questions. Churchill surveyed the hero with some compassion. "You must feel very humble and awkward in my presence," he said.

"Yes, sir," managed Ward.

"Then you can imagine how humble and awkward I feel in yours," returned Churchill.

And so it goes, with our words and our deeds. Our picture of the gruff, verbal warrior dissolves at such a moment. We look both at what a person says and at what he does to get a total picture of what the person is really like.

Fact File

Miracles Happened!

In a document dated A.D. 124, only around thirty years after the death of the apostle John, a man name Quadratus wrote to Hadrian, the Roman emperor at the time, to encourage him to consider the truth of Christianity. That a respected source (Quadratus) should write to so lofty a figure as the emperor of Rome and claim that Jesus did miracles attests to the generally accepted truth of them.

"But the works of our Savior were always present (for they were genuine), namely, those who were healed, those who rose from the dead. They were not only seen in the act of being healed or raised, but they remained always present. And not merely when the Savior was on earth, but after His departure as well. They lived on for a considerable time, so much so that some of them have survived to our own day."

Adapted from Green, *Who Is This Jesus?* 46.

And so it is with God. It is not only important what Jesus said; His deeds must be equally amazing.

Jesus Performed Miracles

In the Scriptures we read of Jesus' giving sight to the blind, hearing to the deaf, strength to the paralyzed, and life to the dead. He stilled storms with a word, fed crowds with a few fish and loaves of bread, and walked on water. Demons fled from Him. A tree withered at His rebuke. Water turned to wine at His word. Miracles followed after Him like a hound dog after a boy going fishing.

Justin Martyr, an early Christian writer, in his book *Apology* (A.D. 150) wrote with confidence, "That he performed these miracles you may easily satisfy yourself from the *Acts of Pontius Pilate*." It was the same with the Jewish leaders. They were not able to deny the reality of the miracles. They were too well known to them to deny. Since they could not deny them, they simply attributed them to the devil ("He casts out demons by

Fact File

Categories of Miracles

- Jesus healed people of physical diseases and infirmities, such as paralysis and deformed limbs. This demonstrated His power over sickness and disease.

- He cast demons out of people. This showed His power over the forces of darkness.

- He stilled storms. This showed His power over nature.

  All types of miracles were intended to give people a reason to believe that He was who He said He was.

the power of Satan," they charged). To the person who assessed the evidence with an open mind, the conclusion was inescapable. Jesus performed miracles not on an isolated basis but on such a widespread basis that it was undeniable, and knowledge of that fact spread throughout that whole part of the world.

Jesus did not perform miracles merely to bedazzle or entertain. He helped people out of a sense of compassion. He wept before raising Lazarus from the dead. Also, He performed miracles in order to help people believe what He was saying. For example, He claimed to be the light of the world, and then gave sight to a blind man. He claimed to be the bread of life, and He fed five thousand with a few loaves. He claimed to be the resurrection and the life, and He raised Lazarus from the dead.

Yes, Jesus' words were amazing, and for His life to be consistent, His deeds had to be amazing, too. As we read the New Testament, we are not disappointed.

Jesus Confronted Religious Leaders

Much of Jesus' life was spent confronting the hypocrisy, jealousy, and error of religious leaders.

The scribes were teachers of the Law. They knew the Law so well that you could ask

Fact File

Religious Leaders

The New Testament refers to three kinds of people in the Jewish religious establishment:

1. The scribes were teachers of the Law.

2. The Pharisees were the religious conservatives in that day.

3. The Sadducees were the religious liberals.

them what the middle verse in the Old Testament was and they could quote it for you. They could tell you the middle letter in the middle verse. The Pharisees were a group of religious leaders who zealously promoted separation of Jews from the Gentiles. The Sadducees were also religious leaders, but they advocated integration with the surrounding life and culture.

The scribes and Pharisees were the religious conservatives of the day, and the Sadducees were the religious liberals. All of them, however, had drifted from true spiritual commitment to God. Following the Law was their way of climbing the ladder of social power, not of leading people to genuine relationships with God.

Some of them accepted Jesus, but the ones who maintained the stronghold in Jerusalem were mean-spirited people who eventually were so jealous of their turf that they were willing to kill Jesus. When you look at the stark list of indictments in Matthew 23 against these religious leaders, it is no wonder that Jesus took them on so forcefully. They were dangerous. They were enemies of the gospel—selfish, jealous, money-grubbing and power-hungry.

Because of the gigantic obstacle these people presented to the gospel, Jesus deliberately initiated scenarios in which He could reveal their hypocrisy. One thing He did was initiate Sabbath controversies, that is, He deliberately did things on the Sabbath that God thought were okay but that the religious leaders objected to (Luke 13:10-17). A second thing He did was to encourage contact with sinners who had repented or might repent (Luke 7:36-39). A third

Fact File

Jesus' Conflicts with Religious Leaders

1. He created Sabbath controversies.

2. He initiated contact with sinners.

3. He challenged their traditions.

thing He did was deliberately challenge their traditions, so He could demonstrate that the traditions violated the Law of Moses (Mark 7:1-13). He did this to reveal their hypocrisy so that they might repent, and so that the multitudes would not follow them if they didn't repent.

Jesus Preached to Many and Discipled a Few

Jesus preached to enormous crowds. In most cases, we don't know how large; the Bible just uses the word "multitudes." However, in Matthew 14:14-21 we read that He preached to five thousand men, aside from women and children. If each couple had two children with them, there were twenty thousand. The actual total is only speculation, but we can guess that it was a very large crowd, perhaps between ten and twenty thousand people, and the Bible gives no indication that this was an unusually large crowd. Jesus took His message far and wide, encouraging people to repent, to believe in Him and accept Him, and to live by faith in obedience to Him.

On the other hand, He often withdrew from public ministry and spent time just with His disciples. He had an outer group of followers that numbered in the hundreds. Then there was a team of seventy people who were more involved in His movement. Finally, He had His twelve disciples who were with Him all the time. And even within the twelve, He was especially close to Peter, James, and John. Building into these people on a life-on-life basis, He was preparing the nucleus of a following that would take the message of salvation to the world after He was crucified.

Jesus Provided an Example for Our Lives

Someone has said the Christian life has not been tried and found wanting—it has been found difficult and not tried. One has only to read the Sermon on the Mount to see how incredibly difficult the Christian life is if one takes it seriously. In America, where it is comparatively easy to be a Christian, the implications often escape us. But move to a poverty-stricken country that is hostile to Christianity, and suddenly the demands of Christ take on a whole new dimension.

▼▼▼▼▼▼▼▼▼

Even a life lived in the hollow of God's hand can sometimes be a difficult life.

▲▲▲▲▲▲▲▲▲▲

Jesus Himself lived a perfect life, of course, and that life showed us how to flesh out the principles of the Sermon on the Mount and His other hard teachings. If we want to know what it means to love God and love our neighbor, we need only look at His life. He proved that even a life lived in the hollow of God's hand can sometimes be a difficult life. Jesus did everything the Father asked of Him, and He ended up on a cross. In return, He asks us to live as He lived, regardless of where it takes us.

First Peter 2:18-25 teaches us that Christ suffered, despite doing only what was right, thus leaving us an example. When He was reviled, He did not revile in return. When He suffered, He did not threaten, but committed Himself to God, who judges righteously. In that and in all other things, He was our example, and we are to follow Him.

Jesus Accomplished Salvation for All Who Believe

The final thing that Jesus did in His life on earth was to accomplish salvation for all who believe. Humanity was cut off from God, destined for an eternity separated from Him. Jesus satisfied all the demands that God the Father had for reconciling humanity to Him. He paid the price for our sin; He died in our place; He offered His righteousness for us.

Since everything necessary to make our salvation possible was done in Jesus through His incarnation, sinless life, crucifixion, resurrection, and ascension into heaven, the only remaining element is that we accept the gift that is offered to us. Some even say that the faith necessary to believe is given as a gift to us by God, while others say that everything short of the act of our will to choose was made possible by Christ's life. All in all, it was Jesus who made our salvation possible, and in Him we are complete before God.

Jesus Prays for Us Today

When Jesus ascended into heaven, He sat down at the right hand of the Father, indicating that His earthly task was completed successfully. Now He intercedes for us in prayer (Heb. 7:24-25). Why? Perhaps Luke 22:31-32 gives us a clue. Jesus was talking with His disciples just hours before His arrest and crucifixion. There was danger for them all, right around the corner. Jesus said to Peter, "Simon, Simon! Indeed, Satan has asked for you, that he may sift you as wheat. But I have prayed for you, that

Think about It

If you don't understand what Jesus did . . .

- You might think that Jesus did not do, or was not able to do, miracles.

- You might think that Jesus was a wimp who never confronted anyone.

- You might think that Jesus went around picking needless fights with religious leaders.

- You might think that Jesus failed when He left behind only eleven disciples.

- You might think that Jesus died needlessly, because we don't really need to be saved from our sins.

your faith should not fail." Perhaps that is what Jesus is doing for us—standing between us and Satan, who wants to destroy us, asking the Father that our faith should not fail.

Conclusion

This, then, is what Jesus spent the bulk of His time doing during His three-year earthly ministry: (1) He performed miracles, not only out of compassion to relieve human suffering but even more to verify that He was the Messiah and to validate the message of salvation He was preaching. (2) He confronted the religious leaders in an attempt to reveal the falseness of their brand of religion and call people to a true relationship with the living God. (3) He prepared for His departure by spreading the message of salvation to the multitudes and by training a team of disciples who were prepared to carry the message of salvation to the world after He was crucified.

 ## Instant Recall

There are six things that Jesus did/does:

1. Performed m_____

2. Confronted religious l_____

3. Preached to m_____, discipled a f_____

4. Provided an e_____ for our lives

5. Accomplished s_____ for those who believe

6. P_____ for us today

 ## Action Line

Read: My book *What You Need to Know about Jesus* has much more helpful information in it. If you want to learn even more about this, read *Who Is This Jesus?* by Michael Green.

Memorize: 1 Peter 2:21.

Pray: Dear Lord, thank You for all You did for me when You came to earth. You had the power and the plan and You provided the example for me. Thank You for backing up Your words with sufficient action. Help me follow You as my example. Amen.

Let Me Ask You

1. Do you have any trouble believing that Jesus performed miracles? Why or why not?

2. Were the Sabbath controversies that infuriated the religious leaders needless provocation, or did they accomplish something important?

3. Why do you think Jesus had only twelve close disciples?

4. What is the biggest thing you would have to change if you were to live life with Jesus as your example?

CHAPTER 7

Chapter at a Glance

- The Holy Spirit is a real person.

- The Holy Spirit is God.

- The Holy Spirit is the third person of the Trinity.

Who Is the Holy Spirit?

Well Said

The Holy Spirit is not religious fervor or a righteous attitude. He is God. He usually stays in the background of our spiritual life, holding things together. But He is no less necessary than gravity to the earth. Without both, everything would go flying apart.

Discovering Pluto

At the time Pluto, our most distant planet, was discovered, we did not have a telescope powerful enough to see it. Astronomer Percival Lowell began searching from his private observatory in Flagstaff, Arizona, for an unknown planet at the far edge of our solar system. He had noticed that something unseen seemed to be influencing Uranus, the most distant planet known to us at that time. He concluded that the only thing that could be making Uranus act that way was if another heavenly body, as yet unseen, were exercising gravitational pull on it. Putting two and two together, he concluded that there must be another planet out there, so far away that it was as yet unseen. His computations and deductions were vindicated when the planet was finally seen by Clyde W. Tombaugh on February 18, 1930.

Discovering Pluto is a lot like learning about the Holy Spirit. We cannot see Him, but we know of His presence because of the influence He exerts. He didn't walk the earth, as Jesus of Nazareth did. He is not the main focus of those of all faiths who believe in a God. Indeed, many who believe in God do not believe in the Holy Spirit. The only way we conclude that there is a Holy Spirit is through the teachings of Scripture and through

Snapshot

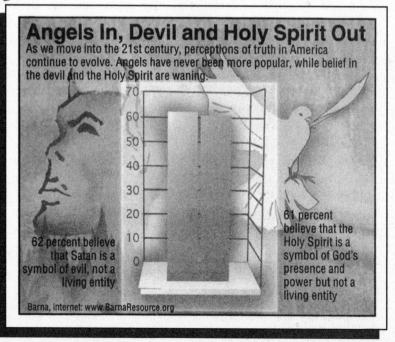

Angels In, Devil and Holy Spirit Out

As we move into the 21st century, perceptions of truth in America continue to evolve. Angels have never been more popular, while belief in the devil and the Holy Spirit are waning.

62 percent believe that Satan is a symbol of evil, not a living entity

61 percent believe that the Holy Spirit is a symbol of God's presence and power but not a living entity

Barna, internet: www.BarnaResource.org

our experience. The Holy Spirit's influence is evident. We can't see Him, but we know of His presence because of the influence He exerts.

Who is the Holy Spirit? To some, He is not a person but an impersonal force like school spirit. To others, He is a mystery, someone or something unknown and perhaps to be feared. However, if we hold to the teachings of the Bible, the mystery is cleared up greatly and we see three major truths emerging.

The Holy Spirit Is a Real Person

My brother and his wife had two children early in their marriage, a boy and a girl. A few years later, on the birth of his third child, my brother quipped, "Well, I always said I wanted three children, one of each—a he, a she, and an it." He said it purely for amusement and we all got a good laugh out of it. All of his children, grown now, think it is funny.

Just as my brother wanted "a he, a she, and an it," many people see God as a He (the Father), another He (the Son), and an It (the Holy Spirit). I suspect the issue goes back to the King James translation of the Bible. *God* is a masculine word in the original language of the Bible; *Jesus* is a masculine word, too; but *Spirit* is a neuter word—a concept rather foreign to English. The word is literally "breath" or "wind," though it was also translated "spirit" or "ghost" in A.D. 1611 when the King James Bible was translated. As a result, the King James Version refers to the Holy Spirit as "it." This, plus general theological uncertainty about the Holy Spirit, has caused some to be confused as to whether He is a real person. He is, of course, and many of the more recent translations of the Bible refer to Him as "He" rather than "it," helping to dispel the impression created by the original King James translation.

There are a number of reasons why we believe in the "personality" of the Holy Spirit. First, the Holy Spirit has the characteristics of a person. He has

- intellect (1 Cor. 2:10-11)
- emotion (Eph. 4:30)
- will (1 Cor. 12:11)

In addition, He does things that only a person would do:

- teaches us (1 Cor. 2:13)
- prays for us (Rom. 8:26)
- performs miracles (Acts 8:39)
- helps us (John 14:26)
- guides us (John 16:13)

Repeatedly, Jesus used the masculine pronoun, "He," when referring to the Holy Spirit (John 16:7-15). Today, those who do not believe the Holy Spirit is a person usually believe that He is merely a force emanating from God the Father. This position can only be held by ignoring or tampering with some verses in the Bible. A high view of *all* of Scripture will lead a person to the conclusion that the Holy Spirit is a person.

The Holy Spirit Is God

Not only is the Holy Spirit a person; He is also God. In Acts 5:3 Peter asked two people caught in a sin why they lied to the Holy Spirit. Then, in verse 4, he said, "You have not lied to men but to God." Peter equated lying to the Holy Spirit with lying to God.

In addition, the Holy Spirit has characteristics that only God has. He is . . .

- eternal (Heb. 9:14)
- all-knowing (1 Cor. 2:10-11)
- everywhere simultaneously (Ps. 139:7)

Also, He did things that only God could do. He . . .

- helped create the world (Gen. 1:2)
- miraculously conceived Jesus (Luke 1:35)
- imparts spiritual life (John 3:8)
- gives life to our resurrected bodies (Rom. 8:11)

Finally, the New Testament treats Him on an equal plane with God the Father and God the Son:

- The Spirit is mentioned in the Great Commission—"Go therefore and make disciples of all nations, baptizing them in the name of the Father and of the Son and of the Holy Spirit" (Matt. 28:19).

- The Spirit is mentioned in Paul's benediction to the Corinthians—"The grace of the Lord Jesus Christ, and the love of God, and the communion of the Holy Spirit be with you all" (2 Cor. 13:14).

▼▼▼▼▼▼▼▼

The Holy Spirit is a real person who cares about me.

▲▲▲▲▲▲▲▲

The complete evidence from Scripture leaves little doubt that the Holy Spirit is a divine person.

The Holy Spirit Is the Third Person of the Trinity

The Holy Spirit is a person; He is God; and He is, therefore, the third person of the Trinity. His role within the Trinity is not as clearly defined or understood as the Father and the Son. The role of the Father is to initiate relationships and plans, and to provide for and protect His own. The role of the Son is to respond, to trust and to obey. The role of the Holy Spirit appears to be a supporting role to the work of the Father and the Son.

John 15:26 says, "When the Helper comes, whom I shall send to you from the Father, . . . He will testify of Me." The phrase "from the Father" has caused a good bit of trouble for some people. In the early days of the church, some people believed that it implied that the Holy Spirit was not God. However, this conclusion is not warranted and in fact flies in the face of the others passages that indicate His deity.

It is true that there is a subordination of role and relationship of the Holy Spirit to the Father, just as there is a subordination of role and relationship of the Son to the Father. But it does not imply a lack of equality with the Father and Son, nor does it imply that the Holy Spirit was a created being rather than an eternal being with the Father and Son. The ancient church councils of Constantino-pie (381) and Chalcedon (451) clarified the deity and equality of the Spirit with the Father and Son, and that doctrine has been safe among Bible-believing Christians ever since.

If these three things are true, then it is good news indeed. It means the Holy Spirit is a real person who cares about me, He has the power to help me, and it is the Holy Spirit's role in the Trinity to help me.

Conclusion

When I was growing up, I had two brothers, one two years older than I and one four years older. Growing up, they were always bigger than I was and knew more than I did, so I concluded that I was short and stupid. I was neither, but no one told me that. We lived in a very small town and one day when I was about six years old and my brothers were eight and ten, the new grocery store owner asked me what my name was.

"Just call me Shorty," I said in dead earnestness.

As it turned out, all three of us are now either a little over or a little under six feet tall, and each of us possesses advanced knowledge in a specialized area. It was a revelation to me when I finally realized I was not short or stupid. There is much more equality among us now that we have grown up than there was when we were still immature.

Think about It

If you don't believe what the Bible teaches about the Holy Spirit . . .

- You may get a twisted notion of who the Holy Spirit is, believing that He is not a real person and not God.

- You may get confused about the trustworthiness of the Bible, because the Bible treats Him as a person and as God.

- You may lose the ability to trust in Him for your daily life because you don't realize He is there to help you.

- You may lose the peace that comes from believing that He is there, He can help, and He wants to help.

A similar point is true with the Father, Son, and Holy Spirit. If we have an immature understanding of them, we might conclude that God the Father is the biggest and best, Jesus is second, and the Holy Spirit brings up the rear. A more mature understanding, however, leads us to a different conclusion. They are equal in personhood, though different in the roles they play. As James Packer wrote, "These three persons are the one God to whom Christians commit themselves."[1]

Let Me Ask You

1. Before you read this chapter, what was your understanding of who the Holy Spirit is?

2. Did your understanding change any? If so, how?

3. What seems like the most important thing to you concerning the fact that the Holy Spirit is a person?

Instant Recall

Three things are true of the Holy Spirit:

1. He is a real p_____.

2. He is G_____.

3. He is the third person of the T_____.

Action Line

Read: My book *What You Need to Know about the Holy Spirit* contains more helpful information about this subject. If you would like to learn even more about the Holy Spirit, read *Keep in Step with the Spirit* by James I. Packer.

Memorize: John 14:16.

Pray: Dear Lord, thank You for sending the Holy Spirit to give me new life and to be my comforter and guide. Help me to grow in my understanding of who He is and in my ability to draw on His strength to live my life. Amen.

What Does the Holy Spirit Do?

Well Said

Wind turns the windmill. Not the other way around. So it is with the Holy Spirit. He does the work of God, not us. But He'll turn us if we let Him.

The Purpose of Light

Washington, D.C., is one of the most beautiful capitals in the world. Perhaps the most spectacular view of the city is at night. All the major sights are illuminated against the backdrop of utter blackness—the White

House, Capitol Building, Washington Monument, Lincoln Memorial, and Jefferson Memorial, all gleaming white, like diamonds on black velvet. You cannot tell where the light is coming from to light up these magnificent buildings.

As you walk around the White House, for example, its impressive architectural features are highlighted perfectly with millions of watts of light, but you cannot see the lights. They are carefully concealed by landscaping and other means. And that is when the lighting engineers have done their best job—when you give no thought to the light, and all attention is drawn to the building.

So it is with the Holy Spirit. Jesus is like the White House; the Holy Spirit is like the lighting around it. The Holy Spirit's job is not to be seen but to throw light on Jesus. It is when you see Jesus most clearly that the Holy Spirit is most at work.

Even though the Holy Spirit is rarely spotlighted in Scripture, His work in our lives is essential. There are a number of things He does that are vital to our salvation and daily lives.

The Holy Spirit Was Active in the Old Testament

The Holy Spirit's role in the Old Testament was different than it is now.

1. He helped create the world (Gen. 1:2).
2. He revealed God's truth to prophets (2 Tim. 3:16-17). In 2 Samuel 23:2 David attributes his own words to the Holy Spirit.
3. He empowered some individuals for service. He indwelt some people some of the time, and empowered them to do what God wanted them to do. Joseph (Gen. 41:38), Joshua (Num. 27:18), and Daniel (Dan. 5:11) were filled with the Holy Spirit.

The Holy Spirit Was Active in the New Testament

The Holy Spirit conceived Jesus in Mary's womb, and revealed to Mary what had happened (Luke 1:35). He gave Jesus power to serve God. He came upon Jesus at His baptism (Luke 3:21-22), and empowered Him to do God's will after that (Luke 4:18-19).

On the day of Pentecost, the Holy Spirit came upon the first believers, appearing as flames of fire, accompanied by a sound of a great, rushing wind. Believers were gifted by the Holy Spirit to speak in tongues so that Jews who were visiting Jerusalem from other countries recognized in their own language what the believers were saying. Finally, the Holy Spirit empowered and led Christians to take the message of salvation to Jerusalem, Judea, Samaria, and the uttermost parts of the earth (Acts 1:8).

Peter, Paul, and the writer to the Hebrews said that Scripture came from the Holy Spirit (Acts 28:25; Heb. 3:7; 10:15-16; 2 Pet. 1:21).

The Holy Spirit Applies Salvation to the Believer

It was the job of Jesus to accomplish salvation for us. This He did with His incarnation, sinless life, death, burial, resurrection, ascension into heaven, and with His present ministry of praying for us. On the other hand, it is the Holy Spirit's job to apply salvation to the believer. He does this through five key ministries to us:

1. **Conviction:** causing us to see our sin and to desire righteousness, leading us to receive Christ as our Savior (John 16:8).
2. **Regeneration:** causing our old, dead spirit to be born again, so that we are now spiritually alive (Titus 3:5).
3. **Indwelling:** coming to live within us to help us live out our new life (1 Cor. 6:19-20).
4. **Baptism:** placing us, spiritually, in the body of Christ (1 Cor. 12:13).
5. **Sealing:** marking us as God's own possession and guaranteeing our eternal salvation (Eph. 1:13-14).

 Insight:

To remember the five major works of the Holy Spirit in our spiritual new birth, think of the acrostic CRIBS. You put new babies in cribs.

The Holy Spirit Is Our Helper

The Holy Spirit is called, in the original Greek New Testament, our *paraklete*. This is translated into English several different ways: comforter, counselor, helper, and even advocate. Jesus said, in John 14.16, "I will pray the Father, and He will give you another Helper." Jesus was the first helper. In 1 John 2.1, Jesus is called the Advocate, which is also the word *paraklete*. Now we have another one who will be with us forever.

As our *paraklete,* the Holy Spirit does a number of things. He . . .

Fact File

What's a Paraclete?

The word *paraklete* comes from two words put together:

para = beside, alongside

kaleo = to call, invite, or summons

Therefore, the literal meaning is "to call or summon someone to come to your side to help."

- helps us have inner assurance of salvation (Rom. 8:16)
- helps us understand the Bible (1 Cor. 2:9-10, 13)
- helps us understand God's ways (Eph. 1:17-18)
- helps us in our prayers (Rom. 8:26-27)
- helps our strength in faith and obedience (Eph. 3:16-19)
- helps guide us (Rom. 8:14)

. . . and helps us in many other ways, some of which we probably aren't aware of and don't understand.

The Holy Spirit Fills Us

In Ephesians 5:18 we are commanded to be filled with the Holy Spirit. There are several different interpretations of what that means. The Pentecostal/charismatic interpretation neither rules out nor requires supernormal experiences such as speaking in tongues. Many believe, however, that one consistent result of any Spirit filling is Spirit-inspired speech, whether tongues or prophecy (Acts 2:4; 4:31; 19:6).

The "victorious Christian life" interpretation is that the filling of the Spirit empowers a person for improved Christian living and greater ministry. There are conditions to being filled, and when they are met, the person is filled with the Spirit: dedicating one's life to the Lord, confessing sin and putting away sins you may be harboring, asking to be filled, and believing that you are filled even though you see or feel no evidence of it.

The "word of Christ" interpretation is that the filling is essentially the same as "let[ting] the word of Christ dwell in you richly" in Colossians 3:16. The results of both "filling" and "letting the word of Christ dwell in you richly" are identical, leading Bible teachers to believe that the causes are the same. To allow the word of Christ to dwell in us richly, we must read it, study it, memorize it, and meditate on it in a spirit of trust and obedience.

Snapshot

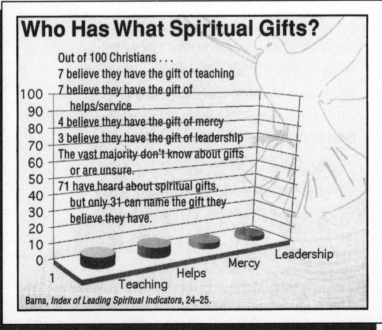

Who Has What Spiritual Gifts?

Out of 100 Christians . . .
7 believe they have the gift of teaching
7 believe they have the gift of helps/service
4 believe they have the gift of mercy
3 believe they have the gift of leadership
The vast majority don't know about gifts or are unsure.
71 have heard about spiritual gifts, but only 31 can name the gift they believe they have.

Teaching   Helps   Mercy   Leadership

Barna, *Index of Leading Spiritual Indicators*, 24–25.

The Holy Spirit Gives Us Spiritual Gifts

A spiritual gift is a God-given ability for ministry to others. Each of us has received a spiritual gift, perhaps more than one. First Peter 4:10 says, "As each one has received a gift, minister it to one another." There is some confusion over the gifts, in part, I think, because there appear to be three different kinds of gifts.

First, there are "office" gifts, which are given to those who serve the church at large in a specific capacity: apostle, prophet, evangelist, or pastor-teacher (Eph. 4:11-12). Some believe that the offices of apostle and prophet have disappeared, now that the foundation of the church has been laid (Eph. 2:21-22), and that only evangelist and pastor-teacher gifts remain.

Others, including Pentecostals, charismatics, and "third wave" Christians (the Pentecostal and char-

Three Kinds of Gifts

Office gifts: people gifted to serve the church with a specific office of apostle, prophet, evangelist, or pastor-teacher.

Service gifts: non-miraculous gifts that serve the well-being of the church in a rather normal way.

Special gifts: miraculous gifts that are a sign to others of the power of God.

ismatic movements were the first two "waves") believe that all four gifts will remain until Jesus returns. They acknowledge, however, that first-generation apostles and prophets were unique in their authority and ability.

Second, there are "service" gifts, which are nonmiraculous gifts that correspond to ministries that all of us should do, but some individuals are gifted for greater impact in those areas. Few people debate the legitimacy of these gifts. Most agree these gifts are alive and well in the church today.

Third are the "special" gifts, which are miraculous or super-normal gifts that appear to be given for the purpose not only of meeting a need of the moment but also for validating the message of Christianity to those who have not previously received the message. We read of these gifts primarily in 1 Corinthians 12:4-11.

In some cases, the exercise of these gifts is said to build up Christians (1 Cor. 14:4-5, 22), yet in Hebrews 2:4 they are said to have been for the purpose of validating the new message of salvation by grace through faith in Jesus.

Christians differ as to whether or not God intends these special gifts to operate today. Pentecostal, charismatic, and "third wave" Christians believe that these gifts were given to the church until Christ returns, both as an expression of the full gospel of Christ as well as to validate the message of the gospel. Mainstream evangelical Christians recognize that these gifts were an expression of compassion and of the coming of the kingdom of God during the time of Christ. However, they generally hold that the gifts were primarily for the purpose of validating the new message of salvation by grace through faith in Jesus, and as that message was gradually established in the world, the purpose of the gifts gradually disappeared. Therefore, so did a proper use of the gifts.

Conclusion

In summary, the Holy Spirit helps us.

My wife, Margie, and I have been helped when we really needed it. People have helped us load our moving truck, let us live with them during times of transition, helped out during times of serious illness, and come close to us when we were lonely. There has been a stream of people who made life easier. When we help others, we are doing what God does every day for us. Whether you help someone in a big way or a small way, you are imitating God.

Instant Recall

1. The Holy Spirit was active in the
   O_____
   T_____ and the
   N_____
   T_____.

2. The Holy Spirit applies
   s_____ to the believer.

3. The Holy Spirit is our h_____.

4. The Holy Spirit f_____ us.

5. The Holy Spirit gives us spiritual g_____.

Let Me Ask You

1. Did you realize that the Holy Spirit did so much in your life? What is the most interesting thing you learned?

2. What ministry of the Holy Spirit means the most to you?

3. What spiritual gift(s) do you think the Holy Spirit may have given you? What would you like to do with it?

Action Line

Read: My book *What You Need to Know about the Holy Spirit* has more helpful information about this subject. If you want to learn even more, read *Keep in Step with the Spirit* by James I. Packer.

Memorize: Titus 3:5.

Pray: Dear Lord, thank You for saving me, for giving me the Holy Spirit, and for helping me live my Christian life. Help me grow in my faith and obedience to You. Amen.

CHAPTER 9

**Chapter
at a Glance**

- The Bible is revealed by God.

- The Bible is inspired by God.

- The Bible is recognized by the church.

How Did We Get the Bible?

Well Said

The Bible is the best gift God has given to man. All the good the Savior gave to the world was communicated through this book. But for it we could not know right from wrong. All things most desirable for man's welfare, here and hereafter, are to be found portrayed in it.

—Abraham Lincoln

The Bible on the Horizon

Just to the west of Jackson Hole, Wyoming, there lies a vast and imposing fortress of stone called the Grand Teton Mountains. Long and narrow, and rising to nearly fourteen thousand feet, they stretch for fifty miles north and south like the saw-toothed backbone of a half-buried prehistoric monster. One of the most photographed places in the United States, these mountains rise abruptly from a flat floor and cast their cold and impersonal yet strikingly beautiful presence in every direction for miles.

The Teton range is virtually impassable. If the summer is warm, there is one pass that will open for a matter of weeks to let you travel east and west over the backbone. Otherwise, you may have to drive fifty or more miles out of your way west from Jackson Hole just to get around one of the largest outcroppings of exposed stone in the world. When you look at the horizon anywhere near the area, the Tetons dominate the landscape.

In the same way, when we scan the horizon of human civilization for the last two thousand years, we see the Bible confronting the traveler like a massive mountain range. The Bible is an enormous historical presence, the dominant piece of literature and a dominant influence in history since the time of Christ. The curious, the earnest, the zealous traveler on life's highway cannot ignore or wish away this vast presence on life's landscape.

Snapshot

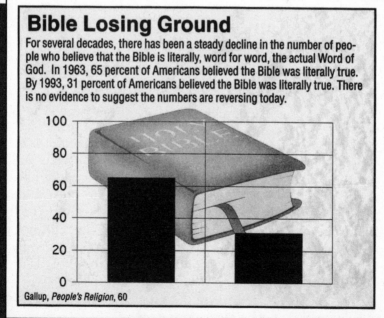

Bible Losing Ground

For several decades, there has been a steady decline in the number of people who believe that the Bible is literally, word for word, the actual Word of God. In 1963, 65 percent of Americans believed the Bible was literally true. By 1993, 31 percent of Americans believed the Bible was literally true. There is no evidence to suggest the numbers are reversing today.

Gallup, *People's Religion*, 60

Two Kinds of Revelation

Nature + providence + conscience = General Revelation

Jesus + Bible = Special Revelation

He or she must ask the question "What is the Bible?" Is it the Word of God?

The Bible Is Revealed by God

Many people are surprised to learn that the Bible did not come to us in one lump delivery, like a package in the mail, but that it was written and compiled over time in what seems to be a rather loosey-goosey fashion. Moses climbed Mount Sinai, enshrouded in clouds, with thunder rolling and lightning flashing, and there the very finger of God wrote the Ten Commandments in stone. That is a process you can have real confidence in. But the rest of the Bible did not come to us in such a neat package. The rest of the Bible was written . . .

- over a period of 1,500 years
- by over forty different authors ranging from farmers to kings
- in mainly two different languages, Hebrew (Old Testament) and Greek (New Testament)
- in many different countries on three continents
- touching on hundreds of different subjects
- but giving us one united message from God!

If mere men wrote the Bible, why do we think it is the Word of God? How can we be sure it doesn't have mistakes in it? How did the writers get their information? Can we really have confidence in the Bible? Many people feel a little uneasy about the process of getting the Bible. God could have dropped a finished Bible out of heaven. The fact that He didn't should not escape us as unimportant. God oversaw the process of giving us the Bible so that we can have confidence that the Bible is the Word of God.

First, God revealed His truth to humanity in two ways: general revelation and special revelation.

General revelation comes to us through three primary sources:

1. Nature. Who has not looked up into the night sky, with stars hanging like so many tiny crystals on black velvet, and not had the thought cross his mind, "There must be a God." That common experience is no accident. God intended for creation to reflect Him, as any piece of art reflects the artist and draws the onlooker's mind from the art to the artist. The beauty, order, magnitude, and intricacy of nature reveal to us that there is a God (Rom. 1:18-20).

2. Providence. God's intervention in the affairs of a people or a person often reveals the truth of God. People who have nearly been killed often feel they have been spared by God for a reason. Nations rise and fall on such tenuous threads that God seems to have a clear role in their welfare (Rom. 8:28).

Fact File

What Does 'Inspiration' Mean?

The word "inspired" comes from two Greek words:

> theo = God

> pneu = to blow, to breathe

Therefore, the word literally is "God-breathed," meaning that the Scripture is a result of God's creative work.

3. Conscience. Romans 2:15 teaches us that God has written His law on the human heart. This explains the inner sense of right and wrong that all people have. Also, there is an inner sense that the supernatural exists, a fact that pulls us to believe in God (Eccl. 3:11). These inner senses make up our conscience, which needs to be informed by Scripture if it is to have its full benefit in our lives. But our conscience tells us that there is a God until or unless we kill the message.

Special revelation is communication that has come to us directly from God. There are two main sources of special revelation.

1. Bible. Without the Bible, we might believe that there was a God, but we would not know who He was, whether He wanted or

Signs of Scripture

In trying to determine if a book or letter was inspired by God, the church used a number of criteria.

1. It had to be written by an apostle or someone close to an apostle.

2. Its content had to be consistent with other recognized Scripture.

3. It had to have been recognized and accepted by the early church.

4. It had to conform to the high standards set by other Scripture.

5. People's lives had to have been changed by it.

expected anything from us, or how to get to know Him. The Bible fills in those gaps, and through the Scripture, we can be led into an understanding of who God is and how to develop a relationship with Him.

2. Jesus. The Bible calls Jesus the Word of God (John 1:1; Rev. 19:13), which reveals a very close connection in the mind of God the Father between the written Word (the Bible) and the living Word (Jesus). Jesus has revealed to us in more complete form than just the Bible could what God is like, how we can be related to Him, and what God expects of us. General revelation tells us that there is a God, but only special revelation is sufficient to save us (Acts 4:12).

The Bible Is Inspired by God

When God revealed His word to humans for the Bible, He supernaturally oversaw the writing down of the Scriptures so that, without the loss of the writers' own personalities, they composed and recorded without error God's revelation in the original manuscripts and letters. The word we use for this process is "inspiration," which is an easily misunderstood word. We commonly speak of artists having been inspired to do a great work. Shakespeare was inspired when he wrote Hamlet. An inspired Beethoven wrote his Fifth Symphony. Michelangelo was inspired when he painted the Sistine Chapel. By these uses of "inspired," we mean simply that the individual reached down within himself or herself and produced a work that was above the ordinary, even for other geniuses.

This is *not* what is meant when we say the Bible is inspired. The word "inspired," when it is used in reference to the Bible, is a technical term meaning "God-breathed" (2 Tim. 3:16). Second Peter 1:20-21 says, "Holy men of God spoke as they were moved by the Holy Spirit." In 2 Samuel 23:2-3, King David, as he lay dying said, "The Spirit of the Lord spoke by me, and His word was on my tongue."

These passages give us a picture of Scripture that came to us from God through men. The writers of Scripture were being supernaturally guided to write what God wanted written, though God did not dictate it. Each man's own personality, background, writing style, and temperament come through. Moses did not write like Isaiah, who did not write like Paul, etc.

There are some who say that only the ideas or concepts are inspired, or that the Bible contains God's inspired Word but that

 Snapshot

The More We Know, the Less We Believe

Historically, in America the higher the education, the less one knows about the Bible. Also, the higher the education, the lower the belief that the Bible is true. There are many people in America today with a Ph.D. in aerodynamics but only a third-grade knowledge of religion.

Gallup, *People's Religion*, 60–61.

Think about It

If you don't understand how we got the Bible . . .

- You may not have the confidence that the Bible is God's Word.

- It may shake your faith when someone questions how God could have authored a book written by mere men.

- You may not grasp the significance of the Bible's unity; it is a mark of divine oversight that such a diverse book could have one consistent message.

- You may not accept the authority the Bible must have for guiding you to heaven as well as for your everyday life.

the Bible has errors in it, and the parts that have errors in it are not God's Word. However, no two people agree completely on which concepts or spots are inspired. There ends up being no final authority for what is true and what is not true.

Therefore, we have to come up with a definition that is as airtight as we can make it.

"The Bible is verbally and totally inspired and without error in the original manuscripts." This definition has a number of implications:

- The individual words, not just the ideas or concepts, are inspired and without error.

- *All* the words are inspired and without error; it is not true that some words are inspired and others not.

- Only the original manuscripts are without error. Minor transcription errors may exist (in fact, they account for less than 1/1,000 of the text), but none affect any doctrine.

- We can have complete confidence in the accuracy of all the Bible.

The Bible Is Recognized by the Church

God sovereignly oversaw a process of men recognizing the books and letters God had inspired and collecting them into one book, the Bible. The collection of books in the Bible is called the canon.

1. Old Testament Canon. Jesus gave His stamp of approval on the thirty-nine books that make up our Old Testament. In Luke 24:44 Jesus referred to all the things that must be fulfilled "which were written in the Law of Moses and the Prophets and the Psalms concerning Me." These three sections make up the entire Old Testament.

2. New Testament Canon. In A.D. 397 the final collection of books and letters that make up the Protestant New Testament was officially recognized at the Council of Carthage. This council of early church leaders did not declare a book to be inspired. It just recognized the inspiration that was already there.

Conclusion

While it is interesting and helpful to know about the formation of the canon of scriptural books, we must trust in the sovereignty of God for their authenticity. If God is going to hold us accountable to truth, He must see to it that we have the truth. God, in His providence, oversaw the process of forming the canon. The witness of the Spirit in the lives of believers who read the Bible, and the change that the Holy Spirit brings about in their lives, is a final telling testimony to the fact that we have the Word of God as He intended us to have it.

 Instant Recall

The Bible is . . .

* r_____ by God

* i_____ by God

* r_____ by the church

 Action Line

Read: My book *What You Need to Know about the Bible* provides more helpful information about this subject. If you want to learn even more, read *God Has Spoken* by James I. Packer.

Memorize: 2 Timothy 3:16-17.

Pray: Dear Lord, thank You for revealing Your truth to us. Thank You for making sure we have a trustworthy message. It is such a comfort to know Your will, and I pray You will help me dedicate my life fully to doing Your will. Amen.

What Is the Story of the Bible?

CHAPTER
10

**Chapter
at a Glance**

- The Old Testament tells the story of God and Israel.

- God provided a temporary solution for sin: sacrifices.

- The New Testament tells the story of Jesus and the church.

- God provided a permanent solution for sin: Jesus.

Well Said

Give me a candle and a Bible and shut me up in a dungeon and I will tell you what the world is doing.

—Cecil Dickard

Biting Off More than You Can Chew

Lady was an amazing dog, a border collie, with that awe-inspiring instinct to herd animals and control anything that moved. She worked the farm animals as I was growing up, and the love of her life was to bring in the cows when it was time to milk, which she did punctually without being told. Her second great love was biting pigs. They can be notoriously difficult to get back in their pen when they get out, but Lady loved it when that happened. It gave her the opportunity to herd, run, chase, and bite with wild abandon.

Her most fruitless habit was biting the tires on the tractor. For some reason, the great black rotating treads seemed to pose some threat to her control of circumstances, and she dedicated herself, with maniacal zeal, to trying to bite the treads of the tractor tire and get them to stop. I tried repeatedly and sternly to get her to stop this deadly game, but to no avail. She never lost the game, thank goodness. But the tractor was so much bigger and more powerful than she was that watching her bite the tires was a preposterous sight.

When it comes to studying and understanding the Bible, many of us feel like Lady biting the tires of the tractor. The Bible is so much bigger and so much more powerful than we are that the thought of our mastering it seems preposterous. However, once

Snapshot

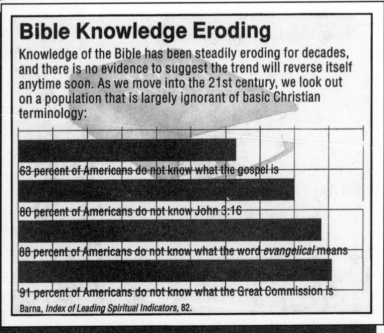

Bible Knowledge Eroding

Knowledge of the Bible has been steadily eroding for decades, and there is no evidence to suggest the trend will reverse itself anytime soon. As we move into the 21st century, we look out on a population that is largely ignorant of basic Christian terminology:

63 percent of Americans do not know what the gospel is

80 percent of Americans do not know John 3:16

88 percent of Americans do not know what the word *evangelical* means

91 percent of Americans do not know what the Great Commission is

Barna, *Index of Leading Spiritual Indicators*, 82.

we get an overall understanding of the story and message of the Bible, it becomes much less intimidating.

The Old Testament Tells the Story of God and Israel

Creation. The story begins when God created Adam and Eve, who were the innocent first members of God's paradise. However, they sinned and as a result were driven out of the Garden of Eden. As their offspring multiplied into the millions, sin also multiplied, and humanity became so sinful that God destroyed the earth with a universal flood. He preserved Noah and his immediate family to repopulate the earth, because they were the only people on earth willing to trust and obey God. Sin kept its hold over humanity, however, and once again, as the population increased, people forgot God.

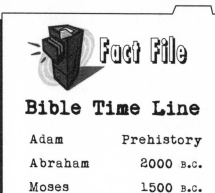

Fact File

Bible Time Line

Adam	Prehistory
Abraham	2000 B.C.
Moses	1500 B.C.
David	1000 B.C.
Ezra	500 B.C.
Jesus	A.D.

Patriarchs. Years later God revealed Himself to Abraham and promised him a nation, many descendants, and a blessing that would extend to everyone on the earth. In believing God, Abraham became the father of a great people, the Hebrews, who were later known as the Jews. God's promises to Abraham were passed down through his son Isaac, his grandson Jacob, and all twelve sons of Jacob. From the twelve sons of Jacob descended the twelve tribes of the Hebrew people, who make up the nation of Israel.

Exodus. A famine hit the land of Canaan (the approximate location of modern Israel), where the Hebrews were living, and they moved to Egypt to get food. In time they became a threat to the Egyptian people because they multiplied so rapidly, and the Egyptians enslaved the Hebrew people for nearly four hundred years. Finally, in response to their cries for deliverance, God raised up Moses to lead them out of Egypt back into the promised land of Canaan.

Kingdom. The Israelites lived in the promised land in a loose governmental system for the next four hundred years. Then a monarchy was established and the Hebrews were ruled by kings for the next four hundred years. During the first 120 years of the monarchy, three famous kings each reigned forty years: Saul, David, and Solomon. Then, as a result of civil conflict over taxation, the northern part of the nation seceded from the monarchy and established its own independent kingdom called Israel. The southern kingdom adopted the name of Judah, after the largest tribe in the southern kingdom.

Exile. Shortly thereafter, Assyria, a nation to the northeast, came and conquered the northern kingdom of Israel and scattered many of the Israelites to the far corners of that part of the world. About one hundred years later, Babylonia invaded and conquered Judah, destroyed Jerusalem, and led thousands of people into captivity in Babylonia.

Return. About seventy years later, Persia defeated Babylonia to rule the entire part of the world from the eastern shore of the Mediterranean to India. The king of Persia allowed the Israelites living in captivity in Babylonia to return to Jerusalem to rebuild it. Fifty thousand people returned under the leadership of three men: Zerubbabel, Ezra, and Nehemiah. They rebuilt the city, rebuilt the temple, and restored public worship of God. They lived that way for the next four hundred years. During that time, Persia fell to Greece, and later Greece fell to Rome. Rome was ruling that part of the world when Jesus was born and the New Testament began.

God Provided a Temporary Solution for Sin: Sacrifices

We all long for abundant life on earth and eternal life in heaven. The only thing that separates humanity from God and this destiny is sin. Separation from God because of sin is called "death" (Rom. 6:23). In the Old Testament, God pictured spiritual death with physical death through a system of animal sacrifice. The Israelites were to kill an animal so that God would forgive the sin. However, the death of the animal itself did not atone for (make up for) the sin. Rather, God required repentance in order to forgive the sin, but the sacrifice of an animal was the sign God required to demonstrate one's repentance. It was possible, however, for someone to sacrifice the animal without having repented in his heart. It is called "hypocrisy." People kept up the show on the outside, even though things were not right on the inside.

The prophet Samuel said, "To obey is better than sacrifice, and to heed than the fat of rams" (1 Sam. 15:22). David said, in Psalm 51:16-17, "You do not desire sacrifice, or else I would give it; You do not delight in burnt offering. The sacrifices of God are a broken spirit, a broken and a contrite heart—these, O God, You will not despise." Jesus called the Pharisees in the New Testament "whitewashed tombs" (Matt.23:27) because they kept up the proper appearance on the outside but inside were unrepentant.

But, if one was repentant, then God prescribed sacrifices that he was to offer. These sacrifices, always costly, usually included the death of an animal, which pictured the spiritual death that sin causes. They were a graphic reminder of the true cost and consequence of sin.

Fact File

The Cost of Sacrifices

The sacrificial system in the Old Testament was expensive. Reflecting today's prices, the following animals would cost, depending on how much a person made, approximately:

1 bull	1 week's wages
1 goat	1 day's wages
1 sheep	1 day's wages
2 doves	1 hour's wages

This visual aid helps us to understand what was at stake with our sin, and what it would take in order for us to have our sins forgiven permanently. If we did not want to have to offer animal sacrifices throughout eternity, something had to happen to permanently remove the need. That "something" was the sacrificial death of Jesus, upon which the New Testament focuses.

The New Testament Tells the Story of Jesus and the Church

Jesus' early life. Jesus was born in Bethlehem near Jerusalem, in keeping with Old Testament prophecy. Then, after a brief time in Egypt to escape King Herod's attempt to kill Him, Jesus and His earthly parents, Mary and Joseph, moved back to

Think about It

Unless you learn the story and message of the Bible . . .

- You will be confused when you try to read or study it, because you won't know the big picture.

- You can be easily led astray by those who teach error.

- You will not take comfort in the fact that the Bible makes sense.

- You will not take hope and encouragement from the good news that pervades the Scriptures.

their hometown in Nazareth in the northern part of the country, just west of the Sea of Galilee. There, with few details from Scripture, Jesus lived an apparently normal childhood until He turned thirty. At the age of thirty (the age that all teachers, by Jewish custom, began their ministry) Jesus left Nazareth and went to Jerusalem. He began His initial ministry there and in the surrounding area of Judea.

Jesus' ministry. Shortly afterward, He relocated north to the area around the Sea of Galilee, making Capernaum His home base. Capernaum was located on the north shore of the Sea of Galilee. Much of His three-year ministry was conducted while He was based at Capernaum, though many events did not actually take place in Capernaum but in the surrounding area. Eventually, He returned to Jerusalem. The religious leaders deeply resented His ministry. They were jealous of His intrusion into their territory and resentful of His making them look bad.

Crucifixion and resurrection. Their hatred was so intense that they eventually crucified Him. Three days later He rose from the dead, then showed Himself to His disciples several times over the next forty days. With His disciples gathered around Him on the Mount of Olives, just east of Jerusalem, He visibly ascended into heaven.

Early church. He had commissioned His disciples to take the new message of salvation through Christ to Jerusalem, to Judea and Samaria (the surrounding regions), and to the uttermost parts of the earth. The fulfillment of this command focused primarily on the apostle Paul, who conducted three missionary journeys to surrounding areas in Asia Minor and Greece. Finally, Paul was arrested and taken to Rome, where he eventually died. Enough disciples remained, however, not only in Jerusalem but also in Asia Minor, Greece, and Rome, that the message not only lived on but mushroomed into a major world religion.

God Provided a Permanent Solution for Sin: Jesus

The New Testament presents in reality what the Old Testament only pictured. In the Old Testament, people sacrificed lambs to cover their sins temporarily. In the New Testament, the Lamb of God, Jesus, was sacrificed so that all sins could be forgiven permanently. Jesus' death, adequate to take away the sins of the whole world, only affects those who accept His offer of forgiveness, repent of their sins, and follow Him. When Jesus said that He had "fulfilled" the law, He meant that no longer was it necessary to keep sacrificing bulls and goats and sheep. Now humanity needed only to rely on the great sacrifice of Jesus on Calvary.

Conclusion

God is self-sufficient and does not need our gifts or service (Acts 17:25). Why, then, does He call us to come to Him? James I. Packer answers that question in his book *God Has Spoken*:

God's purpose in revelation is to *make friends* with us. It was to this end that He created us rational beings, bearing His image, able to think and hear and speak and love; He wanted there to be genuine personal affection and friendship, two-sided, between Himself and us—a relation, not like that between a man and his dog, but like that of a father to his son, or a husband to his wife. Loving friendship between two persons has no ulterior motive; it is an end in itself. And that is God's end in revelation. He speaks to us simply to fulfill the purpose for which we were made; that is, to bring into being a relationship in which He is a friend to us, and we to Him, He finding His joy in giving us gifts and we finding ours in giving Him thanks.[1]

Instant Recall

1. The Old Testament tells the story of G_____ and I_____.

2. God provided a t_____ solution for sin: sacrifices.

3. The New Testament tells the story of J_____ and the c_____.

4. God provided a p_____ solution for sin: Jesus.

Let Me Ask You

1. How did your understanding of the story of the Bible change as a result of reading this chapter?

2. What insights into the relationship between sin and the Old Testament sacrificial system did you gain?

3. What insight into the relationship between the Old Testament sacrificial system and Christ's sacrifice in the New Testament did you gain?

Action Line

Read: My book *What You Need to Know about the Bible* contains more helpful information about this subject. If you want to learn even more, read *God Has Spoken* by James I. Packer.

Memorize: Matthew 28:19-20.

Pray: Dear Lord, thank You that the Bible is a coherent story, that it makes sense. Thank You that You have told us what You are doing in the world and how I fit in. Thank You that You want to make friends with me. Help me to learn Your will and to do it. Amen.

What Are the Recurring Themes in the Bible?

CHAPTER 11

Chapter at a Glance

- We must view the present with eternity in mind.

- God disciplines us when we do wrong.

- Good relationships make life rewarding.

- God fights our spiritual battles for us.

- God sustains us through suffering.

- If God has our hearts, He will also have our money.

Well Said

If the Bible is not true religion, one is very excusable in being deceived, for everything in it is grand and worthy of God. The more I consider the Gospel, the more I am assured there is nothing there which is not beyond the march of events and above the human mind.

—Napoleon Bonaparte

"Mirror, Mirror on the Wall"

In *Snow White and the Seven Dwarfs*, the wicked queen asks her enchanted mirror, "Mirror, mirror on the wall, who's the fairest one of all?" The mirror cannot tell a lie, so for years it said, "You, O queen, are the fairest in the land." But one day the queen asked who was the fairest one of all, and the mirror, unable to tell anything but the truth, said, "Snow White is the fairest of them all." This enraged the queen and set her on a path to destroy Snow White. The plan failed, however. Snow White was rescued by a handsome prince and taken away to live happily ever after.

▼▼▼▼▼▼▼▼

Like a mirror, the Bible tells you the truth every time.

▲▲▲▲▲▲▲▲

Though this is only a fairy tale, it is based on one fundamental truth. A mirror doesn't lie. If your face is dirty, it tells you. If your hair is a mess, it tells you. If your clothes don't fit, it tells you. It will tell you the truth every time.

Like a mirror, the Bible tells you the truth every time (James 1:22-25). It accurately shows you if your attitude is out of place, if your values are a mess, or if your thoughts are dirty.

As we look into the mirror of the Scripture, there are many themes that recur throughout the Bible, demanding that we pay special attention to them. They recur because they are extremely important. In this chapter we will look at six.

We Must View the Present with Eternity in Mind

This world, as the old spiritual song says, is not our home. We are just passing through. That, in essence, is an eternal perspective—living life with the conscious realization that this world is temporary and heaven will be our eternal home, living not for this world but for the next. This is very hard to do because this world is "seen" and the next world is "unseen" and because it is easier to keep in touch with something that is seen than something that is not seen.

Colossians 3:1-3 instructs us to live by remote control: "If then you were raised with Christ, seek those things which are above, where Christ is, sitting at the right hand of God. Set your mind on things above, not on things on the earth."

All the directions, all the commands, all the needful information comes from another place, unseen but real. We live "here" as though citizens of "there." Paul elaborated in 2 Corinthians 4:16-18: "Therefore we do not lose heart. Even though our outward man is perishing, yet the inward man is being renewed day by day. For our light affliction, which is but for a moment, is working for us a far more exceeding and eternal weight of glory, while we do not look at the things which are seen, but at the things which are not seen. For the things which are seen are temporary, but the things which are not seen are eternal."

The "light affliction" to which Paul alluded for him included being beaten with rods, stoned, and shipwrecked; being in danger from rivers, robbers, his countrymen, and Gentiles; being in danger in the city, in the wilderness, and on the sea; knowing labor and hardships, sleepless nights, hunger and thirst, and cold and exposure (2 Cor. 11:25-28). Paul was willing to endure whatever this world brought him because he was pursuing the values of the next.

God promises to meet our true needs in this life and reward us for all service in the next life. We have everything to gain and nothing to lose. It is as C. S. Lewis wrote: if you shoot for the next world, you get this one thrown in; if you shoot for this world, you get neither.

Fact File

The State of Bible Knowledge in America

The Bible knowledge of Americans is an unpredictable potpourri of information. In some areas we are rather astute; in others, embarrassingly ignorant. This condition is attributable to Christian education processes which are not systematic and which incorporate little in the way of knowledge assessment.

Barna, *Index of Leading Spiritual Indicators*, 80.

God Disciplines Us When We Do Wrong

The Bible teaches us that when we sin, we will be disciplined by God, who uses the discipline to turn us from sin. Hebrews 12:5-6 tells us, "Do not make light of the Lord's discipline, and do not lose heart when he rebukes you, because the Lord disciplines those he loves" (NIV). Just as a loving parent does not allow a child to play in the street without disciplining him or her, so God does not allow His children to live in harmful or dangerous ways without disciplining them. He loves His children too much to allow self-destructive behavior and attitudes without trying to correct that behavior or those attitudes.

▼▼▼▼▼▼▼▼▼

Love, joy, peace, patience, kindness, goodness, faithfulness, gentleness, and self-control are the fruit of the Spirit.

▲▲▲▲▲▲▲▲▲

Good Relationships Make Life Rewarding

Unity is one of the great experiences of life. We have all seen the unity of an Olympic team in victory, or the joy of unity in the marriage ceremony, or the unity of soldiers after a successful mission. It is inherently a joyous thing to experience unity with others— perhaps the greatest joy there is in life.

Unity is one of the great themes of the Bible. "Behold, how good and how pleasant it is for brethren to dwell together in unity!" David declared in Psalm 133:1. God wanted the entire nation of Israel to be united in following the Law, and to be one in following Him.

Jesus prayed that "they all [His followers] may be one" (John 17:21). In Ephesians 4:3 we read this command: "[Endeavor] to keep the unity of the Spirit in the bond of peace." The apostle Paul then went on to explain that spiritual gifts are given to the church for the building up of the body of Christ, "till we all come to the unity of the faith" (Eph. 4:13).

In a similar vein, Paul instructed the Christians in Colosse to exercise love toward one another, which is "the bond of perfection" (Col. 3:14). When you consider the interrelatedness of love, peace, and harmony with unity, you see that unity is a dominant theme that runs throughout the Bible. God is one, and He wants His people to be one.

By living in unity, God's children become like Him. Love, joy, peace, patience, kindness, goodness, faithfulness, gentleness, and self-control (Gal. 5:22-23) are the fruit of the Spirit— characteristics of God that we may share. Also, when His children live together in unity, it is a living picture showing the world what God is like. The love, the mutual respect, the deference, the fellowship that are true of God's children as they live together in unity shows the world that God is a God of love, respect, and fellowship, and it creates in the hearts of the people observing this unity a desire to know the God who created the unity.

▼▼▼▼▼▼▼

There are times when life is a battlefield, not a dance floor. It's a war, not a waltz.

▲▲▲▲▲▲▲

God Fights Our Spiritual Battles for Us

Life in modern America can be difficult to understand. From the Declaration of Independence to Walt Disney movies, we have been taught that our pursuit of happiness can bear fruit if we work hard and are persistent. But it isn't always so. There are times when happiness is not what life brings us. There are times when life is a battlefield, not a dance floor. It's a war, not a waltz.

Only God can win the battle we are in, because for us as Christians, all of life is a spiritual battle. It is as Solomon wrote, "The horse is prepared for the day of battle, but deliverance is of the LORD" (Prov. 21:31).

We see dramatic examples of this in the Old Testament. From the crossing of the Red Sea, in which the Lord destroyed the army of Egypt that was coming to destroy Israel, to the collapse of the walls of Jericho to the fight between David and Goliath, God wants to fight the spiritual battles for His children.

Our battles are not fought against invading armies but against the world, the flesh, and the devil (Rom. 7:23; 1 Pet. 5:8; 1 John 5:19). We are powerless to win against these formidable foes, but God wants to fight for us.

Second Corinthians 10:3-4 tells us, "Though we walk in the flesh, we do not war according to the flesh. For the weapons of our warfare are not carnal but mighty in God for pulling down strongholds."

Sometimes God allows us to get in such predicaments that, on a human level, there is no hope. Then He delivers us to prove to us and a watching world that He is faithful and mighty to save. God wants us to understand that we do not have the natural means to emerge victorious from spiritual battle. He is our victory. He is our sufficiency. He wants us to rely on Him.

God Sustains Us through Suffering

Suffering is one of the great themes of the Bible, from beginning to end. It is a thread woven generously throughout the fabric of Scripture. Those who claim that if you are living the Christian life properly you will not experience suffering are not taking the Bible at face value. "For affliction does not come from the dust, nor does trouble spring from the ground; yet man is born to trouble, as the sparks fly upward," said Job's adviser Eliphaz (5:6-7).

Why does life have so much suffering? While the Bible gives some reasons, we do not know the ultimate reason. It is hidden in the mysteries of God and must wait until heaven for the answer.

Where is God when it hurts? Jesus of Nazareth came to earth and suffered everything we will ever suffer. Now He is in heaven, praying to God for us. And He is with us, feeling the same pain we feel.

How does God view our suffering? He views it as a normal part of the human experience on earth, promises sufficient grace for it, and says that in the end all will be well.

How can we endure suffering? By fleeing to the arms of God, as Jesus did when He suffered for us.

If God Has Our Hearts, He Will Also Have Our Money

From God's perspective, money is a test. God uses money to test where our values are, where our hearts are. If our hearts are fixed on things of this earth, we find ourselves pretty tight with our money. If our values are fixed in heaven, we find ourselves trying to find ways in which we can give money to eternal things. Open heart, open wallet; closed heart, closed wallet.

There is nothing in money that will satisfy a person. Whenever money satisfies one desire, it creates two or three more desires. Yet money is the one thing that seems to dominate many of us. We think that if we just have a little more, we will be happy. It is a subtle and formidable trap. Like a duped donkey, we trot mindlessly after the carrot of happiness we will never catch. Matthew 6:19-21 tells us, "Do not lay up for yourselves treasures on earth. . . . For where your treasure is, there your heart will be also." Money is a great servant but a terrible master.

Conclusion

It is important to lock the six recurring themes into our conscious thinking, because the need for them will come up continuously. They are found throughout the Bible because they are found throughout life. As we look into the mirror of the Word, we must adjust our belief and our behavior to reflect these valuable and vital truths.

 Snapshot

What Is the Root of All Evil?

Four out of five people incorrectly believe the Bible teaches that money is the root of all evil. The actual teaching is that the *love* of money is the root of all kinds of evil.

Barna, *Index of Leading Spiritual Indicators*, 80.

Instant Recall:

What are six major themes that recur in the Bible?

1. We must view the
   p_____with
   eternity in mind.

2. God d_____us
   when we do wrong.

3. Good
   r_____
   make life rewarding.

4. God fights our s_____b_____for us.

5. God sustains us through s_____.

6. If God has our hearts, He will also have our
   m_____.

Let Me Ask You

1. Which of the themes in this chapter was the most expected theme to you? Why?

2. Which theme was the most surprising to you? Why?

3. How do you think your life would change if you kept all these themes in your conscious thoughts throughout a typical day?

Action Line

Read: My book *30 Days to Understanding What Christians Believe* has much more helpful information about this subject.

Memorize: Colossians 3:1-2.

Pray: Dear Lord, thank You that You have let us know the really important principles that should guide our lives. Help me to keep them in my conscious thoughts as I live my day, and may they make a difference in my life. Amen.

How Can We Understand the Bible?

CHAPTER
12

Chapter at a Glance

- The Holy Spirit enables us to understand Scripture.

- We must carefully observe what the Bible says.

- We must use responsible principles of interpretation.

- We must apply Scripture to our lives.

Well Said

Disregard the study of God and you sentence yourself to stumble and blunder throughout life, blindfolded, as it were, with no sense of direction and no understanding of what surrounds you.

—James I. Packer

Joining the Battle

A U.S. Army officer once told of the contrast in his pupils during two different eras of teaching at the artillery training school at Fort Sill, Oklahoma. In 1958–1960,

Fact File

How to Understand the Bible

Observation of the text comes first. The key question is, what does it say?

Interpretation of the text comes second. At this point you attempt to answer the question, what does it mean?

Application is the final step. The pertinent question is, what does it mean to me?

a time of world peace, the attitude was so lax that the instructors had a problem getting the men to stay awake to listen. During the 1965–1967 classes, however, the men, hearing the same basic lectures, were alert and took copious notes. The reason? These men knew that in less than six weeks they would be facing the enemy in Vietnam.

If we want the Bible to come alive to us, we must dedicate ourselves to pursuing God and obeying His commands and instructions as well as reaching out to and helping other people for Christ.

The Holy Spirit Enables Us to Understand Scripture

The foundation for effective and meaningful Bible study is spiritual rebirth. We read in 1 Corinthians 2:14, that "the natural man [the non-Christian] does not receive the things of the Spirit of God, for they are foolishness to him; nor can he know them, because they are spiritually discerned." If a person isn't a Christian, he cannot grasp the spiritual truths of the Scripture. He can learn all there is to know about people, places, and events, but grasping the spiritual truths behind them and being changed by them is beyond him. Like an FM radio trying to pick up TV signals, he has no capacity to receive anything.

When a person is born again, he can have the illumining ministry of the Holy Spirit to him. In 1 Corinthians 2:9-10 we read: "Eye has not seen, nor ear heard, nor have entered into the heart of man the things which God has prepared for those who love Him. But God has revealed them to us through His Spirit."

God reveals things to us through His Spirit that we would not know otherwise. This is not the giving of new revelation but rather the enabling of us to understand what He has already revealed in the Scriptures (2 Cor. 3:14-16; 4:6; Eph. 1:17-18; 3:18-19). Such understanding does not always come easily. Proverbs 25:2 says, "It is the glory of God to conceal a matter, but the glory of kings is to search out a matter." Pearls of deeper truth are not often revealed to the careless or ambivalent. But the Holy Spirit *will* open the mind of the Christian to the truth of Scripture as that Christian tackles the Scripture seriously.

In addition to our being spiritually capable of understanding the Bible, we must also exercise personal responsibility if we are to understand the Bible. Effective Bible study involves three steps carried out in a specific order.

We Must Carefully Observe What the Bible Says

We observe the Bible by developing a strategy that forces us to look closely at the text.

1. Basic questions. Rudyard Kipling once wrote,

> I keep six honest serving men
> (They taught me all I knew);
> Their names are What and Why and When
> And How and Where and Who.

As we read the Scripture, we ask ourselves . . .

- *Who?* Who is the author? To whom is he writing? Who is he writing about?

- *What?* What happened and in what order? What ideas are presented?

- *Where?* Where did this take place? Study with a map and every time a place is mentioned, look it up on the map.

- *When?* When was the letter written and when did the events in the text take place? Look it up in a Bible dictionary or handbook. When do certain things in the letter happen in relationship to other events in the letter?

- *Why?* Why does a particular person do or say something? Why is a particular teaching presented?

- *How?* How are things accomplished? How well? By what method?

2. Key words. Look for key words—those words that seem most important for understanding the passage. Repetition of a word, phrase, or clause is often a good clue as to what the author is attempting to communicate.

Comparisons show how things are alike. Connectives used to indicate comparisons include "also," "as," "even so," "just as . . . so," "like," "likewise," and "too." For example, in James 3:3-5 the tongue is compared to the bit in a horse's mouth, a ship's rudder, and a spark that starts a forest fire in that all are small but influential.

▼▼▼▼▼▼▼▼▼

The Bible will never contradict itself.

▲▲▲▲▲▲▲▲▲

Contrasts show how things differ. Sample connectives include "although," "but," "however," "much more," "nevertheless," and "yet." Galatians 5:19-23 contrasts the deeds of the flesh with the fruit of the Spirit.

Repetition signals what is important by mentioning words, people, circumstances, events, and other Scripture.

Volume indicates the importance of something by the amount of space devoted to a matter.

Many other strategies are possible to help a person observe closely the message of the Bible. The key is to read closely and observe the text by these and other strategies that you may learn or know.

We Must Use Responsible Principles of Interpretation

In his poem "The Everlasting Gospel" William Blake wrote, "Both read the Bible day and night/But thou readest black where I read white."

Differences in opinion and interpretation are inevitable, but the more responsible our principles of interpretation are, the more confidence we can have in our understanding of the Bible. Not everything in the Bible can be known with 100 percent certainty. However, we can have confidence that something seems 100 percent certain, 75 percent certain, or 50 percent certain if we are careful to interpret Scripture well.

There are several principles of interpretation that must be followed for *any* passage of Scripture.

1. Consider the context. The meaning of any passage of Scripture will be consistent with what comes before and after the passage. Too often we are guilty of taking brief passages (often verses or portions of verses) out of context and quoting them in support of a position.

In an extreme example that makes the point, a Christian counselor reported that a woman he was counseling told him that God had revealed to her that she was to divorce her husband and marry another man with whom she was romantically involved. She came to this conclusion on the basis of Paul's exhortation in Ephesians 4:24, "Put on the new man."[1] Even a cursory reading of the context makes it clear that Paul was referring to adopting new Christian behavior in light of having become a Christian, and has nothing whatsoever to do with a new husband.

Correct interpretation of a passage requires us to look at (1) the immediate context; (2) the book context; (3) the context of other writings by the same author (if available); (4) the context of the Testament you are studying (Old or New); and (5) the entire Bible context. The Bible will never contradict itself, either in the next paragraph or in the last paragraph.

2. Consider the historical-cultural background. All the books of the Bible were written in a specific time and a specific place by a specific person for specific people. If we are going

Think about It

The first skill you need to develop is to train your mind to *see* when you read a passage—to observe carefully the words, to be on the alert for details. Too many of us are in the habit of reading Scripture without seeing very much, without thinking about the words we are seeing. We read words, but we do not observe what the words are saying. Sometimes we do not even see all the words in a passage. We are lazy observers! Because of inaccurate and careless observations, we often make faulty interpretations and shallow applications.

Oletta Wald, *The Joy of Discovery in Bible Study* (Minneapolis: Augsburg, 1975), 16.

Fact File

When Reading the Bible, Ask If There Is . . .

- an example   to   follow
- a   sin   to   avoid
- a   promise   to   claim
- a   prayer   to   repeat
- a   command   to   obey
- a   condition to   meet
- an error   to   mark
- a   challenge to   face

Howard G Hendricks, *Living by the Book* (Chicago: Moody, 1991), 304.

to understand what was written, it is helpful to know about the historical and cultural background of the writing. For example, to a modern audience there is no surprise at the notion of a "Good Samaritan," but in Jesus' day there was such great hatred toward the Samaritans by Jews that the effect of His description would have been as unsettling as a present-day reference to a "Good Terrorist."

A Bible dictionary, Bible handbook, and Bible commentaries give insight on meaning from history and culture.

3. Consider the word meanings. Each word has a range of meanings. For example, the English word "trunk" may refer to the main stem of a tree, a large piece of luggage, an elephant's nose, a person's torso, or the luggage compartment of an automobile. Also, words change meaning over time. The word that in 1611 the King James Version several times translated as "conversation" is not what we mean by that word today (people talking); instead, it means "manner of life" or "conduct" in today's vocabulary. We must be sure the words we read in our Bible mean the same thing today. One of the easiest ways of doing this is to compare how different translations of the Bible render a given word.

Which words merit more detailed study? Words that you don't understand, words that seem central to what the author is saying, and any words that are repeated or given special emphasis.

It is helpful to consult one or two good commentaries after doing one's own study of the passage. A commentary is a book that helps explain the Bible. Commentaries can be purchased at a Christian bookstore.

We Must Apply Scripture to Our Lives

We apply the Bible by studying it diligently, taking its teachings seriously, and committing to do all that we understand of what God wants of us. We must read the Bible continuously asking the question "So what?" What does this mean to me? What should I do? How should I change?

Conclusion

Let Me Ask You

1. What is the biggest obstacle you have, personally, in studying the Bible? Is it a knowledge of how to do Bible study, or just getting the time? How do you think you can overcome that obstacle more effectively?

2. What seems to be the most important and helpful principle of interpretation to you? Why?

3. Why do you think that it is possible for people to know the Bible well and yet not apply it to their lives? What accounts for the lack of impact of the knowledge on behavior? What do you think is the biggest obstacle in your own life in applying the Bible?

There is much more to know about studying the Bible, but this introduces the basics. We must each be born again and must commit our hearts in faith and obedience to learning the Bible and wanting to do what we learn. Then we study the Bible, observing what it says, interpreting its meaning and applying it to our own lives.

Even though we are responsible to read and study the Scriptures on our own, most of us need the help of a good Bible teacher. This may be a pastor, a Sunday school teacher, or a home Bible study teacher. But most of us must place ourselves under a teacher who will guide this process. Otherwise, we may get overwhelmed and quit. Good teachers can turn Bible study, which is a significant challenge, into a rewarding lifetime pursuit.

Studying the Bible is not just a *good* thing or even an *important* thing; it is an *essential* thing if we hope to achieve our potential in Christ and live in obedience to Him.

Instant Recall

1. The Holy Spirit enables us to u_____Scripture.

2. We must carefully o_____what the Bible says.

3. We must use responsible principles of i_____.

4. We must a_____the truth of Scripture to our lives.

Action Line

Read: My book *30 Days to Understanding the Bible* has much more helpful information about this subject. If you want to learn even more about this subject, read *Living by the Book* by Howard Hendricks.

Memorize: 1 Corinthians 2:14.

Pray: Dear Lord, thank You that You have given me the ability to understand the Scripture. Thank You that the Holy Spirit lives within me, illumining my mind, encouraging my heart, and strengthening my will. Help me to become a true disciple of Your Word. Amen.

Is Humanity Really Lost?

Chapter at a Glance

- Humanity was created in the image of God.

- God's image was corrupted by sin.

- Evidence demonstrates that humanity is lost.

- The Bible declares that humanity is lost.

Well Said

We are not sinners because we sin. We sin because we are sinners.

—Anonymous

Safe at Last!

One time as a teenager I decided, for reasons that no longer seem sufficient, to climb to the top of a city water tower to a catwalk that encircled it. As I got perhaps fifty feet off the ground, I looked down and was seized with panic. Every muscle in my body turned to mush. I began losing my grip. My mouth

The Image of God

The image of God in humanity includes . . .

- a spiritual likeness
- a moral likeness
- an intellectual likeness
- a social likeness

went dry. My mind, involuntarily and relentlessly, replayed a vision of the rung I was holding onto snapping loose from the ladder, sending me plunging backward and upside down to the earth below. I felt sure I was lost . . . a goner! With terror clinging to me like a band of frightened monkeys, I squirmed my way back down to the ground. When my feet touched ground, I had the feeling of having been snatched from disaster.

When I was on the water tower, I was afraid I was lost. But humanity is on the water tower of life. The ladder rung will snap off, sending us to our doom, unless we take steps to be saved.

Humanity Was Created in the Image of God

God did not need to create. There was no lack in Him. Nothing was missing in His life that He needed something to help Him out. Rather, He created all there is for His own glory (Isa. 43:7; Eph. 1:11-12), and our purpose in life is to do all things to the glory of God (1 Cor. 10:31), as well as to have fellowship with God and to enjoy Him forever (Pss. 16:11; 73:25-26).

God created humans in His image. Traditionally, this is referred to with the Latin term *imago Dei* (image of God). This image has been distorted, but not lost, as a result of humanity's sin (Gen. 9:6), and will be perfectly restored when Jesus returns (Rom. 8:29; 1 Cor. 15:49).

But since God does not have a body, the image of God cannot be a physical likeness. So, what does it mean to be created in the image of God?

1. Moral likeness. God has given us an inner sense of right and wrong (Eccl. 3:11; Rom. 2:15). This conscience is intended to prompt us to act in a moral way such that, when we do, we reflect God's moral likeness.

2. Spiritual likeness. We have not only a physical body but also a spirit (John 19:30; Acts 7:59). It is our spirit that is our primary link to God. Our present bodies are corrupted by sin and will never see God. We relate to God spiritually in prayer, in praise, and in worship (John 4:24). Since God is spirit, our spirit reflects His likeness.

3. Intellectual likeness. We have the ability to reason and think logically and to learn in a way that sets us apart from the animal world. Only humans ponder the future, create music, art, and literature, and make scientific and technological advances. Only humans in this sense reflect the image of God.

4. Social likeness. God is a Trinity, that is, there is one God eternally existing in three coeternal and coequal persons. It takes all three members of the Trinity to make up God. Likewise, both male and female make up humanity. It takes the combination of male and female to picture the Trinity. In Genesis 1:27 we read, "God created man in His own image; in the image of God He created him; *male and female He created them*" (italics added). Together, in our maleness and femaleness, humanity reflects the image of God.

There are surely other ways in which humanity could be said to reflect the image of God, but these are major ways that help us see the important truth.

God's Image Was Corrupted by Sin

Humanity was created in the image of God, without sin, and in perfect fellowship and harmony with God. That image has been marred by sin. Adam and Eve rebelled against God in the Garden of Eden. This rebellion contaminated their spirits so that their inner nature tended toward sin (Rom. 7:14-25), and while they were still capable of doing good, they became incapable of not doing wrong. This flawed nature is now passed down to all their descendants (Rom. 5:12-25).

This condition is described as "total depravity," which does not mean that humans are totally bad or even as bad as they could be. Rather, it means that the corruption of humanity is total. We are corrupted not just spiritually but also physically, emotionally, intellectually, socially, and in every other way.

The original sin of Adam and Eve produced universal guilt for all other humans. This might seem unfair until we observe that God has countered that by extending the righteousness of Jesus to all who will accept Him.

Evidence Demonstrates that Humanity Is Lost

1. History suggest that we are lost. The entire story of history tells an endless succession of civilizations that rise on good principles and then fall due to corruption. From ancient Egypt to Israel to Babylonia to Persia to Greece to Rome to Europe to the United States, history is the tale of the rise of great civilizations and their fall because of moral, social, and cultural degeneration. Does this suggest that humanity is basically good?

In our own country, just fifty years ago, the major problems in schools were chewing gum and talking out loud. Today the major problems are physical violence and sexual promiscuity. Who has a solution that can take us back to the days when our problems were so minor? Who knows the path to return us to the time when we all agreed on a moral code that made metal detectors, undercover police, and a call for condom distribution in high schools unnecessary? Who can solve just this one problem in education? No one. Unless God brings renewal, unless God brings a great

Snapshot

Top Five Problems in Public Education in 1950:

1. Chewing gum
2. Talking while the teacher is talking
3. Sassing the teacher
4. Not completing homework
5. Absenteeism

Top Five Problems in Public Education in 1996:

1. Carrying guns to school
2. Teenage pregnancy
3. Drug problems
4. Teenage jobs
5. Crime rate among students

awakening, unless God stirs ou hearts to return to Him and to the principles in His Word, those days will never be seen in America again.

Add to that the profound problems of drug and alcohol abuse, sexually transmitted diseases, physical and sexual abuse, divorce, gang violence, terrorism, and corruption in business and politics, and the problems are compounded beyond comprehension. These are all problems that we cannot solve because they are problems of the heart. Politics and armies cannot change the human heart. We have had over four thousand years of recorded history, and it all suggests that while there is good in humanity, nevertheless humanity is inherently and fatally flawed by sin.

In a Nutshell

The Lostness of the Race

Three lines of evidence, outside the Bible, demonstrate that humanity is lost:

- evidence from history
- evidence from our conscience
- evidence from our experience

2. Our conscience suggests that we are lost. Do you do things sometimes even though you know they are wrong? Do you sometimes fail to do things, even though you know they are right? Are you a perfect human being, even by your own standards, let alone God's? No, you are not incapable of doing good. But at the same time, you are incapable of not doing evil.

I came to the conclusion, early in my Christian experience, that I could make myself do almost anything I wanted to, except *desire* to do only good all the time. My "wanter" is basically flawed. And even if it weren't, I still don't believe I could perform perfectly. It just isn't in me. It isn't in anyone. My conscience tells me that something is wrong with me. My conscience tells me that I am lost and need to be saved.

3. Our experience suggests that we are lost. Most people look to this world to give us a sense of purpose and meaning in life. We may be looking to a career, education, relationships, or toys that we think will make us happy and fulfilled. But many discover that if they get what they want from this world, it doesn't satisfy. An emptiness seeps up from somewhere deep within, and a muffled alarm sounds that will not go away. The phrase "Is this really all there is?" chimes on the hour and grows into a relentless reminder of the futility of life.

But there are others who don't succeed in life. They don't come close to their aspirations. Oscar Wilde once said, "In this world there are only two tragedies. One is not getting what one wants, and the other is getting it." Both people know in some way that things aren't right. They might not describe themselves as "lost," but they would agree that they need an answer from outside themselves, a power greater than themselves.

4. The death of Christ suggests that we are lost. The death that Jesus died on the cross was a truly horrible death. First, there was the physical agony. When He arrived at the place of crucifixion, they drove nails through His hands and feet. But this is worse than we think at first. These nails

The Cruelty of Crucifixion

Crucifixion was one of the most cruel forms of execution ever devised. Typically a person was tied to the cross and might hang there for days. Sometimes, to hasten the death, the legs were broken so they could no longer push themselves up to be able to breathe. They died by suffocation.

Jesus was nailed to the cross and died in only a matter of hours. His legs were not broken.

were not the smooth construction nails that we know today. They were more like small railroad spikes, squared off instead of round, and ragged on the edges. And they nailed them, not through His hands and feet, which would have been bad enough, but through His wrist and ankles, ripping and tearing the flesh and cartilage and dislodging the small bones in those areas.

The only way He could breathe was to push up on His feet, which had the nails driven through them. It was one agony if He did and another agony if He didn't. He hung there for hours until mercifully He died.

Second, there is the spiritual agony. That which is holy (Jesus) must be horrified with that which is unholy (sin). Yet, on the cross, Jesus had the sin of the world placed on Him. It must have offended Him, just as we are offended by ugly, violent, or sordid things that violate our sensibility. Why would Jesus have endured that? After all, He didn't have to. In John 10:18 we hear Him say, "No one takes [my life] from Me, but I lay it down." He could have called ten thousand angels to destroy the world and set Him free.

Why would He have endured the cross if it were not for some colossal reason? Would He have endured it if humanity were basically good and not in need of salvation? Would He have done it if humanity could have had its sin overlooked and gone to heaven anyway? It is unthinkable. The crucifixion is only rational if humanity is lost, if, being motivated by a profound love for us, Jesus decided to die in our place so we could live in His. For me, no other explanation is adequate.

The Bible Declares that Humanity Is Lost

If we take the Bible at face value, we simply cannot avoid the fact that humanity is lost and in need of personal salvation. In Romans, two verses combine with particular force: "All have sinned and fall short of the glory of God" (Rom. 3:23) and "The wages of sin is death, but the gift of God is eternal life in Christ Jesus our Lord" (Rom. 6:23). Many other passages of Scripture reinforce this combined truth (Acts 4:12; Rom. 5:8-10; Eph. 2:8-10), but these two are enough to nail the lid on our coffin. The Bible leaves no room for debate. Humanity is lost and needs to be saved.

Think about It

If you don't believe that humanity is lost . . .

- You have to explain why no good civilizations in history have been able to sustain themselves.

- You have to explain why your own conscience accuses you of guilt.

- You have to explain why your own experience in life fails to convince you that you are basically good.

Conclusion

We see, then, from history, our own conscience, our experience, and Scripture that humanity is unreconciled to God. But if we repent and commit our lives to Christ, our sins are forgiven and we are saved—we live with God and His children in peace, love, and joy in heaven forever.

Instant Recall

1. Humanity was created in the i_____ of God.

2. God's image was c_____ by sin.

3. Evidence demonstrates that humanity is l_____.

4. The B_____ declares that humanity is lost.

Let Me Ask You

1. What evidence have you seen in your own experience or observation that convinces you that humanity is lost?

2. If you were Jesus, would you have been willing to endure what He endured for us if we did not need to be saved?

3. What would you tell someone who did not believe that humanity was lost? What is the most convincing point?

Action Line

Read: My book *What You Need to Know about Salvation* has much more helpful information about this subject.

Memorize Romans 3:23 and 6:23.

Pray: Dear Lord, thank You for saving me. Thank You for not leaving me to try to save myself. Thank You for paying the awful price for my sin. Help me to appreciate it, and give me confidence to share the good news with others. Amen.

How Can We Be Saved?

Chapter at a Glance

- We are predestined to salvation.
- God's grace is the basis of salvation.
- We are saved through faith.
- We repent of sin for salvation.
- We can be assured of our salvation.
- We are eternally secure.
- Christians cannot commit the unpardonable sin.
- Jesus is the only way of salvation.

CHAPTER 14

Well Said

To run and work, the law commands, Yet gives us neither feet nor hands. But better news the gospel brings; It bids us fly, and give us wings.

—Anonymous

Crawling for Salvation

There are two extremes to which people commonly go regarding salvation. One is thinking that everyone has to earn his or her salvation. The other is thinking that everyone will be saved, regardless.

I will never forget, as a young seminary student, standing in the large central square in Mexico City watching a lady crawl on her hands and knees over hard, uneven stone pavement toward the cathedral on the square. She was weeping and praying. Her hands and knees were beginning to bleed. Everyone walked past her as if she were not there.

▼▼▼▼▼▼▼▼▼

Grace is what motivated God to offer us salvation, even though we did not earn it.

▲▲▲▲▲▲▲▲▲

I stood and stared. I wanted somehow to help her but didn't know how. I learned later that that is common in Mexico. People think they have to suffer to prove their sincerity and their worth to God. They think they have to earn their salvation.

On the other hand, others think everyone will go to heaven, regardless of what they do—that they can live like the devil in this life and still go to heaven in the next. This is called "universalism," and it is based on the assumption that God is too loving and kind to send anyone to hell.

Both of these extremes are untrue. The Bible makes it clear that you cannot get to heaven by your own good works (Titus 3:5), and makes it equally true that not everyone is going there (Matt. 7:13-14; Rev. 20:15).

So, if those two instinctive extremes are incorrect, how do we get to heaven?

We Are Predestined to Salvation

"Predestination" is the teaching that God has chosen, before the creation of the world, who will be saved and who will not (John 13:18; Eph. 1:3-14; 2 Thess. 2:13-15).

"Free will" is the opposite teaching, that while certainly some things are predestined, salvation is a result of a person's free will. The Bible seems to teach that people have a free will (Matt. 23:37; John 7:17; Rom. 7:18; etc.) and that God's predestination is based on God's foreknowledge (Rom. 8:29-30; 1 Pet. 1:2). That is, that He looks ahead in time and sees who will accept Him and who won't, and after that foreknowledge, chooses those who will believe.

"Antinomy" is a third position, which holds that these other two truths appear to be mutually exclusive, and that if we hold clearly to one, we violate the other. There-fore, both truths are held simultaneously, in tension, waiting for the coming of Christ when all things will be known and fully understood. In support of this idea, the Trinity is pointed out as another biblical doctrine that seems to be inherently contradictory but that we hold, nevertheless, because otherwise we fall clearly into error.

God's Grace Is the Basis of Salvation

Primarily, grace means "unmerited favor" or "undeserved favor." God loves you and has provided you a way to be spared the normal conse-

Fact File

To Believe Means to Commit

The Greek word for faith is *pistis*. It is usually translated "faith" or "belief." The verb form of the word is *pisteuo*, which means "to believe." It can be translated "commit" or "entrust." In John 2:24 the apostle John wrote, "Jesus did not commit Himself to them, because He knew all men." The word "commit" in this passage is the word *pisteuo*.

quence of sin, which is spiritual death and separation from God. Ephesians 2:8-9 tells us, "By grace you have been saved through faith, and that not of yourselves; it is the gift of God." Titus 3:5 tells us, "Not by works of righteousness which we have done, but according to His mercy He saved us." Good works can't save us. Only His grace can.

We Are Saved through Faith

We are saved *by* grace *through* faith. That is, grace is what motivated God to offer us salvation, even though we did not earn it. But not everyone is saved. We must believe what God says about how to be saved and accept His commands.

Faith does not mean merely to believe information about something. It means to place one's trust in that information. The illustration is often told of a man who strung a tightwire across

Niagara Falls and walked across it pushing a barrel. Then he asked the onlookers who among them thought he could push a person across in the barrel. Everyone raised his hand. Then he asked for volunteers. No one raised a hand. If a person had had biblical faith in the tightrope walker, he would have gotten in the barrel. Biblical faith believes what God has said and acts appropriately.

We Repent of Sin for Salvation

Repentance means "changing one's mind." It is the other side of the coin from faith. If previously we rejected Jesus but now we accept Him, we have repented. We have changed our mind about Jesus. Seen properly, repentance and faith are essentially the same thing. One cannot have true faith without repenting. One cannot repent without true faith.

Fact File

Repentance Means Dying to Self

C. S. Lewis once wrote:

Fallen man is not simply an imperfect creature who needs improvement; he is a rebel who must lay down his arms . . . . This process of surrender— this movement full speed astern—is what Christians call repentance. Now repentance is no fun at all. It is something much harder than merely eating humble pie. It means unlearning all the self-conceit and self-will that we have been training ourselves into for thousands of years. It means killing part of yourself, undergoing a kind of death.

C. S. Lewis, *Mere Christianity* (New York: Macmillan, 1960), 38–39.

We Can Be Assured of Our Salvation

Assurance is the confidence that Christians are, in fact, saved. It is not uncommon for Christians to struggle with doubts as to whether or not they are saved. But Scripture gives assurance that we can know that we are saved:

1. Psalm 130:4—"There is forgiveness with You, that You may be feared." This passage tells us that it is possible to be forgiven.

2. John 6:37—"The one who comes to me I will by no means cast out." We must come to Jesus, believe in Him, and ask Him to save us. He does not ignore our pleadings to be saved.

3. 1 John 5:12—"He who has the Son has life; he who does not have the Son of God does not have life." If we come to Jesus, and as He does not cast us out, we have Jesus and have life.

We Are Eternally Secure

Eternal security is the belief that once Christians are saved they will always be saved. There are some passages that seem to suggest one can lose his or her salvation (Mark 13:14; 1 Cor. 6:27; 15:2; Gal. 5:4; Heb; 6:4-6; 10:28-29), and others that seem to suggest that one cannot (John 10:27-30; Rom. 8:1, 29, 35-39; 11:29; Phil. 1:6; 2 Tim. 1:12; Eph. 1:13-14; 1 Pet. 1:5).

Calvinists (named after John Calvin, a leader of the Protestant Reformation in the 1500s) believe that a person who is genuinely saved cannot lose his salvation. He may "backslide" for a time into sinful behavior, but he will never be lost, since our salvation was dependent upon the grace of God in the first place. Calvinists point to Ephesians, where we see that our salvation is the result of

*   His will, not ours (1:5)

*   His grace, not ours (1:6-7)

*   His purpose, not ours (1:11)

*   His power, not ours (1:12, 14)

*   His calling, not ours (1:18)

According to these passages, it seems that we did not save ourselves; He saves us. We do not keep ourselves; He keeps us. We are not secure in ourselves; we are secure in Him.

Another group (including those called Arminians, after the 16th-century Dutch theologian Jacobus Arminius) believe that it is possible to lose one's salvation, citing the verses referenced above, and making the logical point that if someone accepted Jesus of his own free will, he could reject Him subsequently of his own free will. Add to this the fact that people have claimed and seemingly demonstrated Christ and then have fallen back into flagrant sinful living. The Bible seems to say that people who are settled down and comfortable in flagrant sin will not inherit the kingdom of God.

▼▼▼▼▼▼▼▼

One thing is certain. God will save whoever comes to Him.

▲▲▲▲▲▲▲▲

It seems to me that the eternal security position is the stronger of the two positions. But while earnest Christians disagree on the issue of eternal security, one thing is certain. God will save whoever comes to Him.

Christians Cannot Commit the Unpardonable Sin

In the Gospels Jesus speaks of an unpardonable sin (Matt. 12:32; Mark 3:29-30). Shortly after I became a Christian, when someone told me of the unpardonable sin, I shouted, "I don't want to know what it is!" As long as I didn't know what it was, it might not occur to me to do it. My friend wisely informed me that I could not do it, that only an unwillingness to repent was unpardonable.

In the Gospels, Pharisees, who appeared to know who Jesus was but were unwilling to repent because of jealousy, attributed the work of the Holy Spirit to the devil. Jesus said that was unforgivable. Exactly why is open to debate. Some say that even if the Pharisees later repented, the sin would not be forgiven. That, however, seems inconsistent with the character of God. Rather, it seems less troublesome to say that knowingly attributing the Holy Spirit's work to the devil is a sign of a heart so hardened that it is no longer capable of repentance. If so, it might be an example of the condition Paul described in Romans 1:24, "God . . . gave them up to uncleanness," and 1:26, "God gave them up to vile passions."

If you are a Christian, you need not be concerned with committing the unpardonable sin. If you are concerned about sin and willing to repent, you need not be concerned with committing it. Those who have committed it could not care less. They willingly committed it with their eyes wide open.

Jesus Is the Only Way of Salvation

There are various perspectives on who will be saved and who will be lost:

1. Everyone will be saved and no one lost.
2. Only those who have committed truly awful sins (Hitler, etc.) will be lost.
3. All who are sincere will be saved. It doesn't matter what you believe as long as you are sincere.
4. No one can go to heaven except through Jesus.

All these positions cannot be correct; they are mutually contradictory. If you take the teaching of Scripture at face value, it is quite clear on this matter:

1. Not everyone will be saved (Matt. 25:41 -42).
2. Some who committed awful sins will be saved, and some who did not commit awful sins will be lost (Matt. 26:74-75; Titus 3:5).
3. It does matter what you believe, regardless of how sincere you are (Acts 17:22-31).
4. No one can go to heaven except through Jesus (John 14:6; Acts 4:12).

Conclusion

The doctrine of salvation contains some of the most difficult and controversial teachings in the church. If God is sovereign, how can people be free? What is required for salvation—faith alone? faith plus repentance? faith plus repentance plus sorrow for sin? Is it once saved, always saved? Yet those who hold to a high view of Scripture have always agreed on one central truth: God will save whoever comes to Him in faith. He will not turn anyone away.

Instant Recall

1. We are p_____ to salvation.

2. God's g_____ is the basis of salvation.

3. We are saved through f_____.

4. We repent of sin for s_____.

5. We can be a_____ of our salvation.

6. We are e_____ secure.

7. Christians cannot commit the u_____ sin.

8. Jesus is the o_____ way of salvation.

Action Line

Read: My book *What You Need to Know about Salvation* has much more helpful information about this subject.

Memorize: Ephesians 2:8-9.

Let Me Ask You ?

1. What seems to be the most important implication to you of the fact that you are saved by grace through faith?

2. Have you ever struggled with assurance of your salvation? What help has this chapter given you in your struggle?

3. If there anything in your life for which you need to repent? What do you have to do to fully repent?

Share: Talk over this material with someone—a friend, family member, or someone in your church—in order to learn it better.

Pray: Dear Lord, thank You for Your grace that saves me, and for giving me the faith to accept Your free gift of life Amen.

What Happens When I Am Saved?

I'm not what I want to be,
I'm not what I'm going to be,
But thank God, I'm not what I was.

—Anonymous

Stop the World

If you could stop the world and fix its problems . . . if you could freeze everyone for a time, like stopping a movie halfway through, and correct all the ills . . . if you could build a home and hospital and school for everyone in the world, clothe them, feed them, and put money in the bank for them . . . if you could take guns away from criminals, armies away from dictators, and missiles away from countries . . . if you could hang copies of the Magna Carta, the Declaration of Independence, and the Ten Commandments on every important wall . . . if you could get everything just the way you wanted it, and then let the world start spinning again, it would not be long before it would be in just the same mess it is in today. The problems of the world are not, at the core, problems of economy or education or politics. They are problems of the heart.

Until the human heart is corrected, the troubles of civilization cannot be corrected. The need is not for rehabilitation or reeducation but for regeneration. And that is just what happens when I am saved. A series of things happen in my heart that make all the difference, not just in this life but in the next.

I Am Regenerated

People often discuss what it means to be a Christian. The discussion ranges from what one believes to how "good" one must

 Snapshot

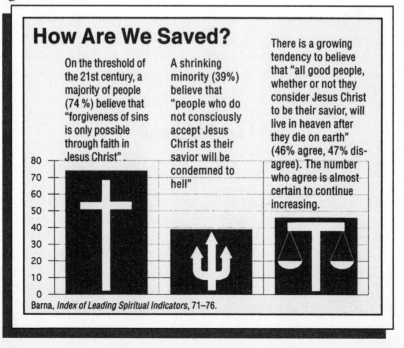

How Are We Saved?

On the threshold of the 21st century, a majority of people (74 %) believe that "forgiveness of sins is only possible through faith in Jesus Christ".

A shrinking minority (39%) believe that "people who do not consciously accept Jesus Christ as their savior will be condemned to hell"

There is a growing tendency to believe that "all good people, whether or not they consider Jesus Christ to be their savior, will live in heaven after they die on earth" (46% agree, 47% disagree). The number who agree is almost certain to continue increasing.

Barna, *Index of Leading Spiritual Indicators*, 71–76.

Redemption

When we take all three of the pertinent words together to form a composite picture of redemption, we see that with Christ's death on the cross believers in Him have been

(1) purchased,

(2) removed from the marketplace of sin, and

(3) set free to live a new life.

be in his or her lifestyle. However, a Christian is someone to whom something very specific has happened. Before this thing happens to him, he is not a Christian, and after this thing has happened to him, he is a Christian. This "thing" is that he is regenerated.

Jesus described it as being born again. In the Gospel of John we read how Nicodemus, a member of the elite religious ruling party, came to Jesus by night to talk with Him. In the course of the conversation, Jesus told him that he must be born again if he was to see the kingdom of heaven (John 3:1-21).

Paul wrote in Ephesians 2:1, "[You] were dead in trespasses and sins." In what way were they dead? Physically? Obviously not. Dead people don't read letters from other people. They were dead spiritually.

Paul went on, "But God, who is rich in mercy, because of His great love with which He loved us, even when we were dead in trespasses, made us alive together with Christ" (Eph. 2:4-5). That is what it means to be born again. It means "to be made alive," spiritually.

I Am Redeemed

Redemption has several dictionary meanings coming from different Greek words that are all translated "redeem." First, it can mean "to purchase from the marketplace." This would be the same word you would use if you were to buy a potato from the local market. The word is *agorazo*, which comes from the word for "marketplace." In relation to our salvation, it means simply to pay the price that our sin demanded (Rev. 5:9).

The second word is the same word, *agorazo*, with the prefix *ex-* added to it. *Ex-* means "out of." So *exagorazo* means not only to pay the purchase price but also to take us out of the market-place. So, in relation to our salvation, it means that not only did Christ pay the price for our sin but also He removed us from the "marketplace" of sin. "Christ has redeemed (*exagorazo*) us from the curse of the law, having become a curse for us" (Gal 3:13).

The third word is an entirely different word, *lutrao*, which means to pay a ransom, so that the "held" one can be freed. "You were not redeemed (*lutrao*) with corruptible things, like silver or gold, from your aimless conduct received by tradition from your fathers, but with the precious blood of Christ, as of a lamb without blemish and without spot" (1 Pet. 1:18-19).

Fact File

Justification

The *Evangelical Dictionary of Biblical Theology* defines justification as "to pronounce, accept, and treat as [righteous], and not . . . liable, and, on the other hand, entitled to all the privileges due to those who have kept the laws." It declares a "verdict of acquittal, and so excluding all possibility of condemnation., Justification thus settles the legal status of the person justified."

Walter A. Elwell, ed., *Evangelical Dictionary of Biblical Theology* (Grand Rapids: Baker, 1984), 593.

I Am Justified

Justification is being declared righteous by God. Being *declared* righteous by God cannot happen unless we *are* righteous in God's eyes. God does not use sleight of hand or smoke and mirrors to get us into heaven. But how can God see us being righteous when we know we have sin in our lives? Does God look the other way when we sin? Does He pretend not to see? How can God declare us righteous if we sin?

Scripture helps us begin to nail down some answers to these questions. Romans 5:1 says, "Having been justified by faith, we have peace with God through our Lord Jesus Christ." How did we gain this peace with God through justification? Romans 4:2-3 tells us: "If Abraham was justified by works, he has something to boast about, but not before God. For what does the Scripture say? *'Abraham believed God, and it was accounted to him for righteousness.'"*

We see, then, that we are justified the way all people of all times have been justified: through faith. As James I. Packer states in his book *Concise Theology*:

> God's justifying judgment seems strange, for pronouncing sinners righteous may appear to be precisely the unjust action on the judge's part that God's own law forbade (Deut. 25:1, Prov. 17:15). Yet it is in fact a just judgment, for its basis is the righteousness of Jesus Christ who as "the last Adam" (1 Cor. 15:45), our representative head acting on our behalf, obeyed the law that bound us and endured the retribution for lawlessness that was our due and so (to use a medieval technical term) "merited" our justification. So we are justified justly, on the basis of justice done (Rom. 3:25-26) and Christ's righteousness reckoned to our account. (Rom. 5:18-19)[1]

When we give our lives to Christ to follow Him, our sins are forgiven, we are born again, and Jesus' righteousness becomes ours. Everything that Christ made possible (forgiveness of sin and the conferring of righteousness to us) is brought forward, in the mind of God, to the moment of our salvation when we are "crucified with Christ" (Gal. 2:20). We have peace with God (Rom. 5:1); we are saved from God's wrath (Rom. 5:9); we are glorified (Rom. 8:30); and we become heirs, having the hope of eternal life (Titus 3:7).

I Am Adopted

Adoption is being taken into and made a legal member of another family, with all the rights and privileges of that family. In Ephesians 1:5 the apostle Paul likened this adoption to the Roman concept of adoption, and said that that which is true of adoption in the Roman world is true of us in the spiritual world. We were absolutely in the power of sin and of the world. We belonged to the family of Adam, lost and without hope. But God, through Jesus, took us out of that family and adopted us into His, and that adoption wipes out the past and makes us new.

We know we are imperfect children. In spite of that, God chose us before the foundation of the world (Eph. 1:5) to be His children. Knowing full well, ahead of time, every sin we would ever commit, He adopted us anyway, clearing our name of all the debts of our old family, Adam's, through the death of Jesus on the cross.

These things are true whether or not we believe them and whether or not we "feel" as though they are true. Just as the earth is round, even though the landscape before us looks

Fact File

Roman Adoption

"When the [Roman] adoption was complete it was complete indeed. The person who had been adopted had all the rights of a legitimate son in his new family and completely lost all rights in his old family. In the eyes of the law he was a new person. So new was he that even all debts and obligations connected with his previous family were abolished as if they had never existed."

William Barclay, *Barclay's Daily Study Bible Commentary* (Raleigh, N.C.: IBM Corp. Pub., 1993), Ephesians 1:5.

flat, we have learned to accept the fact that the earth is round, in spite of what we see. That is exactly what we must do regarding our standing before God. We must accept that He loves us, that we are His children, that we are adopted into His family with all its rights and privileges. We may call Him "Abba," which means "Papa" or "Daddy" (Rom. 8:15). He has chosen us as His children to show love and kindness to us forever.

That is what it means to be adopted. It is not merely a legal term. It is a deeply personal term. It is not just that there is an absence of malice but that there is a presence of love. Envision the best of what earthly families have to offer, and you have a glimpse of what heaven has to offer us as God's children.

I Am United with Christ

To be united with Christ is to become one with Him spiritually. When a woman gets married, the Bible says, she becomes one with her husband (Gen. 2:24). It's like that with us and Christ.

Grace Kelly, one of the true megastars in Hollywood in the 1950s, was one of the most beautiful women in the world. She was courted by Prince Rainier of Monaco, and eventually married him. Even though she was rich, beautiful, and famous, she was considered a "commoner" by royalty. But this commoner became a princess. After a lavish, storybook wedding, Grace Kelly of Hollywood became Princess Grace of Monaco. Prince Rainier's wealth became hers. She dropped her last name and took his. His title became hers. His life of royalty became hers. His destiny became hers as a result of her union with him.

So it is with Christ and us. We become one with Him. We are joined to Him. We become, as the Bible describes it, "in Christ." His wealth, His position, His inheritance, His life becomes ours. The Bible describes elements of our union with Christ:

We are crucified with Him. Galatians 2:20

We died with Him. Colossians 2:20

We are buried with Him. Romans 6:4

We are made alive with Him. Ephesians 2:5

We are raised with Him. Colossians 3:1

We will suffer with Him. Romans 8:17

We are glorified with Him. Romans 8:17

We are joint heirs with Him. Romans 8:17

This is a judicial union with Christ in which God the Father sees us in Christ. When God sees the merit of the cross, He sees Christ and us together. The benefits of Christ's death are credited to us.

Conclusion

If Publisher's Clearing House knocked on our door and gave us a check for $10 million, we would be delirious with joy. Yet the truth of what we have in Christ may not always make us delirious with joy, because it is too much for us to take in. But when we stand before Christ in heaven, able to grasp the marvelous truths of our union with Him, $10 million will seem insignificant by comparison.

Instant Recall

1. I am r_____.
2. I am r_____.
3. I am j_____.
4. I am a_____.
5. I am u_____with Christ.

Action Line

Read: My book *What You Need to Know about Salvation* includes more helpful information about this subject.

Memorize: Romans 5:1.

Pray: Dear Lord, thank You that You have made me to be born again, a new creation in Christ, guiltless before You, and a member of Your family. It is almost too much to take in. Help me to live a life worthy of the position You have given me in Jesus. Amen.

Think about It

1. If you don't know you're regenerated, you may be unclear on what it means to be a Christian, thinking that somehow it has to do with good works or religious activity.

2. If you don't know you're justified, you won't understand that your slate is clear before God, and you won't be able to relax in your relationship with Him.

3. If you don't know you're adopted, you may not have the joy that is possible through knowing God loves you so much.

4. If you don't know you're united with Christ, you may not grasp your importance to God or the wealth and position that is yours.

What Is the Spiritual War?

Well Said

In Scripture the visitation of an angel is always alarming; it has to begin by saying "Fear not." [In the arts] the Victorian angel looks as if it were going to say "There, there."

—C. S. Lewis

Angels at Work

John Paton, a missionary in the New Hebrides Islands, told a story involving the protective care of angels. Hostile natives surrounded his mission headquarters one night, intent on burning out the Patons and killing them. John Paton and his wife prayed all during that terror-filled night that God would deliver them. When daylight came, they were amazed to see the attackers unaccountably leave.

A year later the chief of the tribe was converted to Christ, and Paton, remembering what had happened, asked the chief what had kept him and his men from burning down the house and killing them. The chief replied in surprise, "Who were all those men you had there with you?" The missionary answered, "There were no men there; just my wife and I." The chief argued that they had seen many men standing guard—hundreds of big men in shining garments with drawn swords in their hands. They seemed to circle the mission station, so the natives were afraid to attack. Only then did the Reverend Paton realize that God had sent His angels to protect them.[1]

What do you think when you hear stories like the Reverend Paton's? They are so far beyond our normal experience that most of us are tempted to shake our heads in disbelief. We must conclude that he is a liar or he is deluded or what he said actually happened.

Do we assume he is a liar? He is not known as a liar. Do we accuse him of being deluded? He has shown no signs of delusion in any other area of his life. If we look at his story without a bias against him, we would assume that what he said is true unless evidence demonstrates otherwise.

The Bible tells us that angels, demons, and Satan are real, and that every Christian is in a spiritual battle we will win if we take on God's protection, and which we will lose if we don't.

Angels Are God's Servants

Angels are spirits who live for the most part in another realm than humanity and do the bidding of God. There are a number of observations from the Bible that we can make about what angels are like:

- Angels are created by God to do His will (Ps. 103:20-21; Col. 1:16).

- They are spirit beings who sometimes take on human form, and we do not know they are angels just from looking at them (Gen. 19:1; Heb. 1:14; 13:2). Sometimes they appear in a body that makes it plain they are angels (John 20:12).

- Countless numbers were all created at the same time; there is a fixed number of them; they are without gender, never marry, and live forever (Matt. 22:30; Luke 20:36).

- They are created higher than humans for now, but when we get to heaven, humans will be higher than angels (Ps. 8:5; 1 Cor. 6:3).

- They have great intelligence and power, though their intelligence and power are limited (Ps. 103:20; Isa. 37:36; Mark 13:32; 1 Pet. 1:12).

- They care about what happens to humans, and rejoice when one becomes a Christian (Luke 15:10). Christians may have guardian angels (Matt. 18:10; Heb. 1:14).

We can also make a number of observations from the Bible about what angels do:

- Angels do whatever God wants them to do (Ps. 103:20-21).

- They punish those who rebel against God (1 Chron. 21:15; Acts 12:23).

- Sometimes they defend and protect God's people (1 Kings 19:5; Dan. 6:22; Acts 5:19; 12:8–11).

- They may guide Christians to witness to certain unbelievers (Acts 8:26).

- They will come with Christ when He returns to earth (Matt. 25:31).

- They appear to be organized in a hierarchy of power (Dan. 10:13, 21; Matt. 26:53; Col. 1:16).

- Angels are somehow interested in and connected to the church today (1 Tim. 5:21; 1 Pet. 1:12).

Demons Are Satan's Servants

Demons are good angels who sinned, following Satan in his rebellion against God, and who now oppose the will of God and do the will of Satan. The Bible also gives us information about the character and work of demons:

▼▼▼▼▼▼▼▼

- They were created as good angels, then for some reason did not keep their proper domain but abandoned their own home and rebelled against God, following Satan (Jude 6).

The heart's true loyalties should lie in discovering the will of God and doing it from the heart.

- Demons appear to be organized into an armylike hierarchy. Some demons may have authority over geographic locations, seeming to be the spiritual power behind the empires of Persia, Babylon,

▲▲▲▲▲▲▲▲

and Tyre, while others focus on individuals (Isa. 14:12-15; Ezek. 28:13-19; Dan. 10:13; Eph. 6:12).

- They have a well-developed system of their own "doctrine" that they promote among humans to deceive and destroy them (1 Tim. 4:1-3).

- Demons can possess individuals, inflict physical maladies, cause insanity or derangement, give a person extraordinary strength, have seemingly supernatural abilities, and can take over a person's life and destiny if allowed (Matt. 9:32-33; 10:8; 17:15-18; Mark 6:13; Luke 8:26-31; Acts 16:16-24; Rom. 1:18-25).

Both angels and demons appear to have a role in the spiritual war in which all Christians find themselves (Eph. 6:12). In addition to these usually unseen hosts of heaven, the Bible identifies three other battle fronts in the spiritual war: the world, the flesh, and the devil.

The World Opposes God

By the world (*kosmos*), we do not mean the globe, the earth. Rather, we mean the realm of humanity that is under the control of Satan (Eph. 6:12) and is set in opposition to God (Eph. 2:1-3).

- The dangers of the world include the lust of the flesh, the lust of the eyes, and the pride of life (1 John 2:16).

- Christians are delivered from the world, transferred from the power of darkness into the kingdom of the Son and His love (Col. 1:13).

- Christians can still love the things of the world, that is, things that are outside the will of God for them (1 John 2:15).

- The heart's true loyalties should lie in discovering the will of God and doing it from the heart. Whenever the heart chooses values, attitudes, or behavior over obedience to God, it is worldly, regardless of whether the value, attitude, or behavior is inherently bad (Rom. 6:13).

The Flesh Opposes God

By flesh, we do not mean our physical body but the sinful attitude of the mind that rejects God. It seems to be a force, almost like spiritual gravity, that pulls us to sin.

- Nothing good dwells in the flesh; it opposes the will of God; it wars against the mind of God and makes us captive to sin (Rom. 7:14-25).

- The flesh has illicit passions and desires (Gal. 5:24), works death (Rom. 7:5), and is characterized by lust (Gal. 5:16; 1 Pet. 4:2; 1 John 2:16).

- The works of the flesh include adultery, sexual immorality, hatred, outbursts of wrath, selfish ambition, envy, murder, etc. (Gal. 5:19-21).

- When we become a Christian, we are no longer "after the flesh" (2 Cor. 10:3; Gal. 2:20).

• But we need to be watchful because the flesh can lure us back into its influence (Rom. 6:19).

The Devil Opposes God

The number of people involved in witchcraft, the occult, and Satanism seems to be on a dramatic increase in the United States. There are a number of observations we can make from the Bible about Satan.

• The name Satan means "adversary" or "enemy." The apostle Peter even called him "your adversary the devil" (1 Pet. 5:8).

• He was an angel who rebelled against God and fell into sin, becoming the ultimate evil being in the universe. His sin was pride. He wanted to be like God, meaning he wanted to be equal with God, equal in authority (Isa. 14.13–15; 1 Tim. 3:6).

 Snapshot

We Doubt the Devil

As we enter the 21st century in America,

52 percent of born-again Christians deny Satan's existence

62 percent of adults do not believe the devil is real

72 percent of Catholics say the devil is nonexistent

More women reject his existence than men (64 percent vs. 59 percent)

Barna, Internet: www.BarnaResource.org

Think about It

- If you don't believe that the devil and demons exist, you may underestimate their ability to influence you and be deceived into thoughts or behavior that are not good.

- If you don't realize the dangers of the world and the flesh, you may fall into behavior that is sinful and harmful.

- Some believe that at that time a third of the good angels followed him into rebellion and became demons (Rev. 12:4, 9—angels are often referred to as "stars").

- He has authority over all the demons, and his goal is to set up his own kingdom and rule in place of God (Ezek. 28:13-19).

- Satan deceives us in order to destroy us. Jesus even called him a murderer, a liar, and the father of all lies (John 8:44; Rev. 9:11; 12:9; 20:10).

- Satan blinds the minds of unbelievers so that they might not believe the gospel. He employs demons to try to defeat believers and tempt us to sin (1 Cor. 7:5; 2 Cor. 4:4; Eph. 6:12-12).

- Satan is extremely powerful and is the god of this age and the prince of the power of the air (2 Cor. 4:4; Eph. 2:2).

- Satan is not all-knowing and not able to be in more than one place at a time, and while he's very powerful, his power is limited. He is extremely intelligent and has an army of demons who carry out his orders, making him even more powerful (Job 1:9-12; 2:4-6; Mark 5:12; 1 John 3:8).

- Satan (and presumably his demons) disguises himself as an angel of light to deceive people into thinking that he and/ or his demons are good spirits, when in fact they are evil (2 Cor. 11:14).

- In the end Jesus will triumph over Satan, who will be eternally judged for his unspeakable evil (Rev. 20:10).

Conclusion

The Bible is open and unembarrassed in talking about angels, demons, and Satan. It readily exposes the dangers of the world and the flesh. In years past these ideas used to be suspect, too unsophisticated for moderns to believe, but no longer. In increasing numbers, people are admitting the reality of the unseen world, the power of dark forces, and the ability to choose good or evil.

In the Bible, whenever an angel appeared, the first words out of its mouth were usually "Fear not." They were initially terrifying. They are awesome, powerful beings who usually deliver messages from God that include judgment on actions and attitudes. They are not genies in a bottle, come to give us three wishes. They are messengers of God, come to represent God to us.

Whether angels or demons, they are tor real. Angels may very well have come in and out of your life without your ever knowing it. They may have been invisible, or they may have taken on a human form so that you would not know they were angels.

Also, demonic forces are to be taken seriously. But they can be successfully resisted, for "He who is in you is greater than he who is in the world" (1 John 4:4). We will deal more fully with this subject in a later chapter, but for now we have established the fact that angels, Satan, and demons are indeed for real.

Let Me Ask You

1. Have you ever had an experience in which you suspect an angel might have visited or helped you?

2. What would you say to someone who said he or she didn't believe the devil exists?

3. What is the greatest danger to you, personally, from the world? the flesh? the devil?

Instant Recall

1. A_____ are God's servants.

2. D_____ are Satan's servants.

3. The w_____ opposes God.

4. The f_____ opposes God.

5. The d_____ opposes God.

Action Line

Read: My book *What You Need to Know about Spiritual Warfare* has much more helpful information about this subject.

Memorize: 1 John 2:15-16.

Pray: Dear Lord, thank You that You have warned me against the enemies I face in the spiritual war. Help me to be alert to them and to resist their influence in my life. Thank You for protecting me. Amen.

How Can We Win the Spiritual War?

Chapter at a Glance

- The belt of truth anchors us.

- The breastplate of righteousness protects us.

- The shoes of peace give us stability.

- The shield of faith wards off blows.

- The helmet of salvation guards our head.

- The sword of the Spirit defends and attacks.

Well Said

Humanity falls into two equal and opposite errors concerning the devil. Either they take him altogether too seriously or they do not take him seriously enough.

—C. S. Lewis

Betting on the Snake

When I was a kid, I remember watching a western on television in which a huckster went from town to town with a huge rattlesnake in a glass cage. The man would cover the glass with a blanket and take it into a saloon. There he would tell the people what was under the blanket in the cage and bet that the toughest, bravest man in town would not be able to hold his hand against the glass without jerking it back when the rattlesnake struck.

After all bets were taken, the huckster tore the blanket off to reveal the coiled snake, its rattles buzzing nervously. When it finally struck the glass, the town tough guy jerked his hand back every time. The huckster collected his money and moved on to the next town to repeat the scene. And he almost always won. Why? Because the tough guys didn't trust the glass.

I have often thought what a great metaphor that scenario was for spiritual warfare. The snake represents Satan and the forces of evil. The glass is Jesus. As long as we stay on the right side of the glass, we have nothing to fear. If we go sticking our hand inside the box, there is plenty to fear.

There are two big things to understand about spiritual warfare: First, there is real danger on the wrong side of the glass. Second, we are safe on the right side of the glass, no matter how frightening things seem.

We must submit to God in all things and resist the devil (James 4:7). Specifically, we must put on the spiritual armor He has provided for us (Eph. 6:10-18).

The Belt of Truth Anchors Us

The belt of truth = commitment to God's truth.

The belt of truth refers to the thick leather belt the Roman soldier wore to hold his tunic in place and to which was attached the sheath for his sword. When the Roman soldier "girded his loins," he tucked his long outer robe under his belt so that it would not get in his way when running or fighting.

Peter used the same imagery in 1 Peter 1:13 when he wrote: "Gird up the loins of your mind, be sober, and rest your hope fully upon the grace that is to be brought to you at the revelation of Jesus Christ." This means "Prepare your minds for action. Get ready for combat. Be self-controlled. Get focused."

In the same way, the Christian must prepare himself for spiritual battle by making a total commitment to the truth of Scripture and by setting his mind to follow that truth.

The Breastplate of Righteousness Protects Us

The breastplate of righteousness =
a lifestyle of trusting obedience to God.

The breastplate was an important part of the Roman soldier's battle gear. It was a metal cast of a human torso that protected the upper part of his body, including his heart and lungs, from the swords, arrows, and spears of the enemy.

 Snapshot

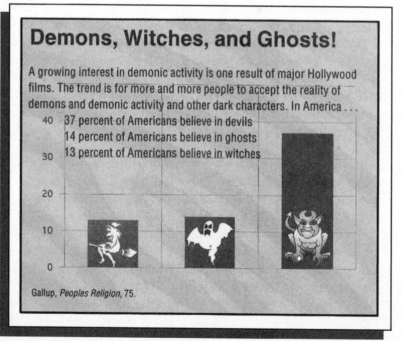

Demons, Witches, and Ghosts!

A growing interest in demonic activity is one result of major Hollywood films. The trend is for more and more people to accept the reality of demons and demonic activity and other dark characters. In America . . .

37 percent of Americans believe in devils
14 percent of Americans believe in ghosts
13 percent of Americans believe in witches

Gallup, *Peoples Religion*, 75.

The spiritual breastplate of righteousness is an equally important piece of armor for our spiritual protection.

- It protects us from the consequences of sin, from the harm and damage and violent ravages of sin.
- It protects us from the hardening and choking of the spiritual arteries that slowly kill the spiritual life.
- It protects us from Satan's deceptive methods by giving us discernment.
- It keeps us from coming under the discipline of God.

The breastplate of righteousness is God's divine protection against the flaming darts and arrows of Satan. One reason God demands that we live righteous lives is to protect us from Satan.

The Shoes of Peace Give Us Stability

The shoes of the gospel of peace = a trusting confidence on the promises of God, and the sense of peace that such trust brings.

The Roman soldier needed good footwear. A soldier who couldn't keep his footing was a vulnerable soldier. Josephus, in the sixth volume of his major work on the *Jewish Wars*, describes the soldiers' footwear as "shoes thickly studded with sharp nails." Thus, they could keep their footing in the worst conditions. The military successes of Alexander the Great and Julius Caesar were due in large measure to their armies' ability to undertake long marches at incredible speed over rough terrain. They could not have done this unless their feet were well shod. The same holds true in the spiritual battle. We must keep our footing, no matter how treacherous the ground.

What does "the gospel of peace" refer to? It is probably not the gospel message of salvation by grace through faith in Christ. What it does refer to, more likely, is the peace of God that is ours when we believe the promises of God and act accordingly. We read Jesus' own words: "Peace I leave with you, My peace I give to you; not as the world gives do I give to you. Let not your heart be troubled, neither let it be afraid" (John 14:27). When we believe God, when we believe what He says and trust Him, then we have the personal, inner peace that enables us to keep our footing in the daily spiritual battle.

The Shield of faith Wards Off Blows

The shield of faith = a life of protection based on our faith in God's character, word, and deeds.

Roman soldiers sometimes used a small, round shield, but the Greek word translated here describes a shield large enough for the soldiers to crouch behind to protect themselves from volleys of arrows coming from enemy archery divisions. The surface of these large shields was either metal or leather over wood, which could repel or withstand flaming missiles. These were arrows that had been soaked in or wrapped with flammable material and were then set on fire and launched by the enemy—they were doubly lethal.

Fact File

Paul's Instructions on Prayer
(Eph. 6:18)

Paul gives us four "alls" to guide us in understanding his instructions on prayer:

1. with all prayer and petition = the scope of prayer

2. at all times in the Spirit = the attitude of prayer

3. with all perseverance and petition = the fervency of prayer

4. for all the saints = the target of prayer

In spiritual warfare the enemy of our soul launches his deadly arrows at us, and it is faith that protects us. Faith is our shield.

The Helmet of Salvation Guards Our Head

The helmet of salvation = a lifestyle of hope that comes from focusing on our ultimate salvation.

The Dimensions of Salvation

Salvation has three dimensions:

- Past salvation delivers us from the *penalty* of sin.

- Present salvation delivers us from the *power* of sin.

- Future salvation delivers us from the *presence* of sin.

The head is a particularly vulnerable spot on the human body. A blow to the arm or leg may be painful, but take a blow to the head and suddenly the stars are out and the birds are singing. A sharp blow to the arm or leg might break a bone; a sharp blow to the head can kill. Roman soldiers wore helmets, for obvious reasons.

In developing his metaphor of spiritual armor, Paul indicated that the helmet is one of the most important pieces, for it is the helmet of salvation.

Salvation has three different dimensions: past, present, and future.

Past. Past salvation delivered us from the penalty of sin. Upon committing our lives to Christ, we were forgiven and cleansed of our sins, spiritually reborn, and made eligible for heaven. We were at that time justified—declared righteous—by God (Rom. 5:1).

Present. We are being freed more and more from the power of sin in our everyday lives. Jesus said, "You shall know the truth, and the truth shall make you free" (John 8:32). As we come to know more and more truth, we are more and more set free from the negative effects of sin. As we live in faithful obedience to God, He frees us from the power and bondage of sin.

Future. Future salvation will deliver us from the presence of sin. When Christ comes again, He will deliver us to our final salvation (Heb. 9:28), and we will go to heaven. The present heaven and earth will be destroyed in a cosmic flash, and a new heaven and earth will be created. All sin will be destroyed and we will live forever in the presence of God, unaffected and untouched by sin, never again knowing anything of sin.

If you would stand firm in the spiritual battle with the powers of darkness, the apostle Paul said, keep your mind fixed on your final and ultimate salvation. Put your heart in the next world while keeping your hands in this one.

The Sword of the Spirit Defends and Attacks

The sword of the spirit = an offensive and defensive use of the Bible in spiritual warfare.

The Roman soldier's sword (*machaira*) was short and double-bladed. This cut-and-thrust weapon, wielded by the heavily armed legionary, was distinct from the large Thracian broadsword (*rhomphaia*). The smaller weapon was used in hand-to-hand combat. It was a weapon of last resort, used in intense warfare.

Commitment to the whole Bible (*logos*) is important in the spiritual warfare, but this occurs when we don the first piece of armor, the belt of truth. When we do that, we accept the truth of the Bible and choose to follow it with integrity. Then, when we take up the sword of the Spirit, we use specific verses (*rhema*) to fend off attacks of the enemy and put him to flight. For example, if we are tempted to get angry, we recite in our minds the verses we have already memorized, "Be swift to hear, slow to speak, slow to wrath; for the wrath of man does not produce the righteousness of God" (James 1:19-20). This is how to use the sword of the Spirit.

Think about It

1. If you don't believe in the absolute truth of Scripture, you cast yourself adrift on a sea of uncertainty, incapable of knowing anything for sure and without any basis for hope.

2. If you don't believe that a righteous life is necessary to pleasing God and being safe in the spiritual war, you will not be willing to make the difficult decisions necessary for victory.

3. If you don't believe and rest in the promises of God, your life is liable to be a constant stream of anxiety and distress.

4. If you don't realize the Christian life is a walk of faith, you will be continually frustrated over God's refusal to bless the things you cherish.

Conclusion

Everything God asks of us, He does so to give something good to us and to keep us from harm. God commands us to put on the spiritual armor because He wants us to equip us for victory in the spiritual war.

Americans pick and choose what commands of God they will take seriously and what they will ignore. If we don't want to be a casualty in this war, we had better quit playing fast and loose with the Christian disciplines and commands of Christ. We had better stop saying, "What can I get away with?" and start saying, "What would Jesus do?" We had better stop crying, "Legalism!" and start crying, "Righteousness!" In spiritual warfare we need the protection of the whole armor of God, not only out of respect for and obedience to God, but also for our own good.

Let Me Ask You

1. If Jesus were to visit you personally today, what do you think He might tell you concerning your preparedness for spiritual warfare?

2. What is the most appealing thing about heaven that helps you put your hope in the next world?

3. Do you know the Bible well enough to use specific verses to help you ward off specific temptations? On a scale of 1 to 10, how do you rate? What do you need to do to increase the number?

Instant Recall

1. The b_____ of truth anchors us.

2. The b_____ of righteousness protects us.

3. The s_____ of peace give us stability.

4. The s_____ of faith wards off blows.

5. The h_____ of salvation guards our head.

6. The s_____ of the spirit defends and attacks.

Action Line

Read: My book *What You Need to Know about Spiritual Warfare* has much more helpful information about this subject.

Memorize: Ephesians 6:11.

Pray: Dear Lord, thank You that You have given us the weapons we need to be victorious in the spiritual war. Help me to take up each piece of armor, and having done that, to stand firm. Amen.

What Is the Church?

Well Said

He cannot have God for his father who does not have the church for his mother.

—Augustine

Stained Glass or Saints?

I was born in the little village of Inwood, Indiana. You'll be lucky to find it on a map. There were only about thirty homes, sheltering perhaps one hundred people, with a gas station, a small grocery store, a post office, a grain elevator, an elementary school, and one church. We lived just a block from the church, which was a large stone-block building with stained-glass windows, solid mahogany pews and altar, and many friendly people. At 8:55 A.M. a bell in the steeple began ringing, calling all the townspeople. Our family emerged from our house like little ducks headed toward the pond, and a few minutes later, we were in our place in church.

From my earliest days, if you were to ask me what the church is, my mind would flash back to a large, gray stone-block building. That image was followed by memories of red and blue light from the stained-glass windows falling across the hardwood floors, giving a soft glow to the interior. The rich wood tones of the pews, pulpit, and altar rail finished the timeless look of it all. That was the church, in my mind.

It came as a bit of a surprise to me when I learned many years later that, biblically speaking, that is *not* the church. The church is not a building. The church is people. We don't *go* to church. We *are* the church. The Bible gives several pictures of the church that help us to understand what it is.

The Church Is Like a Body

The apostle Paul's favorite picture for the church was the body. It is a word picture for the fact that Christians on earth are the hands, feet, and tongue of Christ, that we are to labor, travel, and speak as Christ would if He were in our shoes. Jesus is the head of the body, and each of us makes up our part of His spiritual body on earth. We each have different functions, different abilities, different callings, and different locations. Romans 12:4-5 reads, "Just as each of us has one body with many members, and these members do not all have the same function, so in Christ we who are many form one body, and each member belongs to all the others" (NIV).

We do not become the body when we agree to work together in harmony. We are automatically the body, regardless of whether or not we work together in harmony. The question is only whether we will be a healthy body or an unhealthy one. We are not a member of the body when we decide to join a local church. If we are Christians, we are already members of the body. We are not added to the body or subtracted from the body by our choice. If we belong to Christ, we are members and we belong to each other because we are all in Christ.

Pictures of the Church

The Bible gives three different pictures of the church:

- The church is a body (Rom. 12:4-5).

- The church is a building (Eph. 2:19-22).

- The church is a bride (Rev. 19:6-9).

If Christians ever came to understand and appreciate that truth, it would make us more tolerant of those who are different and more aware of our need for others with diverse abilities. Just as a human body could not function if all its members were the same, so the body of Christ could not function if we were all the same.

The Church Is Like a Building

One of the grandest buildings in Washington, D.C., is the National Cathedral. It is a huge stone cathedral with glorious architectural lines, magnificent stained-glass windows, a lovely altar, and beautiful grounds. When I visited it the first time many years ago, they had already been working on it for many years. It was open to the public, but parts of it were still not finished. We went out to a construction area where we saw stone carvers, some of the last such craftsmen in the world, still chipping away at ornate blocks of granite. Today, the cathedral is still not complete. It will be complete one day, but the task is so huge that the construction life of the cathedral exceeds the life of anyone working on it.

So it is with the universal church. A second picture of the church is that of a spiritual building. The apostle Paul wrote in Ephesians, "You are . . . of the household of God, having been built on the foundation of the apostles and prophets, Jesus Christ Himself being the chief cornerstone, in whom the whole building, being fitted together, grows into a holy temple in the Lord, in whom you also are being built together for a dwelling place of God in the Spirit" (2:19-22).

We can imagine, in our mind's eye, that huge cathedral having a name on each of the stones. Figuratively speaking, one of those stones is Bill, one is Susan, one is James, one is Katherine, and—*glory to God!*—one is Max.

The Church Is Like a Bride

**Church =
Called-Out Ones**

Ek means "out from";
kaleo means "to call."
Together, the two words
mean "called out." It
implies an assembled
group. The same word
would be used whether
or not the meeting was
a religious one.

We have all been to weddings, and what has been the focal point of every one of them? The bride. Everything in the entire service centers on the bride, highlights the bride, honors the bride. The minister is in place, the groom and his attendants stand at the front, ladies come down the aisle, flower girls drop rose petals, heightening the anticipation for the crowning moment: the appearance of the bride. The music swells, everyone's head turns, and the bride, beaming, appears at the back. All stand. She walks down on the arm of her father and the entire gathering turns slowly with her passing. Grandmothers weep quietly, mothers cry openly, fathers bite lips—all for the bride.

Then the vows are given, and the bride is united to the groom. The two become one.

That is the destiny of Christians. Someday in heaven we will be honored as no bride on earth has ever been honored. To think that Jesus would honor us! It is we who should honor Him, and yet a ceremony confirming His marriage to us is conducted in heaven. The apostle John wrote, "Hallelujah! For the Lord our God, the Almighty, reigns. Let us rejoice and be glad and give the glory to Him, for the marriage of the Lamb has come and His bride has made herself ready. . . . Blessed are those who are invited to the marriage supper of the Lamb" (Rev. 19:6, 7, 9, NASB).

Are these not amazing pictures? You are the body of Christ. You are the temple of God in the Spirit. You are the bride of Christ. As the body, you have a task, you are gifted. As a building, you belong, you are possessed and indwelt by the living God, you reflect His glory. As a bride, you are honored, you are owned, you are glorified. By whom? Of all persons, by Jesus!

Is this not too much to take in? It is Cinderella all over again. A handsome prince sees a peasant girl who is in bondage to evil. The prince subdues the power of evil, marries Cinderella, and takes her to his castle to live happily ever after. We are all Cinderella. No matter how hard this life on earth might be for you, take hope. One day you will live in a palace with the King of heaven.

The Church Is Universal

People can become understandably confused about what the church is. Like me, some people are misled into assuming that the church is a building or an organization, rather than a collection of people. In the original language of the New Testament, however, the Greek word for "church" helps us clarify our understanding. *Ekklesia*, translated "church," means an assembly or a group called together for a meeting.

Snapshot

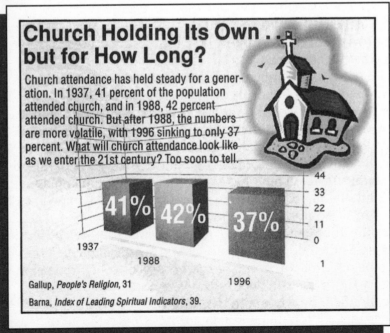

Church Holding Its Own . . . but for How Long?

Church attendance has held steady for a generation. In 1937, 41 percent of the population attended church, and in 1988, 42 percent attended church. But after 1988, the numbers are more volatile, with 1996 sinking to only 37 percent. What will church attendance look like as we enter the 21st century? Too soon to tell.

41% 42% 37%

1937
1988
1996

44
33
22
11
0
1

Gallup, *People's Religion*, 31

Barna, *Index of Leading Spiritual Indicators*, 39.

For instance, in Acts 19, the town clerk of the city of Ephesus was concerned that a riot was going to break out over the apostle Paul's preaching. He urged his fellow citizens, who had gathered to discuss the matter, to remain calm and file legal charges against Paul rather than resort to violence. "And when he had said these things, he dismissed the assembly" (v. 41). The word "assembly" is *ekklesia.*

The word later came to be used of Christians, people who had been called together spiritually to follow Jesus. In the Bible, "the church" never means a building where people meet but rather refers to the people themselves.

The people who are part of the universal church are those who have received Jesus Christ as their personal Savior. Earthly membership in a local congregation, however, is no guarantee of being a part of the spiritual universal church. Someone has said that going into a church building doesn't make you a Christian any more than going into a garage makes you a car or going into a barn makes you a cow. It is not what happens on the outside that matters, but what happens on the inside.

The Church Is Local

A local church is a group of believers who agree together to pursue the ideals of the universal church.

A local church meets regularly. If a group of people are actually to be a church, they must gather regularly. Hebrews 10:24-25 says, "Let us consider one another in order to stir up love and good works, not forsaking the assembling of ourselves together, as is the manner of some." The "gathered" church is commissioned to worship God, to take the message of the Gospel to the entire unsaved world, and to make mature disciples of those who are converted (Matt. 28:18-20).

A local church has qualified leaders. Pastors are key people in the life of a church, necessary to equip the saints for the work of ministry and the spiritual growth of the congregation (Eph. 4:11-12). In addition, elders are to be selected to give spiritual oversight to the congregation and to shepherd them (1 Tim. 3:1-7). Finally, deacons are to look after the physical needs of the congregation (Acts 6:1-6; 1 Tim. 3:8-13). All these people

Think about It

If you don't believe in the ministry of the church...

- You are likely to try to get by in life without going to the church for help.

- You will not realize the importance of baptism, the Lord's Supper, and church discipline.

- You will contribute to a weak church and to a weak personal Christian walk.

must meet the qualifications set down in these passages. (This subject will be dealt with more thoroughly in chapter 20.)

Conclusion

Too many of us have too small a picture of the church. All local churches have their failings because they are made up of imperfect people. Yet we all belong to the church if we belong to Jesus. If our membership were dependent on the value of our personal involvement, many of us would be defrocked.

It was the church that bled and died to keep the message of salvation alive. And we have churches in America today because other Christians gave themselves in life and death to protecting it. Because we have watered down the church to the level of our own commitment and expectations, the church may appear weak and misguided. But when we see the church for what it really is, we ought to lower our heads in humility. If we allow Jesus to function as the head of the church, we see a powerful, dynamic, and visionary entity against which the gates of hell will never prevail, built by the saints of old, whose shoes are bigger than ours.

Instant Recall

1. The church is like a b_____.

2. The church is like a b_____.

3. The church is like a b_____.

4. The church is u_____.

5. The church is l_____.

Action Line

Read: My book *What You Need to Know about the Church* contains more helpful information about this subject. If you want to learn even more, read *The Body* by Charles Colson.

Memorize: Hebrews 10:24-25.

Pray: Dear Lord, thank You that You have created the church, that I can be a part of it not only spiritually but practically, in a local church. Bless Your church, and help me to a helpful member of the body. Amen.

Let Me Ask You

1. Before you read this chapter, if someone had asked you what the church was, what would you have answered?

2. If you could wave a magic wand that make a local church be exactly what you want it to be, what would it be like?

3. How healthy would your church be if every person attending were just like you?

CHAPTER 19

Chapter at a Glance

- The church must instruct.

- The church must fellowship.

- The church must minister.

- The church must worship.

- The church must baptize.

- The church must observe the Lord's Supper.

- The church must exercise discipline.

What Is the Church Supposed to Do?

Well Said

When I first became a Christian . . . I thought that I could do it on my own, by retiring to my rooms and reading theology, and I wouldn't go to [church]. . . . I disliked very much their hymns, which I considered to be fifth-rate poems set to sixth-rate music. But as I went on I saw the great merit of it.

—C. S. Lewis

What's a Church to Do?

We know what many things are supposed to do.

- An army is supposed to fight.
- A band is supposed to play.
- A school is supposed to educate.
- A baseball player is supposed to run, throw, and hit.
- A flower is supposed to grow, bloom, and produce seeds.
- A farmer is supposed to plant, fertilize, and harvest.
- A baby is supposed to eat, sleep, make noise, and spit up.
- A puppy is supposed to eat, sleep, make noise, and spit up.

But what is a church supposed to do? Many of us could run through a list of things our church is currently doing, but is that what the church is *supposed* to do? And is that *everything* the church is supposed to do?

The Church Must Instruct

Knowledge is a tricky thing. It is hard to gain it initially and it is hard to keep it. I once heard the true story of a couple who, after a long and difficult labor, were blessed with their second child, a daughter beautiful and perfect in every way. Later, in the hospital room, the husband looked tenderly through tears at the new little life in his arms. Then he glanced up at his wife, who expected him to utter something truly poetic. Instead, he asked, "What's her name again?"

Perhaps you've never done anything that bad, but we all struggle with gaining enough knowledge and then retaining it. And where is it any more difficult than in learning the Bible? Truth is foundational to Christianity. Jesus said, "You shall know the truth, and the truth shall make you free" (John 8:32). A mindless, contentless faith is not sufficient. Everything we do must be rooted in the truth. Without the foundation of biblical instruction, Christians individually will not mature spiritually, and neither will the church

The Church in Action

Acts 2:41-47 gives us guidance as to what we ought to be doing today.

- *Instruction*: They continued in the apostle's doctrine (v. 42).

- *Fellowship*: They continued in fellowship and in the breaking of bread (v. 42).

- *Ministry:* They sold possessions and divided funds among all as anyone had need, and shared their faith with others who also came to Christ (vv. 45-47).

- *Worship:* They continued in prayer and praising God (vv. 42, 47).

corporately (2 Tim. 3:16-17). If this is true, then the church must instruct its people in the truth, and we see that the first church did.

The Church Must Fellowship

The Christians in the first church, as described in Acts 2, "continued . . . in fellowship"; they "were together." They took care of each other, whenever anyone had need. They continued "with one accord." They "[broke] bread from house to house." They lived as part of each other's lives.

In America we are becoming more and more isolated. In the not-too-distant past, our houses had front porches where people sat and visited when they had the time. Now we have back patios with fences around them. We used to leave our doors unlocked. Now we barricade ourselves behind iron bars and security systems. We used to visit with others when we had the chance. Now we turn on the television and watch it by ourselves. Our culture cuts us off from one another.

It affects even those in the church. We no longer have the normal communal life that used to be part of American culture. True, there are unpleasant and even dangerous people out there who keep us from returning to the old days. But we have developed a living pattern of isolation that not only protects us from dangerous people but also cuts us off from the very people we need in order to live a balanced and healthy life.

The image of a body was well chosen by Jesus to picture the collection of Christians called the church. A body has many different members very unlike each other, yet when they fit together, they form a whole that works quite well. A Christian was never intended to function alone spiritually, any more than an eye, ear, or hand was intended to function alone physically. Christians are created by God to be healthy only as they are in good relationship with other Christians. So if a church is going to function normally and have healthy members, it must encourage, promote, and champion fellowship.

The Church Must Minister

The Holy Spirit had done some remarkable things among the first Christians in Jerusalem, and thousands of people believed the powerful message preached by Peter on the day of Pentecost. These Christians then ministered to one another, fellowshiping, breaking bread together, and dividing possessions to meet one another's needs. But in addition to all that, they reached out to those who had not yet heard. They continued to visit the temple, presumably telling others about their experience, since "the Lord added to the church daily those who were being saved" (v. 47).

> **Christians are created by God to be healthy only as they are in good relationship with other Christians.**

Of course, the church is given much more complete instructions later on in the New Testament regarding its ministry. The apostle Paul wrote in his letter to the Galatians, "As we have opportunity, let us do good to all, especially to those who are of the household of faith" (Gal. 6:10). We minister to one another, and we minister to those who are not of the faith. This is the pattern we see in the first church.

The Church Must Worship

The apostle Luke wrote that the first Christians were "continually devoting themselves to the apostles' teaching and to fellowship, to the breaking of bread and to prayer" (v. 42). Then he mentioned that "everyone kept feeling a sense of awe" (v. 43, NASB) and that they were "praising God" (v. 47). These things are at the heart of corporate worship. The phrase "continually devoting themselves" suggests single-minded faithfulness. When these first Christians met for worship, they were serious about it.

▼▼▼▼▼▼▼▼▼

Immersion in water symbolizes death (being buried in the water) and resurrection (coming back up out of the water).

▲▲▲▲▲▲▲▲▲

The phrase "kept feeling a sense of awe" could be translated "fear came upon every soul." It does not mean "fear" in the sense of being frightened of someone. Rather, it means "awe" or "reverence" or "deep respect." These people had been deeply impressed with the presence of God and His work in their midst. It showed.

However, they were not prune-faced religious scrooges whose very presence dumped a cloud of gloom on others. Verse 46 says that "gladness" characterized their activities, and they favorably impressed all those who saw them.

The Church Must Baptize

Baptism is a symbolic act in which Christians proclaim their belief in Jesus' death and resurrection, and enter into a full relationship of obedience to God. The physical act of baptism is the sprinkling, pouring, or immersing (complete submerging) of a person in water. It is a simple gesture, yet once we understand it, it has deep and profound meaning. God intended it to be a sign of inward cleansing of sin (Acts 22:16) and a sign of receiving spiritual life (Titus 3:5).

Immersion in water symbolizes death (being buried in the water) and resurrection (coming back up out of the water). It is symbolic of our union with Christ (much as the union of a husband in wife in marriage, where the two become one) in His death, burial, and resurrection (Rom. 6:3-7; Col. 2:11-12). Baptism is a fundamental responsibility of the local church.

The Church Must Observe the Lord's Supper

The Lord's Supper is a ceremonial meal of bread and the "fruit of the vine" commemorating the death of Jesus for our sins and celebrating His new covenant with us. The central passage of Scripture dealing with the Lord's Supper is 1 Corinthians 11:23-26, which tells us the following:

1. Jesus instituted the Lord's Supper.
2. It is to be observed in the church until He returns to earth.
3. It is to be a perpetual remembrance of His sacrifice.
4. It symbolizes the new covenant He established with us, to grant us forgiveness of sin and eternal salvation by grace through faith in Jesus Christ.

Snapshot

A Breakdown of Church Attendance

As we enter the 21st century:

- 28 percent of adults never attend church
- 35 percent of adults in the West never attend church
- 34 percent of adults in the Northeast never attend church
- 19 percent of adults in the South never attend church
- 82 percent of adults were formerly regular church attenders

Barna, Internet: www.BarnaResource.org.

Think about It

If you don't believe in the ministry of the church . . .

- You are likely to try to get by in life without going to the church for help.

- You will not realize the importance of baptism, the Lord's Supper, and church discipline.

- You will contribute to a weak church and to a weak personal Christian

Considerable controversy has existed through the centuries over the nature of the elements (the bread and wine). Three views predominate today.

Transubstantiation: This word means "to go beyond the substance." Roman Catholics believe that the substance of the bread and wine are miraculously transformed, actually *becoming* the body and blood of Jesus even though they appear to the eye to be still bread and wine.

Consubstantiation: "Con" means "with." Lutherans believe that Christ's body and blood come to be present *in, with,* and *under* the substance of the bread and wine, which become more than bread and wine. The Eastern Orthodox churches and some Anglican churches believe the same.

Representation: Most Protestants believe that the elements are only a symbolic or ceremonial meal, and/or that by faith the believer, during Communion, enters into a special spiritual union with the risen Christ. They believe that the phrase "this is my body . . . my blood" means that the bread and wine *represent* His body and blood, not that they actually *become* His body and blood, nor that His body and blood come *with* the bread and wine. All Protestants believe that at the Lord's Supper we are giving thanks to Christ for His finished and accepted work of atonement, rather than mystically repeating His crucifixion.

The Church Must Exercise Discipline

Scripture teaches that churches are not to ignore the flagrant sins of its people but are to take biblical steps to deal with them

(1 Cor. 5:1-13; 2 Cor. 2:5-11; 2 Thess. 3:6, 14-15; Titus 1:10-14; 3:9-11). This discipline should occur in an overall ministry of nurture and accountability (Matt. 28:20; John 21:15-17; 2 Tim. 2:14-26; Heb. 13:17). The discipline may be anywhere from personal admonishment to exclusion from the Lord's Supper to excommunication from the church. Sins that are public should be publicly corrected in the church's presence (Gal. 2:11-14; 1 Tim. 5:20). Private sins should be dealt with privately, in hopes that it will not be necessary to ask for the church's public discipline (Matt. 18:15-17). The purpose of all discipline is to encourage repentance, when the church then restores the offender to fellowship again.

Let Me Ask You

1. How committed are you to learning the Bible? How do you think your life is impacted by your Bible knowledge?

2. How do you think you could profit more from relationships with other Christians?

3. Have you been baptized? Do you observe the Lord's Supper?

Conclusion

Certainly, the brief description of the events of the first church do not give us a complete picture of what the church today should do. But it does give us a fundamental picture. If this was their pattern in the earliest days, we might do more today, but we ought not to do less.

Instant Recall

1. The church must i_____.

2. The church must f_____.

3. The church must m_____.

4. The church must w_____.

5. The church must b_____.

6. The church must o_____ the Lord's Supper.

7. The church must exercise d_____.

 Action Line

Read: My book *What You Need to Know about the Church* provides more helpful information about this subject. If you want to learn even more, read *The Purpose Driven Church* by Rick Warren.

Memorize: Acts 2:42.

Pray: Dear Lord, thank You for the church, for the wonderful impact it has on me, on those I care about, and on the world. Bless Your church with vital success, and make me a helpful part. Amen.

Who Can Lead the Church?

CHAPTER
20

Chapter at a Glance

- The church must be governed.

- The church must have pastor-teachers.

- The church must have elders and deacons.

- The leaders of the church must be spiritually mature.

Well Said

*The church is looking for better methods;
God is looking for better men.*

—E. M. Bounds

Rotten at the Core

My wife and I once lived in Marietta, Georgia. The town square is the focal point of this delightful southern community where Sherman once camped during his assault on Atlanta in the Civil War. The square is the size of a city block, outlined by hundred-year-old trees, with grass, flowers, delightful landscaping, and an old statue or two in the center. It is a beautiful piece of history.

My office was just a block off the square, so I drove past it at least once a day. One day after a particularly violent thunderstorm the night before, I drove past the square to see a grand old oak tree twisted grotesquely to the ground. The wind had turned the tree around, split it open, and slammed it to the hard Georgia soil. All the other trees on the square were unharmed.

The first glance told why this tree had gone down while the others had stayed up. The trunk of this tree had rotted. It was hollow in the core. It had looked perfectly healthy, but when the test of adversity came, the tree revealed its inner rottenness by crashing to the ground.

What a parable that is of spiritual leadership, which must be solid to the core. If there is spiritual rottenness at the center, when the winds of temptation or adversity blow, the leader will come crashing to the ground. In the Bible we learn how churches must be led.

The Church Must Be Governed

Over the years, three basic forms of a church government have been developed. *Episcopalian* government is a hierarchical system of governing and decision making in the church in which denominational leaders are the primary authority. *Presbyterian* government is a representative system of governing and decision making in the church in which a board of elders is the primary authority. *Congregational* government is a democratic system of governing and decision making in the church in which the congregation as a whole is the primary authority.

Adherents of each one of these three systems of government can appeal to Scripture to support their position, and if you read only the argument for one form of government, you will be convinced that it is right. But if you read more than one, you may not be sure. Each form seems to have some biblical validation and some strengths and weaknesses.

The Church Must Have Pastor-Teachers

In the early days of our country, the minister was often the best-educated person in town. He was the primary source of information, not only about the Bible but about the world. People gathered in church on Sunday morning with the same sense of expectation that we might turn on the news on television or open up the newspaper or newsmagazine. Knowledge was power, and since the minister had much of the knowledge, he also had much of the power. Today, however, knowledge is largely available to all who want it. There are people in every congregation who may know more about a given subject than the pastor.

Nevertheless, a pastor has a crucial role in the church, and those in the church are spiritually dependent on his ministry. In order to pastor, a man must meet two criteria: he must possess the spiritual gift of pastor-teacher, and he must meet the spiritual qualifications of an elder established in 1 Timothy 3:1-7 and Titus 1:5-9, which we will look at later in the chapter. If he possesses these two qualifications, he can be used by God to pastor a church, regardless of what everyone else in the congregation knows. Church leadership is essentially spiritual leadership by one who is divinely gifted for the task.

Snapshot

Pastors Are Better Than Lawyers!

- 9 percent of Americans think the clergy are doing an excellent job
- 58 percent think they are going a good job
- 7 percent think they are not doing a good job

This places pastors among the highest-rated professionals in the nation, below judges and doctors but above teachers, lawyers, and business executives.

Barna, *Index of Leading Spiritual Indicators*, 46.

The ministry of pastor-teacher is not clearly articulated in Scripture. In fact, the only use of the term is found in Ephesians 4:11. The word "pastor" means "shepherd," and the word is used as "shepherd" elsewhere in the New Testament. The primary task of the pastor, in addition to the general responsibilities of shepherding the flock, is to "[equip] the saints for the work of ministry, for the edifying of the body of Christ" (Eph. 4:12). Other than that general description, the function of the ministry is not described or defined.

▼▼▼▼▼▼▼▼▼

The primary task of the pastor, in addition to shepherding the flock, is to equip the saints for the work of ministry.

▲▲▲▲▲▲▲▲▲

Not all are in agreement on the term "pastor-teacher." Ephesians 4:11 reads, "He gave some as apostles, and some as prophets, and some as evangelists, and some as pastors and teachers" (NASB). Some people believe there are five positions described in this passage. However, there are two words in Greek translated "and": *kai* and *de*. Inserting those words in their proper place, and also including the definite article that is in the Greek, this passage reads: "He gave some as *the* apostles, *kai* some as *the* prophets, *kai* some as *the* evangelists, *kai* some as *the* pastors *de* teachers." This suggests strongly that the pastor and teacher should be connected, referring to one person.

Seen this way, there is no such thing as a pastor. There is only a pastor-teacher, though for cultural reasons, there is no problem with calling a person a "pastor" rather than the more cumbersome "pastor-teacher."

The Church Must Have Elders and Deacons

The word for "elder" means to shepherd the congregation (1 Pet. 5:2), to oversee its affairs, to preach and teach (1 Tim. 5:17), and to guard the moral purity of the congregation (Titus 1:9). An elder, just as a pastor-teacher, should also meet the spiritual maturity qualifications established in 1 Timothy 3:1-7 and Titus 1:5-9.

A deacon's task is not as clearly understood from Scripture as an elder's. The word for "deacon" means "to serve," and a major use of the word for "deacon" has to do with waiting on tables. So, whatever a deacon is to do, it falls within the general category of serving. It is possible that the ministry of deacons was first seen in Acts 6:1-6, when widows and orphans were being overlooked in the daily distribution of food. So the church was instructed to choose men full of wisdom and of the Holy Spirit, and they were to oversee the proper distribution of food while the apostles devoted themselves to prayer and the ministry of the word.

Whether or not deacons are supposed to be functioning in every church is not clear, but if a church chooses to have deacons, they must be spiritually mature. Their qualifications are clearly spelled out in 1 Timothy 3:8-13.

The Leaders of the Church Must Be Spiritually Mature

While no mention is made of the spiritual-maturity qualifications of a pastor-teacher, it seems that if an elder must be spiritually mature, it would be just as important for a pastor to be spiritually mature. In fact, the wording of 1 Timothy 3:1-7 ("above reproach," NASB) suggests that these marks of maturity are for everyone in the church to strive toward, not just elders. While some of the traits refer to "abilities" such as "able to teach," in all the moral qualifications, we are all equally to strive for them. It is just that, in order to be an elder, a person must meet the qualifications.

Think about It

If we don't believe what the Bible says about church leaders . . .

- A church might be controlled by rampant individualism where there is little cooperation and everyone is does what is right in his own eyes.

- Or a church might be controlled by a single domineering pastor.

- A church might be governed by an elder board or pastor who do not meet the qualifications, thus stunting the growth of the entire congregation at best, and leading to moral failure at worst.

Therefore, we can say that all three positions of leadership in the church must meet the qualifications of an elder. To encompass all three positions in a way that does not get too cumbersome verbally, I will refer to these three spiritual leadership ministries as "holding a spiritual office" in the church.

To get a picture of a spiritually mature person, we can merge the two lists in Timothy and Titus, which are very similar but not identical. The actual terms used vary depending on which translation of the Bible is used. For our purposes, we will use the New American Standard Bible. Because there is overlap between the words on the two lists and similarities of meaning among several words, we will be examining only twenty of the characteristics listed in the two passages:

1. "Above reproach": This qualification is generally regarded as a summary qualification, with the remaining qualifications being a description of what it means to be "above reproach." It means that you have a good reputation because you have no major character faults.

2. "Husband of one wife": to be faithful to one's wife in thought, word, and deed.

3. "Temperate": to be self-controlled and moderate in attitude and actions.

4. "Prudent": to be skilled in managing practical affairs.

5. "Respectable": to be proper in behavior.

6. "Hospitable": to be kind to strangers.

7. "Able to teach": to be qualified, by virtue of one's life, knowledge, and ability to communicate, to teach others.

8. "Not addicted to wine": not to drink alcoholic beverages habitually or compulsively.

9. "Not self-willed": not to be demanding of your own way.

10. "Not quick-tempered": to control your anger and express anger only at the things that anger God.

11. "Not . . . pugnacious": not to be a fighter, either verbally or physically.

12. "Gentle": to treat others with care, so as to soothe and not to hurt.

13. "Uncontentious": not to be quarrelsome or argumentative.

14. "Free from the love of money": not to want money more than you want the will of God.

15. "One who manages his own household well": to lead one's family with care and diligence.

16. "Not a new convert": to be of sufficient spiritual age.

17. "Love what is good": to choose good rather than evil.

18. "Just": to give equal weight to all people and actions.

19. "Devout": to earnestly pursue one's faith.

20. "Self-controlled": to be personally disciplined in all things.

Let Me Ask You

1. Does your church take the need for spiritually mature leadership seriously? What has been the result?

2. Who are the most effective leaders in your church? What do you think has made them effective?

3. Which qualities of an elder are strongest in your life? Which are weakest? What can you do to strengthen your weaknesses and use your strengths?

Conclusion

We have taken a number of pages just to say one thing: spiritual leaders in the church must be spiritually mature. Water seeks its own level. A congregation will rise no higher, as a whole, than its leadership. If the leadership is shallow and hypocritical, most mature people will not be willing to stay there; they will move on. The only people who will stay under that kind of leadership are people who are willing to put up with shallowness and hypocrisy.

Paul did the church a great favor by spelling out in detail what a spiritual leader must be like. Those of us who lead must measure ourselves by that standard and be willing to step aside, perhaps just temporarily, until our lives are a basic (not perfect) reflection of these character qualities. Those of us who follow must require that our leaders manifest these qualities. If they do not, we must put ourselves under the spiritual leadership of those who do.

Instant Recall

1. The church must be g_____.

2. The church must have p_____ -t_____.

3. The church must have e_____ and d _____.

4. The leaders of the church must be spiritually m_____.

Action Line

Read: My book *What You Need to Know about the Church* offers more helpful information about this subject. If you want to learn even more, read *The Body* by Charles Colson.

Memorize: Ephesians 4:11-12.

Pray: Dear Lord, thank You that You have designed for church leaders to reflect Your character, and to lead us as You would. Help me to reflect these characteristics in my life. Amen.

What Does the Future Hold?

Well Said

The only way to wait for the Second Coming is to watch that you do what you should do, so that when he comes it is a matter of indifference.

—Oswald Chambers

Seeing the End from the Beginning

A number of years ago, my wife and I watched *Jane Eyre*, a movie adaptation of Charlotte Brontë's classic novel. There is a frightening scene in it in which a hideous, demented woman steals into Jane Eyre's bedroom one night and threatens her with harm. The scene had my nerves vibrating like high-tension electrical wires in a strong wind. The scene passes with no harm and the movies proceeds to its conclusion.

Some years later we watched the same movie with my brother and sister-in-law. Since I had seen the movie before, the frightening scene no longer held suspense for me. But I noticed out of the corner of my eye that my sister-in-law was showing the same signs of strain that I showed on my first viewing—muscles tense, jaw tight, eyes wide.

I could not help but reflect on the difference it makes when you know the end of a story. The fear, the tension, the anxiety are gone. And so it is with life. When we know the end from the beginning, it takes away the fear, the anxiety, the tension. That is the value of Bible prophecy. We can read the last chapter and discover that we win.

There Are Nine Key Terms in Bible Prophecy

It is helpful to get generally familiar with the important terms of Bible prophecy. The following are nine key terms:

1. **The Second Coming** is the return of Christ to the earth at an unknown time in the future (John 14:3).

2. **The Rapture** is the sudden departure of all Christians to meet Christ in the air (1 Thess. 4:16-17).

3. **The Millennium** refers to a period of time in which Christ reigns on earth in righteousness (Rev. 20:1-10).

4. **The Great Tribulation** is a period of intense, unprecedented suffering (Mark 13:19).

5. **The Antichrist** embodies evil and is the key agent of Satan's resistance to the plan of God in the last days (1 John 2:18-22).

6. **The judgment seat of Christ** is the place where all Christians will receive their reward for the quality of their life on earth (2 Cor. 5:10).

7. **The great white throne judgment** is the place where all who have rejected God receive the punishment for their unbelief and their life on earth (Rev. 20:11-15).

8. **Heaven** is the ultimate destination of all people who truly believed in God and committed their lives to Him (Acts 1:9).

9. **Hell** is the ultimate destination of all people who did not truly believe in God and commit their lives to Him (Matt. 10:28).

Later in the chapter we will put these events together in a time line so that they will be more fully understood. Right now, the goal is to get you generally familiar with them so that when we begin talking about them later, it will not be totally new information.

There Are Differences in Understanding Bible Prophecy

Understanding Bible prophecy can be a very difficult thing, for a number of reasons. First, some prophecies are intended to be understood literally and some symbolically. For example, Micah 5:2 says that the Messiah was to be born in Bethlehem—obviously a literal prophecy. On the other hand, in Revelation 6:13 we read, "The stars of heaven fell to the earth." This is literally impossible and clearly intended to be taken figuratively.

Another complication is that some prophecies have both an immediate and a future fulfillment. In Isaiah 7:14 it is prophesied that a virgin will give birth to a child, which was a sign not only regarding a coming invasion of Israel but also of the Messiah to come many years later.

Finally, some people are by temperament, upbringing, and/or education inclined to interpret prophecy literally, and some are predisposed to interpret it figuratively. All these factors, plus the passing of time, make it very difficult to know for sure when you have properly understood a prophecy. We should read prophecy in its historical, grammatical, and literary context, relying on the whole context of Scripture for its meaning, to be sure we don't make any obvious mistakes. Beyond that, we must proceed with caution, knowing that there may be other godly, intelligent, and well-educated people who may have a different understanding of a prophetic passage.

There Are Different Perspectives on the Rapture

First Thessalonians 4:16-17 says that at some time in the future (perhaps any day) the Lord will appear suddenly and call to heaven all Christians on earth. From an earthly perspective, they will all simply disappear.

Also the Bible says that the earth will undergo a Great Tribulation, a time of unprecedented suffering on earth, lasting for seven years, after which Jesus will return to earth. He will also establish a thousand-year reign of righteousness on earth. After all these events culminate, history will come to an end.

There are, however, several different interpretations of these events.

Figurative. The Great Tribulation is not a specific period of time between the Rapture and the Second Coming of Christ, but rather is a symbolic reference to the suffering that is taking place on earth right now. The Rapture occurs essentially at the same moment as the Second Coming.

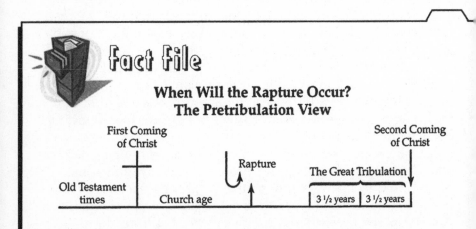

Fact File

When Will the Rapture Occur?
The Pretribulation View

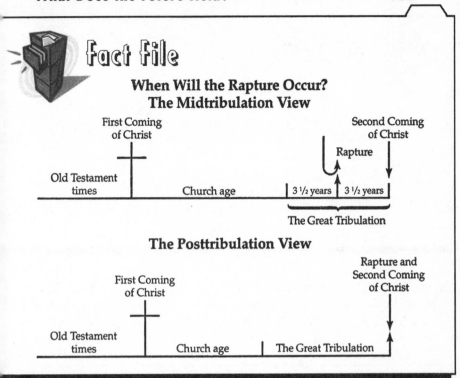

Fact File

When Will the Rapture Occur?
The Midtribulation View

First Coming of Christ

Second Coming of Christ

Rapture

Old Testament times

Church age

3 ½ years | 3 ½ years

The Great Tribulation

The Posttribulation View

First Coming of Christ

Rapture and Second Coming of Christ

Old Testament times

Church age

The Great Tribulation

Pretribulation. The Rapture occurs any day, followed right away by a seven-year Great Tribulation, followed by the Second Coming of Christ, followed by the Millennium.

Midtribulation. The Great Tribulation begins. After three and a half years, the Rapture occurs, followed by the remaining three and a half years of the Great Tribulation, followed by the Millennium.

Posttribulation. The Great Tribulation ends, followed by the Rapture and the Second Coming, followed by the Millennium.

There Are Different Perspectives on the Millennium

Just as there are differing views on the Tribulation and the Rapture, so there are differing views on the Millennium.

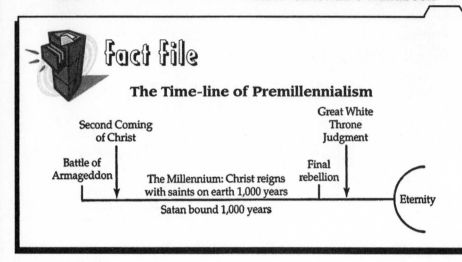

Fact File

The Time-line of Premillennialism

Second Coming
of Christ

Great White
Throne
Judgment

Battle of
Armageddon

Final
rebellion

The Millennium: Christ reigns
with saints on earth 1,000 years

Eternity

Satan bound 1,000 years

Premillennialism. The Second Coming of Christ will be followed immediately by a literal period of one thousand years during which Christ will rule over the world as its political leader.

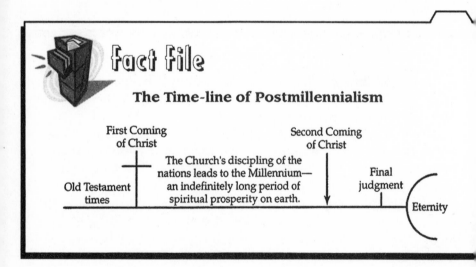

Fact File

The Time-line of Postmillennialism

First Coming
of Christ

Second Coming
of Christ

The Church's discipling of the
nations leads to the Millennium—
an indefinitely long period of
spiritual prosperity on earth.

Final
judgment

Old Testament
times

Eternity

Postmillennialism. The Gospel will spread throughout the earth, creating a better and better world, after which Jesus will return to bring this age to a close and usher in eternity.

Amillennialism. The thousand-year reign of Christ is symbolic of the ultimate triumph of God's righteousness and goodness

The Time-line of Amillennialism

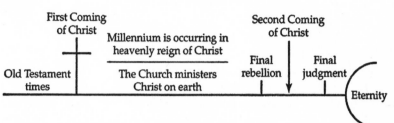

in the world. There is no literal thousand-year reign of Christ on earth, but Christ is now ruling and expanding His rule on earth.

There Is a Core of Essentials We Agree Upon

Though not all Bible teachers and scholars agree upon the particulars of Bible prophecy, nevertheless, among those who believe that the whole Bible is the inspired Word of God, there are a number of things upon which we all agree:

1. Jesus is coming again, and when He does, God will set all things right. In the end all will be well for God's people. In the meantime we must live in light of His return.

2. Jesus is the ultimate focal point of all prophecy. The Old Testament looked forward to His coming; the New Testament looked back at His coming; unfulfilled prophecy looks forward to His coming again.

3. Holiness should be the end result of prophecy. The Bible was not given merely to satisfy our curiosity, but to tell us how to live.

4. We must be personally committed to the Great Commission. If the end is coming, must we not warn others?

5. God is sovereign and, in spite of seeming evidence to the contrary, is guiding history to a meaningful conclusion, just as He said he would.

Conclusion

God is often misunderstood. The world is a mess, and people don't understand why He doesn't fix it. Christians wonder why they are not spared the calamity that falls on non-Christians (accidents, disease, natural disasters, persecution, etc.). God seems content to (from our perspective) plod along, letting the world run its course. In the meantime He woos the world with love, relentlessly pursuing those who ignore Him or shake their fists in His face.

Christians are, of course, His body, His physical presence on earth. He woos the world through us, so we have a great challenge to do a good job. He uses the weak things to overpower the

Snapshot

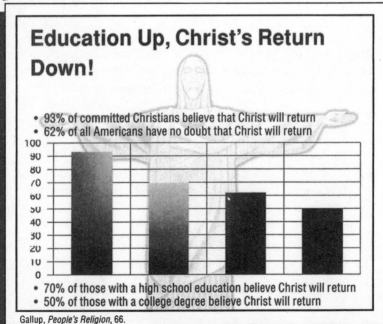

Education Up, Christ's Return Down!

- 93% of committed Christians believe that Christ will return
- 62% of all Americans have no doubt that Christ will return

- 70% of those with a high school education believe Christ will return
- 50% of those with a college degree believe Christ will return

Gallup, *People's Religion*, 66.

mighty, and the foolish things to confound the wise.

During the hardest times, Bible prophecy matters the most. It tells us that God will make everything all right, that justice may seem deferred but will not be denied, that the good and gracious purposes for which God created the world will all be fulfilled. Through Jesus, God has already entered the suffering of the world, already borne the world's sin, and already landed the knockout punch on the devil and on the evil he and human sin have produced. Through the Resurrection of Jesus Christ, death itself has already been reversed and its paralyzing power of fear already disabled among those who receive the life of God here and now.

Bible prophecy helps us glimpse the certainties of God's future so that we may live wisely, righteously, passionately, and boldly today. It urges us, as we look for the coming of the Lord, to answer the question of 2 Peter 3:11: "What manner of persons ought [we] to be?"

Bible prophecy assures us that God will not leave a job half done but will complete the new creation begun in Jesus. One day the righteous, saving reign of God will no longer be a matter of faith but of full sight. And so the church of every age prays, "Even so, come, Lord Jesus! (Rev. 22:20).

Instant Recall

Think about It

If you don't believe what God has revealed about the future . . .

- You may get fearful or depressed at evil in the world, wondering how good can ever triumph.

- You may be tempted to live a sinful lifestyle, not believing that you will ever be held accountable for your actions.

- If you don't have heaven to look forward to, you have little reason for joy in life and you lose a major reason for hanging in there when the going gets tough.

1. There are n_____ key terms in Bible prophecy.

2. There are d_____ in understanding Bible prophecy.

3. There are different perspective on the R_____.

4. There are different perspective on the M_____.

5. There is a core of e_____ we agree upon.

Action Line

Read: My book *What You Need to Know about Bible Prophecy* in-cludes far more helpful information about this subject.

Memorize: John 14:3.

Pray: Dear Lord, thank You that You have told us how the future will unfold. Thank You that in the end all will be well. Help us to live for You during the hard times until then. Amen.

Let Me Ask You

1. What areas in your life would you want to see improved if you knew for sure that Jesus was coming back soon?

2. What would you have to do or change in order to say that you were fulfilling your part in the Great Commission?

3. When people see trouble in the world and are dismayed, what can you tell them when they wonder where God is?

What Is Hell?

Well Said

The safest road to hell is the gradual one—the gentle slope, soft underfoot, without sudden turnings, without milestones, without signposts.

—C. S. Lewis

The Eternal Campfire

I remember as a young child gazing into the hottest coals of a campfire at night and imagining that that was a miniature picture of hell. Inside the unburned outer logs, inside the flaming edges, inside the hottest coals was a near-white-hot center that made my face burn from several feet away. While I do not recommend my action, out of curiosity I dropped a bug into that small inferno and saw it writhe in agony for a moment, then be consumed. My mouth gaped. I couldn't imagine that destiny. But it was even worse. My understanding was that anyone going to hell would writhe in agony in that white-hot center of the great Eternal Campfire but would *never be consumed!* My mind drew back. It was unthinkable.

In fact, many people draw back from the possibility of hell. It is the single most disagreeable doctrine of Christianity and the reason many people give for rejecting Christianity. None of that affects the truth, however. There either is a hell or there isn't, regardless of whether people like it. So our challenge is to discover what the Bible says about hell rather than to nurture our own preferences.

No matter what a person understands hell to be like in its specifics, we know that in the Bible it is always described in ominous and foreboding terms as a place of torment to be avoided at all costs. If you don't like going to the dentist, you want nothing whatsoever to do with hell.

Today, of course, the concept of hell has fallen into disfavor among those who do not believe in any literal hell and is often an awkward subject among those who do. One does not hear much of hell anymore from anyone. Some people are revising the traditional concepts of hell, suggesting that there is no literal fire, as has been traditionally held, while still others are suggesting that hell is a temporary place, or that all will eventually be saved from hell.

Some Believe Hell Is a Literal Place

Literalists believe that hell is a place of endless, conscious physical, spiritual, and emotional suffering in literal fire for those who have rejected God in their earthly life.

There are a number of Bible passages that appear to speak of hell as a literal place of torment for unbelievers who have died (Matt. 13:42, 50; 25:14-30; Luke 12:47-48). The most vivid, perhaps, is Revelation 14:9-11, where we read, "If anyone worships the beast, . . . he shall be tormented with fire and brimstone. . . . And the smoke of their torment ascends forever and ever; and they have no rest day or night." Also we read in Revelation 20:10 that the devil himself will be "cast into the lake of fire and brimstone where the beast and the false prophet are. And they will be tormented day and night forever and ever." These passages by themselves seem to suggest a physical place dominated by fire where unbelievers will spend eternity.

Some see this as necessary retribution for their sins. While God bestows infinite grace on those who believe in Him, He must on the other hand inflict eternal punishment on those who reject Him. Others see the agony as self-inflicted, rather than active retribution. If a person will not accept God and will not go to heaven (love, peace, joy), then by default he or she gets the opposite of God and heaven (hate, pain, suffering).

Sensitive literalists struggle with this grave truth. They hold to it not because they desire it but because they believe the Bible teaches it. This has been the majority position of the Christian church for two thousand years.

Some Believe Hell Is a Metaphor for Suffering

Fact File

The Great Garbage Dump

The word translated "hell" in the New Testament comes from the Greek word *Gehenna*. It is derived from the name of the valley of Hinnom, located just south of Jerusalem, which was a city garbage dump that burned twenty-four hours a day every day. In this dreadful place, human sacrifices were once offered to the god Molech (2 Kings 23:10). It was used as a burial place for criminals and for burning garbage. It came to be a metaphor for the everlasting state of the unsaved.

Metaphoricalists believe that hell is a place of endless, conscious emotional and spiritual suffering for those who have rejected God in their earthly life.

Those who hold to the metaphorical interpretation of hell believe that hell is a place of eternal torment but do not believe that the torment is physical. They do not believe there is any literal fire. Rather, the fire stands for the torment that is a natural consequence of having rejected God and been separated from Him forever.

Some passages in the Bible are clearly intended to be metaphorical, while others are clearly not. However, there are some in the middle about which we may be unsure, and whether one ends up understanding hell to be literal physical suffering or spiritual and emotional suffering depends on how one interprets that middle category of verses that might not be completely clear to some.

For example, the metaphorical view finds it significant that heaven is described in terms familiar in first-century culture. Until the time of gunpowder, all major cities were protected by high, thick walls and sturdy gates, with signs often placed above the gates. Therefore, in Revelation, when heaven is described, it is described in terms relevant to that culture: unimaginably high and unbelievably thick walls. Of course, there is no need for walls in heaven, but that is the way it is pictured anyway. The implication is that heaven is a safe place.

Fact File

A Metaphor

A metaphor is the use of a word picture to compare with something literal. "The evening of one's life" uses the picture of the closing of day to indicate the closing of one's life. As a metaphor, the fire, brimstone, and physical torment of hell could be a picture of emotional and spiritual torment.

Heaven is also a beautiful place, so it is described in terms that first-century people would find impressive, with pearls and gold. It is also described as a place of bounty and rest, which would appeal to a culture bound to poverty and labor. And if heaven is described in powerful images not intended to be literal but symbolic, the metaphoricalists reason, so it must be with hell. The images of hell are the ones that would be the most dramatic and shocking to first-century people but are not to be taken literally. The literal truth behind the horrible imagery created by the prophetic language is that hell is a place of profound misery where the unsaved are separated from the presence of God forever and suffer whatever is the opposite of God and heaven for eternity.

So the metaphorical interpretation of hell does not picture it as a belching inferno with humans writhing in agony in the midst of fire that gives no light. Rather, the unsaved will be cast from the presence of God forever, without any hope of restoration, experiencing an eternity of no peace, no love, no joy, no fellowship.

Some Believe Hell Is Temporary

Conditionalists believe that hell is a place of conscious suffering for those who have rejected God in their earthly life but that it does not last forever. They see both the literal and metaphorical views of hell as inconsistent with the character of God, and not required by the rules of interpretation.

First, in the Old Testament, the words used to describe the destiny of those who reject God overwhelmingly point to a final, irreversible termination of existence in hell, not eternal conscious punishment. In Psalm 37, for example, we read that the wicked will fade like grass and wither like the herb, that they will be cut off and be no more, that they will perish and vanish like smoke, and that they will be altogether destroyed. The prophet Malachi repeated the same imagery (Mal. 4:1).

Second, the Gospels continue this imagery of final destruction. Jesus spoke of judgment in terms that could be understood as final destruction when He warned about God's ability to destroy body and soul in hell (Matt. 10:28). John the Baptist pictured individuals as dry wood about to be thrown into the fire and as chaff about to be burned up (Matt. 3:10, 12). The wicked would be burned up just like weeds thrown into the fire (Matt. 13:30, 42, 49-50). Terms like "destroyed" and "burned up" give the impression that the unbeliever can expect to be destroyed by the wrath of God.

Third, the apostle Paul continued this imagery when he said that everlasting destruction would come upon unrepentant sinners (2 Thess. 1:9), and that God would destroy the wicked (1 Cor. 3:17;

Think about It

If you don't believe hell exists . . .

- You might go merrily on your way, oblivious to the unspeakable calamity that awaits you in hell.

- You eliminate a compelling reason for becoming a Christian.

- You will fail to warn others of the danger, since you see none yourself.

Phil. 1:28). "Their destiny is destruction" (NIV) he stated plainly in Philippians 3:19. Peter spoke of the "destruction of ungodly men" (2 Peter 3:7, NIV) and of false teachers who brought upon themselves "swift destruction" (2:1, 3). He said that they would be like the cities of Sodom and Gomorrah that were burned to ashes, destroyed (2:6), and that they would perish like the ancient world perished in the great flood (3:6-7).

It is possible to conclude that the Bible can reasonably be read to teach the final destruction of the wicked. To the conditionalist, the concept of eternal conscious punishment seems neither just nor required by an exegesis of the biblical texts dealing with hell.

Of course, the literalists and metaphoricalists point to a passage such as Revelation 14:10-11: "If anyone worships the beast and his image, and receives his mark on his forehead or on his hand, he himself shall also drink of the wine of the wrath of God. . . . And he shall be tormented with fire and brimstone. . . . And the smoke of their torment ascends forever and ever; and they have no rest day or night."

 Snapshot

Hell Is Cooling Off!

A shrinking percentage of Americans believe that hell is a literal place or that they have any real danger of going there. As the 21st century begins . . .

- 4 of 10 believe hell is a state of separation from God
- 3 of 10 believe hell is a literal place
- 2 of 10 believe hell is a symbolic term
- 6 of 10 believe that good people will go to heaven
- 4 of 10 believe that if a person does not consciously accept Christ as his savior, he will be condemned to hell.

Barna, *Index of Leading Spiritual Indicators*, 74–75.

Conditionalists admit this as the most difficult passage to reconcile but point out that while the smoke goes up forever, the text does not say the wicked are tormented forever. It says that they have no relief from their suffering as long as the suffering lasts, but it does not say how long it lasts. And they contend that this is only one difficult passage to reconcile, while the literalists and metaphoricalists have many more than that.

Let Me Ask You

1. What to you is the most foreboding aspect of hell?

2. What role did hell have in your becoming a Christian?

3. Why do you think most people don't talk about hell anymore?

Conclusion

So here we have a stalemate, according to the three views. None is willing to admit a knockout punch from the others. Of course, biblical interpreters are faced with similar difficulties throughout the Bible with issues such as the free will of man and the sovereignty of God, Calvinism and Arminianism, dispensationalism and Reformed doctrine, premillennialism and amillennialism, etc. While it is a serious issue and one in which people might hold strong beliefs enthusiastically championed, it is not an issue that ought to create enmity between people who otherwise believe in the inspiration of Scripture, the perfect character of God, the deity of Christ and the Holy Spirit, the resurrection, the depravity of humanity, salvation by grace through faith in Jesus, the Great Commission, and the Second Coming of Christ.

Instant Recall

1. Some believe that hell is a l_____ place.

2. Some believe that hell is a m_____ for suffering.

3. Some believe that hell is t_____.

Action Line

Read: My book *What You Need to Know about Bible Prophecy* contains more helpful information about this subject.

Memorize: Mark 8:36.

Pray: Dear Lord, thank You that You have made it possible for us to escape the torment of hell. Thank You that Jesus paid the price for my sin so that I do not have to. Amen.

What Is Heaven?

Homesick for Heaven

Vance Havner, a venerable old preacher of a previous generation, once said, "I'm homesick for heaven. It's the hope of heaven that has kept me alive this long." Another time he said, "There are a lot of questions the Bible doesn't answer about the Hereafter. But I think one reason is illustrated by the story of a boy sitting down to a bowl of spinach when there's a chocolate cake at the end of the table. He's going to have a rough time eating that spinach when his eyes are on the cake. And if the Lord had explained everything to us about what's ours to come, I think we'd have a rough time with our spinach down here."

CHAPTER 23

Chapter at a Glance

- Heaven is a real place.
- Heaven is beautiful.
- We will worship God.
- We will fellowship with God.
- We will fellowship with one another.
- We will reign with Jesus.
- We will have marvelous abilities.

And so it is. The Bible tells us that there is a heaven and gives us some indication of what it is to be like but does not come close to satisfying our curiosity. However, we can be greatly enriched by discovering what little the Bible does tell us about that great place.

To answer the questions we have about heaven, we can look at specific Scripture passages as well as do a little educated speculating.

▼▼▼▼▼▼▼▼▼

Heaven is a real place, not a state of mind or a condition of peace or a retirement village for disembodied spirits.

▲▲▲▲▲▲▲▲▲

Heaven Is a Real Place

It seems, from the biblical language, that heaven is a real place, not a state of mind or a condition of peace or a retirement village for disembodied spirits. When Jesus revealed Himself to His disciples after His resurrection, He appeared in a real body, capable of talking, walking, and eating (John 21:1-23). And the apostle Paul taught that our bodies will be like His (Phil. 3:21). The indication, then, is that we will live physical lives rather than haunt shadowy corners of the universe.

This conclusion is strengthened by the understanding that God created heaven (Gen. 1:1) and Jesus went there after He was resurrected (John 14:1-3). When Jesus ascended into heaven (Acts 1:9), the whole point seems to be that He went to a specific place. Similar impressions are made in the story of the stoning of Stephen, the first Christian martyr (Acts 7), and the account of the apostle Paul's having visited the third heaven (2 Cor. 12:1-10).

Since we will have resurrection bodies like Jesus', it seems perfectly reasonable to conclude that there is a place where these rather physical bodies can function in a rather physical place.

Heaven Is Beautiful

A renewed earth will be part of heaven, along with a celestial city, the New Jerusalem (Rev. 21). One of the most striking features about the renewed earth is that it will have no oceans

(Rev. 21:1). Beyond that, we can only speculate. New Jerusalem is described as a place prepared as a bride adorned for her husband (Rev. 21:4), drawing on the descriptions of the original creation in Genesis 1—2. Clearly, what little we know about it now still makes it a grand paradise, even if it is beyond our comprehension.

The Bible describes it as a city of immense size compared to earth. It is described as being nearly fifteen hundred miles long, wide, and high (Rev. 21:16). To get some feel for this, when you see pictures of astronauts orbiting the globe, with the earth *w-a-y* down there, the astronauts are only approximately two hundred miles above the earth. The New Jerusalem would be seven times higher than that.

In addition to its outer size, there are twelve stories inside this giant cube, so each story would have a ceiling approximately one hundred miles above the "streets of gold." No one will feel cramped in there. The city is described as having walls constructed of immense precious jewels (Rev. 21:18-21), with the gates of the city constructed of single, immense pearls (Rev. 21:21).

It sounds more beautiful and immense than Yosemite Valley or the Swiss Alps or the Grand Canyon. If we marvel at those stupendous sights, what will we do when we see heaven?

▼▼▼▼▼▼▼▼

In heaven you are surrounded with beauty that makes Yosemite Valley look like a flat wall mural.

▲▲▲▲▲▲▲▲

We will eat and drink at the marriage supper of the Lamb (Rev. 19:9). Jesus will once again share the cup with His disciples in heaven (Luke 22:18), a river of the water of life will flow from the throne of God and of the Lamb through the middle of the streets of heaven (Rev. 22:1). The tree of life will bear twelve kinds of fruit, one kind each month (Rev. 22:2). While some believe these are symbolic representations of fellowship and life, there are many Bible teachers who understand them to be literal, even while they suggest larger spiritual truths.

Finally, it is a place where "God will wipe away every tear" and "there shall be no more death, nor sorrow, nor crying. There shall be no more pain" (Rev. 21:4). There we will be able to drink from the fountain of the water of life freely (Rev. 21:6). It is a city that has the "glory of God" and its radiance is like a rare jewel (Rev. 21:11). Yes, it is a place of great beauty.

We Will Worship God

I know what it's like to be bored in church. I remember as a four- or five-year-old child being scolded by my grandmother because, instead of "behaving" and paying attention in church, I had found an empty pew all to myself and I had laid down, crawled, twisted, squirmed, banged my shoes against the solid mahogany pews, and made a general distraction out of myself. I have never done that again, on the outside. But on the inside, I have done it many times. The most recent was not long ago!

Therefore, I realize that to say, right off the bat, that the first thing we will do in heaven is to worship God will not make heaven seem very appealing to some. They already have a mind-deadening picture of our sitting around on clouds picking

 Snapshot

How Good Do You Have to Be to Go to Heaven?

4 of 10 believe that if a person does not consciously accept Christ as his Savior, he will be condemned to hell

JESUS

EARTH   HELL   HEAVEN

6 in 10 believe that you get to heaven by enough good works
9 in 10 believe that eventually God will judge everyone

GOOD WORKS

EARTH   HELL   HEAVEN

Barna, *Index of Leading Spritural Indicators*, 71.

listlessly at our harp strings, trying, after a million years, to think of a new tune.

On the other hand, have you ever been in a really big worship service where everything that was going on was really terrific and everyone meant what was being said, sung, and prayed? In my seminary days, when the seminary chapel was filled with glorious voices singing "All Hail the Power of Jesus' Name," I was deeply filled. I was not bored. I have been in conferences where thousands of people have done the same with well-known hymns, and it too was deeply moving. I was not bored. The more people present and the more deeply they believe what they are singing, the more moving it is.

Now transfer your thoughts to heaven. There are millions upon millions of voices. Each one is more beautiful than any voice on earth. The triune God is there. You are surrounded with beauty that makes Yosemite Valley look like a flat wall mural. All the people sing with deeper conviction and meaning than you have ever heard on earth. God is on the throne and there is an emerald-green rainbow around the throne. Lightning and thunder flash and boom in the background. Sitting around the throne are dignitaries dressed in beautiful white robes with gold crowns. Angels hover in the air. Jesus is there. Many angels (ten thousand times ten thousand) sing with deafening grandeur. Ever been to a grand performance of the *Messiah* with a two-hundred voice choir and a fifty-piece orchestra? It will sound like Alvin and the Chipmunks by comparison.

You will not be bored.

We Will Fellowship with God

In addition to worshiping the triune God, we will also fellowship with God. The apostle John wrote, "Beloved, now we are children of God; and it has not yet been revealed what we shall be, but we know that when He is revealed, we shall be like Him, for we shall see Him as He is" (1 John 3:2). Who is the one person in the world you would most like to meet? A famous musician? A statesman? A king or queen? The girl or boy next door? If you could meet that person, after longing so earnestly to meet him or her, your life would be complete for that moment. You would be

Think about It

If you don't believe biblical truths about heaven . . .

- You lose one of the great motivations and sources of strength for enduring the difficulties of this life, because you have nothing lasting to look forward to.

- You have no great hope to share with others as to how God will set things right in the future.

- You cannot see how all the difficulties of this life will be worth it when you see Jesus.

satisfied for that one hour or day that you got to talk to Billy Graham or Itzhak Perlman or Queen Elizabeth. Perhaps you would like to meet some distant historical figure, such as the apostle Paul or George Washington or Abraham Lincoln. You would not be looking out the window or glancing at your watch. You would be, for that moment, complete, satisfied, totally occupied with the presence of that person. So it will be when we meet Jesus. We will be complete, satisfied in His presence forever.

We Will Fellowship with One Another

Bible teacher J. Vernon McGee used to say, "To live above with saints we love, oh, that will be glory. To live below with saints we know, well, that's another story." And so it is. Fellowship down here is often imperfect. But up there, not so. It will be perfect.

The apostle Paul urged us to "keep the unity of the Spirit in the bond of peace" (Eph. 4:3). In heaven we will experience unimpeded unity and fellowship with all the other members of the body of Christ.

Have you ever been in a quiet intimate conversation with good friends and felt as though you were experiencing something special? Have you ever had special friends with whom intimate conversation was quite natural? Have you ever been with a host of other people rooting for an athletic team or filling sandbags during a flood, or helped a family whose home had been burned, feeling a sense of bonding with the people you were working with? Heaven will be all that, I believe, and much, much more. In the Bible we read of things like great feasts (Matt. 8:11), a wonderful wedding ceremony (Rev. 19:7-9), and glorious worship experiences (Rev. 5:8–14; 19:1-8). It will be all for one and one for all!

We Will Reign with Jesus

If you have trouble keeping your checkbook balanced and your Day-Timer up to date, you can't imagine reigning with Christ in heaven. But it will happen. When you get your new body, it will come with capacities never imagined on earth. Same with your mind. "[Christ] will transform our lowly bodies so that they will be like his glorious body" (Phil. 3:21 NIV).

We don't know what it means to reign with Christ, but we have some hints. In 1 Corinthians 6 Paul tells us "that the saints will judge the world" (v. 2) and "shall judge angels" (v. 3).

In addition, in Romans 8:16-17 we read, "The Spirit Himself bears witness with our spirit that we are children of God, and if children, then heirs—heirs of God and joint heirs with Christ," and "we shall also reign with Him" (2 Tim. 2:12).

▼▼▼▼▼▼▼▼▼

When you get your new body, it will come with capacities never imagined on earth.

▲▲▲▲▲▲▲▲▲

We Will Have Marvelous Abilities

Sin will be done away with, and we will be free to become all that God wants us to be. What all that includes is not yet known, but C. S. Lewis once wrote that if we were to see our glorified selves walking down the street, we would be tempted to fall at our feet and worship ourselves. I suspect he is right.

If our bodies are like Jesus' resurrection body, we will be able to appear and disappear at will, to pass through walls or doors without limitation, to rise from the ground unbound by gravity, and apparently to travel at the speed of thought. We will never forget. We will never hit our heads against a brick wall. We will never hunger or thirst or mourn or cry.

Conclusion

What will we be like in heaven? We will be like a desperately thirsty person who has finally gotten a glass of water. Like a hungry person who has finally eaten his fill. Like a lonely person who has finally been reunited with loved ones. Like a person in the gallows who just received a pardon.

Let Me Ask You

1. What was your concept of heaven before reading this chapter? How has it changed?

2. What role did heaven play in your decision to become a Christian?

3. What role do you think heaven should play in talking to others about becoming a Christian?

Instant Recall

1. Heaven is r_____ place.

2. Heaven is b_____.

3. We will w_____ God.

4. We will f_____ with God.

5. We will f_____ with one another.

6. We will r_____ with Jesus.

7. We will have marvelous a_____.

Action Line

Read: My book *What You Need to Know about Bible Prophecy* has much more helpful information about this subject.

Memorize: 2 Peter 3:13.

Pray: Dear Lord, thank You for the hope of heaven. Thank You that one day all the longings of our hearts on earth will be fulfilled at Your feet in heaven. Keep me looking forward to it all my life. Amen.

Part 2

Why Do We Believe It?

Why Believe in Truth?

CHAPTER 24

Well Said

Truth is incontrovertible. Panic may resent it; ignorance may deride it; malice may distort it; but there it is.

—Winston Churchill

"That, My Friend, Is A"

A man came to his old friend, a music teacher, and said, "What's the good news today?" The old teacher stood up silently, walked across the room, picked up a tuning fork, and struck it. As the pure note sounded in the room, the teacher said, "That is A. It is A today; it was A five thousand years ago;

and it will be A ten thousand years from now. The soprano upstairs sings off-key; the tenor across the hall flats on his high notes; and the piano downstairs is out of tune." He struck the note again and said, "That is A, my friend, and that's the good news for today."

Today, however, A is being ignored, denied, or forgotten, and with it the music of life. Fewer and fewer people believe that truth exists, or if it does, that it can be known. Perhaps that is because we often see what we want to see and miss what we don't want to see. Winston Churchill once said that men occasionally stumble over the truth but that most of them pick themselves up and hurry off as though nothing had happened.

Fact File

Every Man for Himself!

Some American college students refuse to condemn Hitler for the Holocaust. After all, they say, from the Nazi point of view, Hitler believed he was doing the right thing. "Who is to say it was morally wrong?"

John Leo, "A no-fault Holocaust." *U.S. News & World Report*, July 27,1997.

The Bible, however, declares itself to be A. Listen to it, hold to it, and music can be made. Ignore it, and get noise.

Many People Don't Believe in Truth

Confusion over truth is the fundamental crisis of our age. With truth we can fashion answers to the perplexing problems of modern life. Without it we are doomed to stumble along in blindness, hitting our heads on low beams and our knees on sharp corners and eventually pitching headlong off a cliff.

Perhaps the dominant opinion, at least in educational and intellectual circles today, is that universal truth does not exist or cannot be known. This view of truth is called postmodernism, and as a result of postmodernism, everyone is doing what is right in his or her own eyes. The result is that American culture is falling apart.

The clash over right and wrong plays itself out daily on television talk shows. Every day guests defend practices and beliefs that would only be discussed privately—and then only rarely—forty years ago. Everything is defended by statements like "Who are you to tell me what is right?" or "I am happy in what I am doing, and it is not hurting anybody, so why does it matter to you?"

Tolerance is perhaps the most important virtue to postmodern society, and intolerance the most serious vice. One can violate the Ten Commandments and no one blinks an eye. If one dares to question the truth or moral value of someone's views or actions, that is intolerable.

The Bible Declares that It Is True

The Bible teaches that truth exists and can be known. God has revealed truth through His prophets, apostles, and Son, and this truth is preserved for us in inspired Scripture. So we do not share the postmodern anxiety about truth. In the Gospel of John, Jesus says, "I am . . . the truth" (14:6), not "a truth"; "You shall know the truth, and the truth shall set you free" (John 8:32); and "When He, the Spirit of truth, has come, He will guide you into all truth (John 16:13).

The apostle Paul was equally unambiguous when he wrote, "The truth is in Jesus" (Eph. 4:21) and "God our Savior . . . desires all men to be saved and to come to the knowledge of the truth" (1 Tim. 2:3-4).

We must admit that we do not have a perfect grasp of the truth that God has given us. Godly, well-informed, and intelligent Christians disagree over many things in the Bible, such as the sovereignty of God and the free will of man and how we should baptize. Therefore, we should not overstate our case when discussing truth. We may believe something to be true (such as how to baptize) without being able to prove to someone else that it is true.

As Francis Schaeffer used to say, we must be careful to say all that Scripture says, and we must be equally careful not to say more than Scripture says. As 1 Corinthians 13:9-13 teaches, it is not until we stand before Jesus that we will know and understand

Truth

There are three avenues by which we may know truth:

- reason
- faith
- experience

truth perfectly. When presenting truth, we should have a certain humility that acknowledges our imperfect grasp of truth and that treats others with respect even if we do not agree with them.

Nevertheless, we do not determine our own truth, as postmodernists claim. Instead, we accept and practice the truth as it is revealed in Jesus, who is the truth. And in areas outside God's special revelation through Jesus and the Scriptures, we reject as false any claims to truth that are not in harmony with what we understand of revealed truth.

We Can Know Truth

Reason. Many Christians are influenced by fact-based knowledge and careful reasoning based on that knowledge. It is important to them that their faith be rooted in facts and that it be reasonable. Christian apologetics, the study and practice of defending our faith, has been heavily influenced by rationalism, the belief that truth is grasped by reason, even though Christians believe that God is the ultimate source of truth. This means that Christian apologetics can use reason, but it should not be limited only to what the human mind can understand. Thomas Aquinas was significantly shaped by the rationalism of Aristotle, and so he offered us five proofs for God's existence. Josh McDowell, a well-known contemporary evangelical leader, loves to present careful reasons and historical evidences in defense of Christian beliefs.

Faith. Some Christians, on the other hand, have been influenced by an outlook known as fideism. This view is prominent in Reformed or Calvinistic theology and in some Catholic writers. It says that we find truth by first trusting in God and then following His revelation as the accurate map of all reality. This quote from C. S. Lewis expresses the fideist's perspective (although Lewis himself did not rely only on fideism in his defense of the faith): "I believe in Christianity as I believe in the sun—not only because I see it, but because *by it I see everything else"* (emphasis mine). Human reason is fallible and gives no ultimate certainty. Faith rests in the God who alone is the anchor of truth.

Cornelius Van Til, a famous Christian apologist, advanced a version of fideism in contending that one's presuppositions determine everything. Van Til, who taught for forty years at Westminster Theological Seminary, believed that unless one presupposes that God has given truth, there is no way for humans to be certain of anything. For Van Til, only the assumption that God is sovereign and has revealed the truth in the Bible will save humanity from the otherwise confusing voices of human reason. From the Lewis quote, Van Til would emphasize that only by the light of God's revelation—and not by human reason—could he truly see or understand anything else.

 Snapshot

Americans Believe the Bible, but Don't Always Let It Influence Them

- 60 percent believe the Bible is absolutely true, but . . .
- 23 percent believe that religious beliefs and teaching are the single most significant influence on belief of whether or not absolute moral truth exists
- 15 percent said the Bible is the most significant influence
- 13 percent said their family is the most significant influence
- 10 percent said their experience is the most significant influence
- 7 percent said intuition and emotion are the most significant influence

Barna, *Index of Leading Spiritual Indicators*, 17.

Experience. Still other Christ-ians emphasize experience in defending their faith. They might refer to their conversion experience as proof for their faith, or talk about a mystical moment in their lives or an answer to prayer, or share an example of divine healing. Still others might talk about a time when they believe God gave them precise, accurate knowledge about a future event or about another person's need as evidence that God is real. Or they may rely on a deep sense of intuition that the gospel has what J. B. Phillips called "the ring of truth" to it.

Balance. As we look at each of these three avenues for perceiving truth, we can see value in each of them. At times, fact-based information is important to us, while at other times faith provides the light by which we can see the truth; and at still other times, our experience validates truth to us. So it is with those to whom we share our faith.

Along with presenting biblical truth in an appropriate way, we must personally live out a biblical lifestyle. Whether one is dealing with a modern or postmodern person, the openness to a religious position depends on truth claims being wedded with an attractive lifestyle. People are more turned off by a person they can't handle than a doctrine that they can't swallow.

Fact File

Why Reject Truth?

Aldous Huxley, author of *Brave New World,* is a good example of someone who embraced a non-Christian view of life and the meaninglessness that went with rejecting objective truth. He states why clearly:

> For myself, as, no doubt, for most of my contemporaries, the philosophy of meaninglessness was essentially an instrument of liberation. . . . We objected to . . . morality because it interfered with our sexual freedom. . . . We don't know [objective truth] because we don't want to know. It is our will that decides how and upon what subjects we shall use our intelligence. Those who detect no meaning in the world generally do so because, for one reason or another, it suits their [desires] that the world should be meaningless.

Aldous Huxley, *Ends and Means* (New York: Harper, 1937), 273.

People May Deny Truth because They Don't Want to Know It

Where does the contemporary denial of truth come from? How has it come to be so prevalent? What accounts for this historic and ominous shift in thinking? Many people today have this mindset because they have been indoctrinated and deceived by those who have taught them. They are, perhaps, innocent "believers." Others hold to this mindset because they want to. It fits their personal agenda, and if so, there are none so blind as those who will not see.

In order to discover truth about God, one has to be willing to go where the truth takes him. Truth, then, demands a response. If one is not willing to go where the evidence leads, he is liable never to find God. And at the bottom of his soul, perhaps he doesn't want to.

Conclusion

Obviously, Christian confidence about truth will not automatically lead people to Christ. Jesus said, "No one can come to Me unless the Father who sent Me draws Him" (John 6:44). Ultimately, whether or not people acknowledge and respond to truth is a matter between them and God. Nor will the defense of Christian truth claims necessarily win acceptance. However, we are commanded in Scripture to defend our faith and to present the truth as the Bible sees it.

Think about It

If you don't believe in absolute truth . . .

- You are cast adrift on a sea of uncertainty to make your way through this life by trial and error as best you can.

- You have no hope for life beyond the grave.

Instant Recall

1. Many people don't believe in t_____.

2. The B_____ declares that it is true.

3. We can know truth through r_____, f_____, and e_____.

4. People may d_____ truth because they don't want to know it.

Action Line

Read: My book *What You Need to Know about Defending Your Faith* has much more helpful information about this subject.

Memorize: John 8:32.

Pray: Dear Lord, thank You that we can know truth and that with it You will set us free. Give me insight to grasp truth and courage to live it. Amen.

Let Me Ask You

1. What would you tell someone who wanted to know if truth existed, or if it were possible to know truth?

2. Do you think there is any truth you have not accepted because you don't want to be held accountable to it?

3. How well do you think you balance truth with an authentic Christian lifestyle?

Why Believe in God?

Well Said

I can see how it might be possible for a man to look down upon the earth and be an atheist, but I cannot conceive how he could look up into the heavens and say there is no God.

—Abraham Lincoln

Indiana Max

Imagine I am an archaeologist and I am tramping through the jungle of Guatemala with my crew of assistants. We are hacking our way through nearly impenetrable vegetation toward a site that I believe is an undiscovered Maya ruin. The heat, the snakes, the mosquitoes, and the constant din of a million crawling creatures almost drive us back. Finally, feet burning, eyes stinging, muscles screaming, we hack our way through a wall of hundred-year-old vines, and on the other side, rising like a great green diamond out of the jungle floor, is a huge pyramid, covered with lush tropical undergrowth, right where I thought it would be. We set up camp and settle in for the long haul—years of exploring and digging. The adventure has only begun.

Fact File

Key Definitions

Atheist: Someone who says there is no God.
Agnostic: Someone who says he doesn't know if there is a God.
Pantheist: Someone who says that everything is God and God is in everything.

How did I know this ruin was here? Well, I was flying over the jungle one day and I saw a simple, square-based hill that betrayed intelligence and design. Nature doesn't produce square-based hills. I took an exact reading of latitude and longitude and began making mental preparations for my return trip. That's how I found that ancient ruin.

Why would *anyone* believe in God? For the same reason we believe there is an ancient Mayan ruin in the middle of the Central American jungle. When you see something that seems to have design and purpose to it, it is reasonable to suspect there is intelligence behind it. The universe reflects design and intelligence.

There Are four Good Reasons to Believe in God

Reason 1. Every effect must have an adequate cause, and God is the only "cause" great enough to account for the existence of the universe. "Every house is built by someone, but He who built all things is God" (Heb. 3:4).

The square-based mounds on the jungle floor in Central America had to have an adequate explanation. So it is with the universe. It is here and it seems to have design and purpose.

So how do we explain it? The theory of evolution gives an explanation for life on earth that doesn't require a God, but it can't explain where the universe came from. We have two choices. The first is that God created the universe. This option many reject out of hand. The other is that the universe came into existence by itself, which seems clearly impossible. It is no greater act of faith to believe in God than to believe what you must if you do not believe in God.

Reason 2. The order and purpose in the universe suggest an intelligent creator behind it. "Since the creation of the world His invisible attributes are clearly seen, being understood by the things that are made, even His eternal power and Godhead, so that they are without excuse" (Rom. 1:20).

Not only is the universe here and therefore to be accounted for, but also the universe has order, design, and apparent purpose behind it. It is the difference between all the parts of a watch lying in a jumbled heap on a table, and having the watch all put together and running. It is one thing to have to explain where

Snapshot

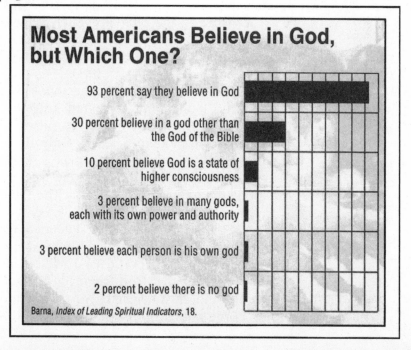

Most Americans Believe in God, but Which One?

93 percent say they believe in God

30 percent believe in a god other than the God of the Bible

10 percent believe God is a state of higher consciousness

3 percent believe in many gods, each with its own power and authority

3 percent believe each person is his own god

2 percent believe there is no god

Barna, *Index of Leading Spiritual Indicators*, 18.

Think about It

If you don't know the arguments for the existence of God . . .

- You might fall into ancient heresies already identified and discredited in church history.

- You might be deceived by a present-day cult or false religion.

- You would lose a chance to strengthen your own faith and walk with God.

- You won't be as able to share intelligently with others.

the jumble of parts came from; it is quite a greater thing to explain how they all got put together and working in such a way as to tell time. Not only is the universe here, but it also runs like a precision watch. If a square hill in a jungle *suggests* a Mayan civilization, then the universe *shouts* of a God.

Reason 3. Humanity is higher than the animals, and being created in the image of God explains why. "The work of the law [is] written in their hearts, their conscience also bearing witness" (Rom. 2:15).

Humanity is different from the animals. People long to know who they are. They long to know where they came from. They long to know where they are going. They long for purpose and meaning in life while they are here on earth. They are far more intelligent than other animals. They have a moral code. They have a sense of a spiritual domain. All civilizations in all of history have had a religion. These things are not true of animals.

Reason 4. The Bible accurately reflects nature and humanity. "The heavens declare the glory of God; and the firmament [sky] shows His handiwork" (Ps. 19:1).

The Bible is not a science textbook. But if it is true, it ought not to contradict science. Nor does it. In fact, Scripture has provided the basis for modern science. Only those who believe that the universe makes sense, that it is governed by predictable laws, would expend the effort to investigate it. The Bible gave modern scientists this confidence.

As Psalm 19:1 says, God intended for the intricacy and design of the universe to point to Him. The apostle Paul in Romans 1:18-20 tells us that God has made Himself known to us through nature and an inner, intuitive recognition of God. This seems to be borne out by our experience. Who has not sat under the vast expanse of stars on a moonless night and had the intuitive thought well up in him, *There must be a God*. Because the Bible is accurate when it speaks of physical things, it suggests that we can trust it when it speaks of spiritual things. And the Bible declares that there is a God !

We Cannot Prove God's Existence

"Without faith it is impossible to please Him, for he who comes to God must believe that He is, and that He is a rewarder of those who diligently seek Him" (Heb. 11:6).

You do not find God in the laboratory, where you look for *proof* in test tubes or computer models. Rather, you find Him in the courtroom, where you look for *evidence* to persuade beyond a reasonable doubt. In the courtroom of nature and history, there is enough evidence for His existence to convince the willing mind beyond reasonable doubt.

Of course, if one does not want to believe, he can find reasons not to. Unbelief never has enough evidence. So it boils down to faith. If one wants to find God, he can.

Not only are there logical, philosophical reasons to believe in Him, but also there is powerful physical evidence to suggest that

Fact File

Scientist: "I Believe the Impossible!"

George Wahl, former Harvard professor and Nobel Prize winner in biology once said,

There are only two possibilities as to how life arose: One is spontaneous generation—a rising evolution. The other is a supernatural act of God. There is no third possibility. Spontaneous generation was scientifically disproved 120 years ago by Pasteur and others. This leaves us with only one logical conclusion—that life arose as a supernatural act. I will not accept that, philosophically, because I do not want to believe in God. Therefore, I choose to believe that which I know is scientifically impossible.

the theory of evolution is not sufficient to explain the complexity of the universe. There are major scientists who are increasingly expressing doubt about the theory of evolution. On the other hand, there are those—scientists and others—who agree that the theory of evolution does not explain the universe, but the only alternative, creation, is so unpalatable that they are willing to believe something (evolution) that does not seem scientifically possible.

Conclusion

Whatever you believe, you believe by faith. If you believe in God, you believe by faith. If you do not believe in God, you are still exercising faith. So the question isn't "Will I have faith or not?" but rather "Where will I place my faith, in God or in evolution?"

Why believe in God? Because He is the most likely explanation for the existence of the universe—its complexity, purpose, and design—and for the uniqueness of humanity.

Let Me Ask You

1. Did you believe in God before you read this chapter? If you did, why did you? Did this chapter add to the reasons why you believed, or merely confirm why you already believed?

2. If you did not believe in God before reading this chapter, how has this information affected your perspective?

3. Can you think of another reason why you believe in God?

4. If a child wanted to know if there were a God, what would you tell him or her?

5. How might your family history and personal life experiences influence your belief in God and what He might be like? How might they affect your ability to trust Him?

Instant Recall

There are four big reasons to believe in God:

1. He explains the o_____ of the universe.

2. He explains why the universe has d_____ and beauty.

3. He explains the s_____ of humanity over animals.

4. Since the Bible has never been proven wrong in material matters, it can be trusted when it speaks of s_____ matters.

Action Line

Read: My book *What You Need to Know about God* has much more helpful information about this subject. If you want to learn even more about this, read *My God* by Michael Green.

Memorize: Psalm 19:1 and Hebrews 11:6.

Pray: Dear Lord, thank You for giving me the faith to believe in You. Thank You for giving us reasons to believe in You. Help me to grow in my knowledge and trust. Amen.

Why Believe Jesus Is God?

Well Said

Alexander, Caesar, Charlemagne, and I myself have founded great empires. . . . But Jesus alone founded His empire upon love, and to this very day, millions would die for Him. Jesus Christ was more than a man.

—Napoleon Bonaparte

Jesus Was a Great Moral Teacher

Few people doubt that Jesus of Nazareth lived. The evidence, when understood, is simply too overwhelming. However, it is one thing to believe that Jesus of Nazareth was a historical figure, but it is quite another to believe that He was God. Many people believe He was a great moral teacher. Why? Look at the greatness of His teachings! "Do to others as you would have them do to you," He said. "Love your neighbor as yourself." "Love your enemies." These three sentences alone, if followed, would stop all war, all crime, all deliberate violence, and all of man's inhumanity to man. It would eliminate the majority of suffering we see in the world today. Indeed, Jesus was a great moral teacher.

However, we cannot say that He was *only* a great moral teacher. He said too many other things to allow us to stop there. He also said He was God. He claimed to be able to forgive sins. He said that no one could get to heaven except through Him. He said He was coming again to judge evil in the world and to reign forever in heaven. He said that His Father would judge you and send you to hell unless you accepted Him. He said one outrageous thing after another that prohibit us from saying He was merely a great moral teacher. If these teachings were not true, including His being God,

Snapshot

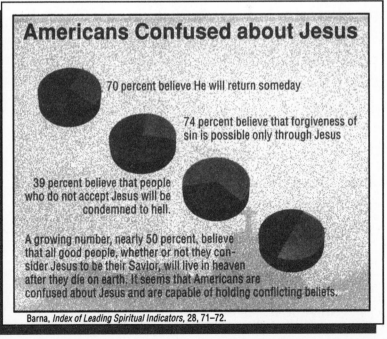

Americans Confused about Jesus

70 percent believe He will return someday

74 percent believe that forgiveness of sin is possible only through Jesus

39 percent believe that people who do not accept Jesus will be condemned to hell.

A growing number, nearly 50 percent, believe that all good people, whether or not they consider Jesus to be their Savior, will live in heaven after they die on earth. It seems that Americans are confused about Jesus and are capable of holding conflicting beliefs.

Barna, *Index of Leading Spiritual Indicators*, 28, 71–72.

▼▼▼▼▼▼▼▼

**If we were to
cover the entire
state of Texas
two feet deep
in silver dollars,
paint one red,
blindfold
a person and
tell him to
pick up one
silver dollar,
his chances
of getting the
marked silver
dollar are
approximately
the same as a
person fulfilling
eight major
prophecies of
the Messiah by
accident.**

▲▲▲▲▲▲▲▲▲

then the one thing that is certain about Him is that He was *not* a great moral teacher.

There are a number of reasons to believe that Jesus was also God.

Jesus Fulfilled All Prophecies as the Messiah

A prophecy is a prediction of the future. Jesus' birth and life were not random. He did not come helter-skelter, any old way, and claim to be God. Rather, His birth, His life, and His death all conform to statements carefully predicted about Him hundreds and sometimes thousands of years before He was born.

1. **Prophecy:** The Messiah would be born of a virgin (Isa. 7:14).
   Fulfillment: Jesus was born of the virgin Mary (Matt. 1:17-25).
2. **Prophecy:** The Messiah would be an ancestor of King David (Jer. 23:5).
   Fulfillment: Jesus is in the lineage of David (Luke 3:23, 31).
3. **Prophecy:** The Messiah would be born in Bethlehem (Mic. 5:2).
   Fulfillment: Jesus was born in Bethlehem (Luke 2:11).
4. **Prophecy:** The Messiah would be betrayed by a friend (Ps. 41:9).
   Fulfillment: Jesus was betrayed by Judas Iscariot, one of His twelve disciples (Matt. 10:4).
5. **Prophecy:** The Messiah would be tortured and crucified (Isa. 53:5).
   Fulfillment: Jesus was beaten and then crucified (Matt. 27:26).

6. **Prophecy:** The Messiah would rise from the dead (Ps. 16:10).

Fulfillment: Jesus rose from the dead (Matt. 28:5-6).

We could go on and on with many more prophecies and fulfillments. These major ones give an idea of Jesus' remarkable life as it fulfilled one after another of the prophecies that told of the Messiah. Josh McDowell writes that if we were to cover the entire state of Texas two feet deep in silver dollars, paint one red, blindfold a person and tell him to pick up one silver dollar, his chances of getting the marked silver dollar are approximately the same as a person fulfilling eight major prophecies of the Messiah by accident.[1]

Jesus' Words Were the Words of God

Admittedly, some of the things Jesus said were startling. If He were not God, they were outrageous words indeed!

1. Jesus claimed to be God. After Jesus had been arrested, prior to His crucifixion, the high priest who was interrogating Him said, "'I put You under oath by the living God: Tell us if You are the Christ, the Son of God.' Jesus said to him, 'It is as you said. Nevertheless, I say to you, hereafter you will see the Son of Man sitting at the right hand of the Power, and coming on the clouds of heaven.' Then the high priest tore his clothes, saying, 'He has spoken blasphemy! What further need do we have of witnesses? Look, now you have heard His blasphemy! What do you think?' The other religious leaders answered, 'He is deserving of death!'" (Matt. 26:63-66).

This entire incident makes no sense whatsoever unless we understand that both Jesus and the religious leaders understood that Jesus was claiming to be God.

2. Jesus claimed things that only God can do. Jesus claimed to forgive sin and give salvation (Matt. 9:2-3; Luke 7:48-50). Only God can forgive sin. Only God can give salvation.

3. Jesus promised things that only God can promise. Jesus promised that He would give eternal life to those who followed Him (John 3:36), that they would never perish, and that nobody would be able to pluck them from His hand (John 10:27-29). He promised that He would come again to close out history and judge the world for sin and righteousness (Matt. 25:31-33).

Jesus' Actions Were the Actions of God

We move now from the words of Jesus to the deeds of Jesus. The two most obvious deeds of Jesus that point toward His being God are His miracles, each of which was a claim to divinity, and the fact that He accepted the worship of men and women.

John the Baptist sent a message asking if Jesus was the one who was to come (meaning the Messiah) or if there was another. Jesus' reply was "Go and tell John the things which you hear and see: The blind see and the lame walk; the lepers are cleansed and the deaf hear; the dead are raised up and the poor have the gospel preached to them. And blessed is he who is not offended because of Me" (Matt. 11:4-6; see Isa. 29:18; 35:4-6).

Second, He accepted the worship of people. What kind of evil, what kind of delusion, what kind of warp would have to lie in the soul of one who would accept the worship of others if He were not God? In the Jewish culture, where to recognize any other god was blasphemy (Command-ment 1: You shall have no other gods before Me!), no serious Jew would give a thought to worshiping anyone except the one they believed to be God. Jesus was God.

If the Resurrection Is True, Jesus Is God

The Bible makes it clear that Jesus died. All Gospel accounts and many references in the epistles state this clearly. And it makes it clear that the tomb was empty after three days. So the question is, what happened to the body? In his book, *Who Moved the Stone?*, Frank Morison argues powerfully that the Resurrection is the only credible explanation for why the tomb was empty and what happened to Jesus' body.

1. The theft theory. The earliest attempt to explain away Christ's resurrection was that His body was stolen. Some way had to be found to explain the empty tomb, so the Jewish leaders bribed the Roman guards to report that Jesus' body had been stolen while the soldiers had slept (Matt. 28:11-15). This, however, is not a credible theory. The enemies of Jesus had no motive whatever for removing the body. It would have been to the advantage of the Jews and Romans for the body to remain where it was, so that they could prove that Jesus was dead. The friends of Jesus could not have stolen the body. It was guarded by

Roman soldiers who would have paid with their lives if the body were stolen.

2. *The swoon theory.* This theory asserts that Christ did not really die on the cross. Rather, Christ appeared to be dead but had only swooned from exhaustion, pain, and loss of blood. He revived when laid in the cool tomb. After leaving the tomb, He appeared to His disciples, who mistakenly concluded He had risen from the dead.

Suppose for a minute that the Roman executioners were wrong and Jesus had somehow survived and was buried alive. How likely would He have been to have endured another thirty-six hours in a cold, damp tomb without food, water, or medical attention? Would He have survived being wound in heavy, spice-laden grave clothes weighing an estimated seventy pounds? Would He have had the strength to free Himself from the grave clothes, roll away the heavy stone sealing the mouth of the tomb, overpower the Roman guards, and then walk on feet that had been mutilated with nails?

It is impossible that one who had just emerged from the tomb half dead, who staggered around in need of medical attention, could have ever convinced the disciples that He was the bread of life or inspired them to lay down their lives for Him. The only reason this theory received any credence whatsoever was that people were eager to have some way of explaining away the resurrection so that they did not have to believe it.

3. *The hallucination theory.* According to this theory, the disciples so longed for their dead master that they imagined that they saw Him and heard Him speak to them. It is incredible that a large group of people would have the same hallucination. This theory is a late theory and not widely held.

If you apply the same tests to the Resurrection as you would to any other historical event, you come away concluding that the Resurrection of Jesus actually happened. Only those who do not *want* to believe it come to another conclusion and must twist the arm of historical research to do it.

Only if we apply one test of accuracy to all other historical events and a different test to the Resurrection do we disagree that it actually happened. Why would anyone do this? Some do so because they do not understand the impact of historical accuracy tests. Others may do it because, for reasons of their own, they do not want to believe in the Resurrection and must therefore come up with whatever theory they can to explain it away.

Conclusion

Think of the greatest person you have ever heard of. Has anyone done anything to come within a hundred miles of Jesus? Has Alexander the Great? Plato? Socrates? Joan of Arc? Gandhi? George Washington? Abraham Lincoln? Think about it. Any one of them falls so far short of Jesus that it is like comparing a boxing kangaroo to a neurosurgeon. Their deeds fall so short of the actions of Jesus they cannot be in the same category of being. These are not the deeds of a man. They are the deeds of God.

Instant Recall

1. Jesus fulfilled all p_____ as the Messiah.

2. Jesus' w_____ were the words of God.

3. Jesus' a_____ were the actions of God.

4. If the Resurrection is true, Jesus is G_____.

Action Line

Read: My book *What You Need to Know about Jesus* has much more helpful information about this subject. If you want to learn even more, read *Who Is this Jesus?* by Michael Green.

Memorize: John 1:1.

Think about It

If you don't believe Jesus is God . . .

- You must admit that the Bible is full of lies.

- Jesus is not who He said He is, and He can offer you no hope for this life or the next.

- There is no such thing as right or wrong. You can do whatever society will let you get away with. And so can everyone else.

Pray: Dear Lord, thank You for sending Jesus to earth for our sake. Thank You that He was a believable, credible historical figure, that we do not have to commit intellectual suicide to believe in Him. Thank You for giving us the faith to receive Him. Amen.

Let Me Ask You

1. Why do you think people are willing to believe Jesus was a great moral teacher, even though many of the things He said were so outrageous that He could not be merely a great moral teacher?

2. Some people claim Jesus manipulated circumstances to make it look as though He fulfilled many prophecies, even though He really was not the Messiah. How do you respond to that?

3. Why do you think God chose the Resurrection to be the pivotal event in history?

Why Believe the Bible?

Well Said

Defend the Bible? I would just as soon defend a lion. Just turn the Bible loose. It will defend itself.

—Charles Haddon Spurgeon

The Search for Truth

We are living in an incongruous time in history. On the one hand, many people do not believe in absolute truth. On the other hand, they are hungering for truth as never before. Every year the hottest-selling tabloids that infest the checkout lanes of grocery stores are the year-end editions that contain all the prophecies for the upcoming year. The prophecies range from the goofy to the bizarre to the absurd—and virtually never come true. Yet "inquiring minds" scoop them up as though they were gold nuggets.

The search for truth takes people in various directions—crystals, reincarnation, the horoscope—yet many others are turning to the Bible. This is especially true as one looks at the global scene rather than just the American scene. The world seems to be polarizing. On the one hand, the world is plummeting to new cultural, social, and spiritual depths, while on the other hand many are turning to Christ and the Bible in record numbers.

The Bible has weathered criticism and neglect and today stands stronger than ever. Billions of Bibles have been distributed, and millions more are being distributed every year. What could possibly account for this astonishing hunger for, longevity of,

Snapshot

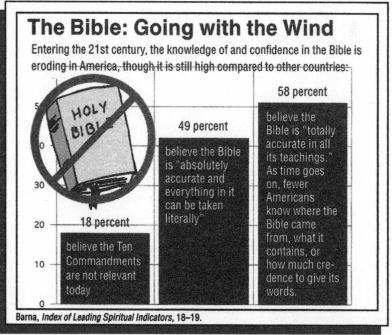

The Bible: Going with the Wind

Entering the 21st century, the knowledge of and confidence in the Bible is eroding in America, though it is still high compared to other countries:

58 percent believe the Bible is "totally accurate in all its teachings." As time goes on, fewer Americans know where the Bible came from, what it contains, or how much credence to give its words.

49 percent believe the Bible is "absolutely accurate and everything in it can be taken literally"

18 percent believe the Ten Commandments are not relevant today

Barna, *Index of Leading Spiritual Indicators*, 18–19.

and indestructibility of the Bible? The answer is that the Bible is the Word of God. There are several key reasons to believe this is true.

The Bible, as Originally Written, Was Without Error

If there were mistakes in the Bible, and if the Bible were the Word of God, then God would be the author of mistakes. If God were the author of mistakes, then He would not be what the Bible claims He is, and He would be unreliable. We must have confidence that there are no mistakes in the Bible.

▼▼▼▼▼▼▼▼

There is nothing in the Bible that has ever been proved wrong.

▲▲▲▲▲▲▲▲▲

There is nothing in the Bible that has ever been proved wrong. The significance of this is that if the Bible is utterly reliable on earthly matters, it is reasonable to trust it on heavenly matters.

People often are told, or get the impression, that there are errors or contradictions in the Bible. But everything that seems to be an error or contradiction can be explained credibly. For example, the four Gospels differ in their account as to what was written on a sign that was nailed to the cross above Jesus' head when He was crucified. Matthew says, "This is Jesus, the king of the Jews." Mark says, "The king of the Jews." Luke says, "This is the king of the Jews." John says, "Jesus of Nazareth, the king of the Jews." True, all of these are different. However, none of these accounts say that this was all that was written on the sign. The whole thing can be reconciled by realizing that the sign contained everything that was written: "This is Jesus of Nazareth the king of the Jews." From this full statement, each author, for reasons of his own, articulated only part of the statement, but there is no error.

I may tell my wife that I am going to the post office. When I get home, I tell her that I picked up a screwdriver at the hardware store. Did I lie to her by not telling her I was going to the hardware store? No. I did go to the post office, and I did not tell her that I was *only* going to the post office. I did not give her all the truth, but everything I gave her was true.

People say that the Bible is a book of mythology or that it is filled with contradictions and riddled with errors. But this has never been demonstrated. Whether in matters of science, history, geography, or internal consistency, it has never been demonstrated that the Bible is wrong. There are some apparent or momentary items that initially seemed to be inaccurate but they have all been credibly harmonized. Many people who claim the Bible contains errors often have not come to that conclusion as a result of their own study but have borrowed that conclusion from a fellow worker or professor in college or a relative who made the claim. It is not true. There is not one apparent error or contradiction that cannot credibly be explained.

Fact File

The Extent of Variations

Bruce Metzger, a New Testament scholar who taught at Princeton, has said that out of the twenty thousand lines in the New Testament, only forty lines are up for debate today. Everything else is a given, and none of the variances affect the Christian faith.

Quoted by McDowell, *Evidence That Demands a Verdict*, 53.

Today's Bible Is Essentially the Same as the Original

While the original Bible may have contained no errors, the Bible has gone through centuries of copying. There are some discrepancies in the various ancient manuscripts, but those discrepancies are insignificant and have no bearing on any doctrine. There are variations in spelling and inconsistencies in numbers, but they are few, minor, and affect no doctrine.

There are two other matters that are important in establishing the reliability of the ancient manuscript from which we get our English Bible. First, there are many of them. There are over five thousand ancient manuscripts of the New Testament! By comparison, there are only ten copies of Caesar's *Gallic Wars*. In addition to the New Testament documents, we have over ten thousand ancient manuscripts or parts of manuscripts of the Old Testament. The sheer volume of manuscripts makes it easier to verify the truth and accuracy of the manuscripts. They all say exactly the same thing, with insignificant exceptions. Our Bible today is reliable.

In addition, we have very old manuscripts. The New Testament was completed no later than A.D. 100. The earliest known manuscript that contains most of the New Testament dates to about A.D. 200, a span of only about one hundred years. By comparison, Caesar's *Gallic Wars* was written about 60 B.C., yet the earliest existing manuscript we have is dated A.D. 900, nearly one thousand years older. This is typical. The Bible has unmatched manuscript credibility.

Archaeology Supports the Credibility of the Bible

Many of the attacks on the accuracy of the Bible were begun prior to modern archaeology. As travel has become easier and scholars more curious, archaeologists have begun to peel away the earth's surface to reveal ancient cities, painted tombs, solid gold likenesses of rulers, jars, money, and items needed for the afterlife, tablets of stone and clay telling the story of a

Fact File

The Reappearance of Belshazzar

Belshazzar, named in the book of Daniel as the last king of Babylon, was nowhere to be found in Babylonian records. In fact, all known Babylonian records listed Nabonidus as the last king. Then it was discovered in archaeological records that Nabonidus left Babylon for ten years and went to Arabia. His son Belshazzar ruled as king in his place. Nabonidus never abdicated his throne, so he was listed as the king of record. But Belshazzar ruled as king in Babylon in his place during the time of Daniel. In this way archaeology explained the apparent discrepancy between the biblical record and the previous Babylonian record.

Paul E. Little, *Know Why You Believe* (Chicago: InterVarsity, 1968), 95.

people or a city, etc. As this evidence began to amass, references to biblical places and people became not unusual. In a number of cases, people or places that skeptics had written off as fanciful mistakes in the Bible were now confirmed. In fact, many things that were questioned by scholars in the eighteenth and nineteenth centuries have now been verified as factual, both cities and things in those cities, as well as rulers and important people.

More than a century of biblical excavations at over twenty-five thousand sites have repeatedly confirmed the accuracy of the Bible. After working in the field for many years, noted archaeologist Nelson Glueck said, "It may be stated categorically that no archaeological discovery has ever controverted a biblical reference."[1]

Fulfilled Prophecies Support the Credibility of the Bible

The Bible is the only book in the world that has specific prophecies made hundreds of years earlier that have been clearly fulfilled. The prophecies that validated the divinity of Jesus (chapter 26) are exactly the same as those that validate that the Bible is the Word of God.

These, of course, are only prophecies dealing with Jesus. But there are many more prophecies in the Bible that were fulfilled, and the Bible itself makes it clear that fulfilled prophecy is one of the evidences of the supernatural origin of the word of its prophets (Jer. 28:9). If a prophet ever spoke anything that did not come true, he was not a true prophet (Deut. 18:21-22) and was to be stoned.

Think about It

Unless you believe the Bible is true . . .

- The lights go out. You are in the dark. You have no moral compass to guide you, and no hope beyond the grave.

- You have no answers to the significant questions in life: Who am I? Where did I come from? Why am I here? Where am I going?

- You are alone. You have no meaning in life and no explanation for the world around you.

The odds of these prophecies being accidentally fulfilled are virtually zero. Just look at the record of the psychics in the tabloid papers. No one is able, on any level of credibility, to prophesy things that come true. Yet the Bible is full of such prophecies. They create a set of odds so remarkable that they validate that the Bible is the Word of God.

Changed Lives Support the Credibility of the Bible

Most of the twelve disciples died terrible deaths because of their faith. Would they die

Let Me Ask You

1. Did you believe the Bible before reading this chapter? How has this chapter influenced your thinking?

2. When you compare the grocery store tabloids with Bible prophecy, how does it affect your perception of the Bible's credibility?

3. Does the change in your own life support the credibility of the Bible in your mind? Why or why not?

dreadful deaths for something they knew to be a lie? They said, in essence, "Go ahead and kill me if you want to, but I know it is true."

The same is true of many people who followed in their footsteps over the last two thousand years. *Foxe's Book of Martyrs* is an account of the deaths of many early Christians for their faith. The stories send a chill into the bones of anyone who reads them. People being sawed in half, fed to wild animals, forced to stand unprotected in the cold until they froze to death, and all they had to do to escape all of this was deny Jesus. This they would not do.

Millions of people's lives over the centuries have been dramatically changed as a result of becoming a Christian and following the Bible.

Conclusion

The greatest nonevent of the twentieth century was the death of Christianity. It didn't happen. The theory of evolution, the establishment of Marxism, and the rise of scientific knowledge were supposed to drive the final nails in the coffin of Christianity. Just the opposite is true. Evolution is a theory in chaos, Marxism has collapsed under its own weight, and science is only confirming Christian truths, rather than disproving them. The Bible stands taller than it ever has. It has never been so demonstrably true, nor so universally accepted. Truth has a ring to it truer than a tuning fork at middle C, and a power to it stronger than a hurricane. To multiplied millions of people worldwide, the Bible is ringing true, and its power is changing lives, to the glory of God.

Instant Recall

1. The Bible, as originally written, was without e_____.

2. Today's Bible is essentially the s_____ as the original.

3. A_____ supports the credibility of the Bible.

4. Fulfilled p_____ support the credibility of the Bible.

5. Changed l_____ support the credibility of the Bible.

Action Line

Read: My book *What You Need to Know about the Bible* has much more helpful information about this subject. If you want to learn even more, read *God Has Spoken* by James I. Packer.

Memorize: Hebrews 4:12.

Pray: Dear Lord, thank You that the Bible can be trusted. Thank You that my life is one of the millions that have been changed, in testimony to its power and authenticity. Help me always to do it justice in my life. Amen.

How Can I Believe in Spite of the Pain?

Well Said

If God were a pagan god, . . . our grief would force Him down to earth. But . . . our God came to be among us. Shake your fist at Him, spit in His face, scourge Him, and finally crucify Him; what does it matter?. . . It's already been done to Him.

—George Bernanos

Why Do Bad Things Happen to Good People?

Fact File

Roll Call of Infamy

- Hitler killed 6 million Jews.
- Stalin killed 40 million Russians.
- Mao killed 70 million Chinese.

The problem of human suffering is perhaps the single greatest problem that people have with God. Dorothy Sayers once wrote, "The only question worth discussing is 'Why do the righteous suffer?'" How can God be good and still allow His children to suffer? The temptation is to conclude that either God must not be all good, in which case He doesn't care about the evil, or else He is not all powerful, and He can't do anything about it.

We don't understand why His will and our will don't coincide more often. Why won't things work out? Why won't He bless us? Why can't I be happy? Why won't He relieve the pain? Why won't He correct the wrong? Why won't He take compassion on me and visit me either with an end to my suffering or with a greater measure of grace? Whether it is in a pointed and painful area or a dull and confusing area, it is the problem of pain. Why does God allow suffering? What does He want from me?

Not only do we wrestle with it on a very personal level, if we are suffering, but we also must wrestle with it on a global/historical level. We are not the only ones to suffer. Suffering is universal.

Hitler exterminated six million Jews and is therefore generally regarded as the most evil man in history, but he has competition. In terms of numbers of people who suffered at his hands, he is dwarfed by others. Before him, Joseph Stalin, the father of modern communism, is commonly believed to have killed as many as forty million of his own countrymen.

But Hitler and Stalin together do not reach the depths of Chairman Mao of China, responsible for the deaths of perhaps as many as seventy million Chinese.

In sum, 116 million people killed at the hands of dedicated atheists.[1]

What a ghastly record of just one evil in the world: armed revolution. There are the additional evils of crime, domestic abuse, discrimination, famine, epidemics, earthquakes, and floods and other natural disasters. The amount of evil and suffering in the world is profound, mind-numbing. If one thinks about it on the individual level, for there is the real tragedy, the sensitive soul could not take it in.

▼▼▼▼▼▼▼▼

When we wish that God would destroy evil in the world, we are making a death wish.

▲▲▲▲▲▲▲▲

This has become a significant problem for Christianity in the eyes of many. They believe that the suffering in the world is incompatible with an all-good, all-powerful God. Is it?

God Did Not Create Evil

Evil originated with Satan and entered the world with Adam and Eve (Gen. 3; Ezek. 28:15). The Bible studiously avoids attributing the responsibility for sin and evil to God. Satan and Adam and Eve are clearly held accountable for their choices. We might wrestle with why God created a system in which evil was possible, but sin is the consequence of free will, and without free will, no creation would be meaningful. We are ultimately left with a decision of faith, to believe that God is not morally culpable for the presence of sin in the world.

God Cannot Remove Evil without Destroying Humanity

When we wish that God would destroy evil in the world, we are making a death wish. He cannot destroy all evil without destroying us. When we ask, "Why do the innocent suffer?" the answer is "There are no innocent." Romans tells us that all have sinned and come short of the glory of God.

"All right," we counter, "why do the good suffer?" When we ask this, we want Mother Teresa not to suffer, but it is understandable if Hitler does. But if Mother Teresa is white and Hitler is black, as you move from one to the other, you never cross a line between black and white. You only move through infinite gradations of gray. At some point you would have to draw a line between one person who had committed ninety-nine sins who goes to heaven and one who had committed one hundred sins who goes to hell. Is that fair? God must either allow evil to exist or else destroy all humanity.

We Must Reconcile Our Pain with God's Character

1. We lack information. When attempting to reconcile pain with God's character, we can safely assume that there is still some information we don't have.

Five Key Truths

Five truths help us reconcile our pain with God's character:

1. We lack information.

2. We lack understanding.

3. We must see things from God's point of view.

4. We must recognize that God enters our pain.

5. We must believe that our suffering matters.

New discoveries are being made every day based on information that is new. At the time of this writing, cloning is a new phenomenon, as is the ability to choose the gender of one's baby by artificial insemination. Without commenting on the ethics of those issues, the point is, we are able to do them now because we have gained information that we didn't have a decade ago. It will seem old hat in another decade.

When we get to heaven, we will have complete information.

2. We lack understanding. It may not be that we lack information but that we lack understanding, because of limited intellectual or spiritual capacity. If we do not understand other things in this finite world, should it come as a surprise to us that we do not comprehend everything in the infinite world? Many of us don't understand electricity or computer manuals or the theory of relativity. But just because we don't understand them does not mean they are not true, or that they are not understood by others with greater understanding.

▼▼▼▼▼▼▼▼

Where is God when it hurts? He is on the cross, taking to Himself in Christ the pain, agony, and terror of all the suffering of all the world for all time.

▲▲▲▲▲▲▲▲

3. We must see things from God's point of view. We do not yet fully see things from God's point of view. He is not out to get us, nor is He out to neglect us. He is out to make us like Him, to make friends with us, to create in us a capacity to know and enjoy Him. And for reasons hidden deep in the mysteries of His will, He allows and uses pain to achieve those purposes.

4. We must recognize that God enters our pain. Scripture says, "God was in Christ reconciling the world to Himself" (2 Cor. 5:19). Where is God when it hurts? He is on the cross, taking to Himself in Christ the pain, agony, and terror of all the suffering of all the world for all time. We are united with Christ. When we suffer, God the Father suffers. When we are in pain, God feels and hears and cares.

No, God does not escape. He has chosen not to escape. Even from heaven, when I hurt, God hurts. And so I no longer cry out, "God, why don't you make it stop hurting?" He is hurting with me. And so there must be a reason for it that lies beyond me.

5. We must believe that our suffering matters. The Bible hints that the suffering we go through, which makes no sense to us at all, is perhaps a cosmic drama in which we are not alone, though in our pain we feel very much alone. If the book of Job is any indication, perhaps at that moment we feel most alone the eyes of heaven and hell are focused most sharply on us to witness the triumph of the grace of God. At that point at which we feel most removed from reality and purpose in this world, we are the most involved in reality and purpose in the next world.

There is more to life than we see. There is more going on than we understand. When you suffer, take heart. Your life matters. God knows you and loves you. When you hurt, He cares.

When you are lonely, He cares. When you are confused and fearful, He cares. He is not off in some other corner of the universe paying attention to something that really matters. He is living within your heart, calling and hoping that your faith will remain strong in the struggle. And He promises to set all things straight one day. What a celebration that will be!

In the End All Will Be Well

Eventually, God will destroy all evil and end the suffering of His children. He has provided a way for humanity to be saved from sin. God Himself came to earth, was born as Jesus of Nazareth, and died for our sins so that we would not have to. He paid our price for us. Whatever the mystery behind the existence of sin, there is sufficient evidence to uphold the goodness of God. Had He stayed in heaven, leaving us to grovel in our own pain and find our own way to heaven, we might feel we had a stronger case against God. But because He came and entered our condition—became sin for us, that we might become the righteousness of God (2 Cor. 5:21)—God's goodness is vindicated to all but the most skeptical.

Think about It

If you don't believe what Scripture says about suffering . . .

- You may not have the internal strength to cope with suffering.

- You may get angry with God for not delivering you.

- You may not be able to help others who are suffering.

John Newton, author of the hymn "Amazing Grace," once said, "Many have puzzled themselves about the origin of evil. I am content to observe that there is evil, and that there is a way to escape from it, and with this I begin and end." Some might consider that statement insufficient explanation, but it carries a valid point. If God claims He is not the author of evil, and if He sent His Son to die for us to give us a way to escape the eternal consequences of evil, is there not sufficient evidence to vindicate the character of God?

God Can Use Suffering for Good

While evil and suffering are not good in themselves, they can be used for good. In a fallen world, pain can be a gift to turn us from an action so that we do not experience even greater pain.

1. Giving spiritual enlightenment. Pain can also be used for spiritual purposes. In 2 Corinthians 1:1-11 we learn that we can gain three things from suffering:

- the ability to comfort others
- wisdom to trust not in ourselves but in God, who can see us through our difficulties
- the opportunity to give thanks in all things because of God's mercy and grace.

2. Creating spiritual growth. There are times when God uses discipline in the lives of His spiritual children for their good. The book of Hebrews (12:10-11) tells us there are two benefits we can experience from suffering:

- We can receive encouragement because discipline assures us that we are, in fact, children of God.
- We can share in God's holiness and reap the reward of righteousness.

3. Conveying eternal glory. A final good that God can bring out of suffering is to give us eternal rewards for our earthly suffering. In fact, bad as the suffering of this world may be, the apostle Paul told us that the glories of heaven will make our earthly suffering seem easy by comparison (2 Cor. 4:17-18).

Conclusion

Ultimately, the reason for suffering must dissolve into mystery. There is no way for us to grasp it fully this side of heaven. For most of us, understanding usually comes after the difficulty is over and we look back. So it will be with life. When we look back, we will understand and we will accept. God's character and power will be intact. And we will realize that we are not qualified to be God ourselves, and there are times when we must simply bow to Him and let Him be God.

Instant Recall

1. God did not create e_____.

2. God cannot remove evil without destroying h_____.

3. We must r_____ our pain with God's character.

4. In the end all will be w_____.

5. God can use suffering for g_____.

Let Me Ask You

1. When you compare yourself with others who have suffered terribly (refugees in the Third World, Jews during World War II), have you really suffered much?

2. Do you find yourself complaining for relatively trivial things? If so, how can you change?

3. What Scripture verse has been most helpful to you in coping with suffering?

Action Line

Read: My book *What You Need to Know about Defending Your Faith* has much more helpful information about this subject. If you want to learn even more, read *Where Is God When It Hurts?* by Philip Yancey.

Memorize: Hebrews 12:11.

Share: Discuss this material with someone—a friend, a family member, or someone in your church—in order to learn it better.

Pray: Dear Lord, thank You that You can use suffering to accomplish good. Thank You that Jesus entered into our suffering. Thank You that in the end all will be well. Amen.

Part 3

▼▼▼▼▼▼▼▼▼▼▼▼▼▼▼▼▼

How Should We Live?

▲▲▲▲▲▲▲▲▲▲▲▲▲▲▲▲▲▲

How Do I Make the "Great Wager"?

CHAPTER
29

Chapter at a Glance

- Some people don't want to believe in God.

- Some people do want to believe in God.

- We all wager our lives on whether or not God exists.

- The "great wager" is made by faith.

Well Said

Granted that faith cannot be proved, what harm will come to you if you gamble on its truth and it proves false?. . . If you gain, you gain all; if you lose, you lose nothing.

—Blaise Pascal

Life Is a Gamble

Life is uncertain. I remember a number of years ago hearing of a couple in England who were terrified of nuclear war. They searched the globe looking for a safe place to live, and finally settled on the Falkland Islands, a remote British crown colony off the coast of Argentina, not far from Antarctica. Not long afterward, in 1982, Argentina, who also claimed sovereignty over the islands, sent troops to seize the islands. In response, England dispatched a large naval task force to retake the islands. After intense naval and air battles, the Argentine military surrendered. Heavy losses were suffered on both sides.

Sometimes you can't win for losing. You travel to one of the remotest inhabitable locations on earth, and war comes thundering to your doorstep. This is a small example of the fact that much of life is a gamble. Sometimes the odds are great, sometimes slim, but almost everything is a calculated risk. We all gamble when we get on an airplane. We gamble when we take a new prescription drug. We gamble when we leave our house in the morning.

Not only do we all gamble *in* life; we all gamble *with* life. That is, we are all betting on whether there is a God or whether there isn't. Someone once asked Aldous Huxley, a renowned humanist, why he and his other intellectual friends were so eager to embrace what was then the new theory of evolution. He said that they desired a liberation from morality. "We objected to the morality because it interfered with our sexual freedom."[1]

On the other hand, I am betting on God. If someone were to ask me why I believe the Bible, on one level it is because I *want* to believe the Bible. Everything will be better if the Bible is true.

If we want to believe in God, we have sufficient evidence to convince ourselves, and we have good company. The same is true if we don't want to believe. So, what is the rationale for belief? Some do not believe in God because they do not want to, and interpret all the evidence accordingly.

Some People Don't Want to Believe in God

There are a number of reasons why some don't want to believe in the God of the Bible.

1. Intellectual opposition. Alister McGrath has written of intellectual barriers in his book *Intellectuals Don't Need God,* and these thoughts are drawn largely from his book.[2]

a. Christianity is merely a hangover from the intellectual Dark Ages. It is not relevant to a modern world.

b. Christianity is merely a wish fulfillment, not supported by the facts.

c. Suffering seems incompatible with the idea of a loving God.

d. All religions lead to God.

e. Christianity is based on a series of unjustifiable, outdated, and incredible events that can no longer be taken seriously.

2. The failure of Christians or Christianity. The failure of individuals as well as the church as a whole to live up to expectations is a major claim for unbelief. From something as individual as "all the hypocrites in the church" to revulsion over the institutional failings of the church for the last two thousand years (the Crusades, the Inquisition, modern televangelists, etc.), many, as a reason to reject God, point to the failure of Christians and/or the church to live up to expectations.

3. Pride or inferiority. There are some people who won't give themselves over to God because, in their pride, they are unwilling to believe or admit that they need God. "There's nothing wrong with me. I don't need to be saved!" they cry. Others don't give themselves over to God because of a sense of inadequacy and inferiority. They say something such as "Why would God want a worm like me?" This is often said quite sincerely and with great emotional anguish.

> **Many people believe in God because, when they look at the starry heavens on a clear night, something deep within them cries out, "There must be a God."**

4. Carnality. There are those who are unwilling to give their lives to God because they don't want to stop sinning. As long as they believe that God doesn't exist or that He doesn't condemn people for sins or there is no sin, they don't have to give up anything they currently have or are doing.

Some People Do Want to Believe in God

There are people who are inclined to believe in God for a number of reasons.

1. To escape hell. Avoiding punishment is often the easiest to understand and the most compelling reason to want to believe in God. A fear of death and the afterlife persuade many to believe in God.

2. Hope of heaven. Some want to believe in God not so much because they fear hell but because they want heaven. They want to look forward to an eternity in the presence of God and other good people, without the pain, heartache, and tears of this life.

3. Intuitive belief. Many people believe in God because, when they look at the starry heavens on a clear night, something deep within them cries out, "There must be a God." Also for some, when they search their own inner thoughts for an explanation of where humanity came from, why we are here, where we are going, nothing satisfies except that there is a supreme creator-God.

4. Purpose and meaning. For others, there is no purpose or meaning in life unless there is God. If we are just the result of a biological accident, then life has no meaning. If we are created and can know God, there is possibility for meaning.

5. The credibility of the Bible. The Bible is a remarkable book. It records prophecies, a plausible explanation for the world, and a keen understanding of the nature of humanity. When we obey it, we benefit; when we violate it, we suffer. It provides a compelling reason to believe in God.

6. The life of Jesus. Jesus was the most important person ever to have lived. His teachings are profound, His life exemplary, His works remarkable, His death and resurrection so unexplainable that many people believe in God because of Him.

We All Wager Our Lives on Whether or Not God Exists

In his classic writing *Pensèes (Thoughts)*, Blaise Pascal wrote that either God is or He is not but that you cannot prove God or disprove Him, so on what basis do we believe in Him? He encouraged us to "wager" with our lives. That is, to "bet" that God exists

Fact File

To Understand the Wager . . .

There are four basic points to understand in making the "great wager."

1. **Created:** God created us for fellowship with Him. He wants us to have a rich meaningful life on earth and eternal life in heaven (John 3:16; 10:10).
2. **Separated:** We are all separated from God by sin. As a result, we are hampered in this life and are destined to an eternity separated from Him (Rom. 3:23; 6:23).
3. **Called:** Jesus is the only way we can be reconciled to God, restored to more meaningful life on earth, and given eternal life in heaven. He died for our sin and rose from the dead to give us new life (Rom. 5:8; 1 Cor. 15:3-6). He appeals to us to believe in a receive Him (John 1:1, 12).
4. **Restored:** When we believe in Jesus (which includes repenting of our sin), receive Him into our lives, and commit our lives to living for Him, we are forgiven of our sins and given eternal life (John 1:1, 12; Eph. 2:8-9).

and to live accordingly, rather than to "bet" that He doesn't exist and live according to that. His argument had the following points.

1. We do not have the option of not wagering. If we do not wager that God exists, then by default we are wagering that He does not. Since we are all going to die, and since, if God exists, we must answer to Him for our lives, we automatically wager against Him unless we wager in favor of Him.

2. If you wager that God exists and you are right, you win everything. You win a meaningful, purposeful life on earth and

Think about It

If you don't understand the "great wager" . . .

- You might not realize that not to accept God is the same as rejecting Him, that you don't have the option of not wagering on God.

- You might put off the wager, thinking you have plenty of time, and then run out of time.

- You might lead others astray. Just because you're willing not to bet on God doesn't mean that you should encourage others not to bet on Him.

eternal happiness in heaven. If you wager that God exists and you are wrong, you have lost little, perhaps nothing.

3. If you wager that God does not exist and you are right, you have gained little. The life of an unbeliever is no richer on earth than the life of a believer. Often it is much worse. But if you wager that God does not exist and you are wrong, then you face eternal destruction in hell.

Does it not make sense, then, that the safest position is to wager your life on the belief that God does exist, and to follow Him in faith? There is everything to gain if you do, and everything to lose if you don't.

The "Great Wager" Is Made by Faith

Pascal then went on to suggest what a person should do if he decides he wants to believe but doesn't. He writes that if your head (intellect) tells you to believe but your heart (faith) is unwilling to go along, it is because of your desires, since your intellect tells you to believe. So he suggested that, rather than amassing additional intellectual reasons to believe, diminish your desires. Learn from those who have faith. Begin acting as if you did believe. Begin living a good life and attending worship services. As you do, faith will grow on you. You can "act" your way into "believing," said Pascal.

Another suggestion I would add to this one is to ask God for faith. We see an example of such a request in the Bible. In Mark 9:20-24 an anguished father brought his son to Jesus and asked Him to heal him from demon possession. Jesus said, "If you can believe, all things are possible to him who believes." The father cried out, "Lord, I believe; help my unbelief!"

If someone prayed to Jesus, "Lord, my head tells me it is reasonable to believe in You, but I just don't seem to be moved to do so. Help me place my faith in You," it is hard for me to believe that God would not honor that prayer. In the Gospel of John, Jesus said, "The one who comes to Me I will by no means cast out" (6:37). If anyone came to Jesus with this prayer, He would not turn her away.

Let Me Ask You

1. Does faith in God come easily to you or not? Why do you think that is?

2. What, to you, are the most compelling reasons to believe in God?

3. Does the "great wager" seem reasonable to you? Why or why not?

Conclusion

If you believe that Jesus is the Son of God, that He died for your sins, rose from the dead as victor over death . . . if you believe you are a sinner, separated from God, and that you cannot save yourself, that you must be forgiven of your sins to be reconciled to God and given eternal life . . . if you are willing to turn from your old life of sin to follow Jesus . . . then you can simply tell God all of that, ask Him to forgive your sin, give you eternal life, and help you to become the person He wants you to be.

Make the "great wager." Bet your life on God. You have everything to gain and nothing to lose if you do, little to gain and everything to lose if you don't.

Instant Recall

1. Some people d_____ want to believe in God.

2. Some people do w_____ to believe in God.

3. We all w_____ our lives on whether or not God exists.

4. The "great wager" is made by f_____.

Action Line

Read: My book *What You Need to Know about Defending Your Faith* has much more helpful information about this subject.

Memorize: Hebrews 11:6.

Pray: Dear Lord, thank You that if I come to Jesus, I will not be turned away. Thank You that You are willing to save me from my sin and give me eternal life. Help me to give my life to You completely. Amen.

How Do I Maintain Spiritual Health?

CHAPTER 30

Chapter at a Glance

- There are things I must not do.

- There are things I must do.

Well Said

Salvation is free, but discipleship costs us everything we have.

—Billy Graham

You Are What You Eat

The old saying "you are what you eat" is being proved correct. Scientific studies have proved that dietary fiber (or lack of it), high cholesterol, fat calories, cigarette smoke, alcohol, stress, and a sedentary lifestyle all have a direct link to modern diseases, especially heart disease, stroke, and cancer.

If I want to be physically healthy, there are a number of things I must do: I must eat properly, exercise regularly, get sufficient sleep, and maintain a positive outlook on life. But that is not all. On the other hand, there are things I must not do. I must not abuse my body with alcohol, drugs, and tobacco; I must not succumb to stress in my life; and I must not worry.

▼▼▼▼▼▼▼▼

If we want to be spiritually healthy, we must eliminate spiritually destructive things from our lives.

▲▲▲▲▲▲▲▲

The same is true if I want to be spiritually healthy. There are some things that I must do, and there are some things I must not do.

There Are Things I Must Not Do

When we talk about things we must not do to be spiritually healthy, we are in danger of slipping into legalism. Legalism is placing demands on ourselves or others that God doesn't place on us. However, just as it is not legalistic for a doctor to tell someone he must stop smoking or he will die, so it is not legalistic to tell someone she must stop spiritually destructive behavior.

If we want to be spiritually healthy, we must eliminate spiritually destructive things from our lives.

Media. David said, "I will set nothing wicked before my eyes" (Ps. 101:3). Philippians 4:8 says, "Whatever things are true, whatever things are noble, whatever things are just, whatever things are pure, whatever things are lovely, whatever things are of good report, if there is any virtue and if there is anything praiseworthy—meditate on these things." Ephesians 5:12 tells us that it is "shameful even to speak of those things which are done by them in secret." This is in a context talking about fornication, uncleanness, filthiness, foolish talking, and coarse jesting. These things are "works of darkness." The terms sound as though they are describing prime-time television. And if it is shameful even speak of these things, how much more shameful is it to sit down and watch it for entertainment?

Television may be the single most destructive influence in the history of the human race. Nearly everyone agrees that television is loaded with trash, but very few people will stop watching it. Nor is there a significant difference between the viewing habits of churched and unchurched people. Not only is the programming terrible, but many of the commercials and promotions for other programs are unwatchable by someone wanting to keep a pure mind.

A major step forward for all Christians would be to eliminate television. One can make a logical argument for watching selectively, but few people are able to do so with wisdom and maturity. Cable and satellite television are both better and worse than network programming. While some programming on cable and satellite is much better than network, without discernment and determination, they make a bad situation

In a Nutshell

For Health

For my spiritual health,
I must eliminate:

- harmful media
- harmful relationships
- harmful activities
- harmful attitudes

For my spiritual health,
I must encourage:

- worship (individual and corporate)
- growth (knowledge, character, and ministry)
- impact (evangelism and humanitarianism)

worse. A total break, I believe, is helpful and perhaps necessary to even gain the discernment to decide what can be watched and what should be avoided. It is legalistic to forbid television watching for the minority with the spiritual maturity to control it, but abstinence may be essential for the vast majority.

Similar arguments apply to movies, music (especially rock and rap), literature, and things available on the Internet. More Christians are defeated by media today, I believe, than any other single influence. I have no doubt that if television were eliminated from the earth, Satan would come up with something else alarmingly destructive, but today media is our great battle. All other battles are exacerbated by it.

Relationships. First Corinthians 15:33 says, "Bad company corrupts good character" (NIV). If there are people we relate to who have a detrimental effect on our character, we must alter or end the relationship. Flirtatious, negative, or corrupting relationships stand in the way of our devotion to Christ. We sometimes tell ourselves that we can help others, but unless we are very mature already, we risk being reduced to their level rather than elevating them to our level.

Activities and recreation. Alcohol and drugs not only have a terrible effect on us physically; they are equally damaging spiritually. If you abuse alcohol or drugs, you must stop. Hard as it may be, there is no other answer.

If you engage in other activities that discourage or interfere with a committed Christian lifestyle, they must be altered or eliminated. You may have a hobby that is not inherently harmful but gets in the way of your Christian responsibilities; it must be controlled or eliminated.

Attitudes and values. We may have resident attitudes and values that are distinctly unbiblical. If so, they need to go. Racial prejudice, a sarcastic spirit, a complaining heart, a loose tongue, etc.—all are unbiblical and need to be corrected.

There Are Things I Must Do

In addition to not doing harmful things, there are helpful things we must do if we are to be spiritually healthy.

1. Worship. We must worship God individually, on a daily basis (John 4:23-24). This includes praying to Him, reading Scripture, perhaps reading a devotional booklet, perhaps listening to or singing music. A sample guide to personal worship, with Scripture, is included at the end of this chapter. In addition, we must exercise the individual spiritual disciplines(see chapter 36).

We must also worship God with other Christians on a regular basis (Heb. 10:24-25). This means we must find a good church and commit ourselves to it. The church should have a high view of Scripture, commitment to Christian character, and a concern for the lost. In addition, we must exercise the corporate spiritual disciplines (see chapter 36).

2. Growth. There are three things a person must do if he is to grow spiritually. First, he must gain a mature knowledge of the Bible (2 Tim. 3:16-17). Therefore, he must study the Scripture seriously under the ministry of a skilled Bible teacher. A Bible study through a church or other ministry is essential.

The second thing we must do is to develop relationships with those who are more mature than we are spiritually (1 Cor. 11:1). The Christian life is more easily caught than taught. Whether in a formal discipleship relationship in which you meet with someone who specifically helps you in your Christian growth, or whether in an informal personal relationship with someone who is spiritually mature, life-on-life influence is essential for spiritual growth. Fellowship with other Christians in general has a beneficial impact on the Christian life.

Last, we must discover our spiritual gift and learn how to use it (1 Pet. 4:10). The church needs us and we need the church. Only as we help each other and minister to the needs of one another will we all grow to spiritual maturity (Eph. 4:12-16).

▼▼▼▼▼▼▼▼▼

Dietrich Bonhoeffer once said, "When Jesus calls us to discipleship, he bids us come and die."

▲▲▲▲▲▲▲▲▲

3. Impact. We must all commit ourselves to sharing the gospel with those who need to hear (Matt. 28.19-20). Christ has commissioned us all to spread the gospel to the world, and we must do what we are gifted and called to do to fulfill the Great Commission.

Furthermore, the world should be a better place because a Christian has lived (Gal. 6:10). We must be concerned for those in need and do what we can to alleviate suffering and help establish kingdom principles in the world.

Conclusion

All Christians are greatly influenced by the age in which they live. Today we are living in an undisciplined, self-centered, "feel-good" age. The result is that we are pulled to an anemic, half-hearted form of Christian experience. If we want to break free from this devastating gravitational pull, we must determine that we are going to work harder and be more committed to the Christian life than run-of-the-mill Christians. Certainly, our hard work does not gain us favorable status with God. That is granted to us automatically because we are in Christ. But the Christian life is a life of discipline.

Jesus' followers are called "disciples," that is, "disciplined ones"—persons who take up their cross and follow Jesus. Dietrich Bonhoeffer once said, "When Jesus calls us to discipleship, he bids us come and die." Yet in the paradox of spiritual reality, when we give up our life, we find it.

We must make a ruthless and fearless inventory of our lives, do away with the harmful and pursue with single-mindedness the helpful.

 ## Instant Recall

1. In the pursuit of spiritual health, there are things I must n_____ do.

2. In the pursuit of spiritual health, there are things I must d_____ .

 ## Action Line

Read: My books *30 Days to Understanding the Christian Life* and *What You Need to Know about Spiritual Growth* have much more helpful information about this subject. If you want to learn even more, read *Ordering Your Private World* by Gordon MacDonald.

Memorize: Romans 12:1-2.

Pray: Dear Lord, thank You that You have made it possible for me to grow, to become more and more like You. Help me have a clear vision and full commitment for a life of total dedication to You. May you bless me with spiritual health. Amen.

Scriptural Guide to Daily Worship

"I spent the first twenty-five years of my life wanting more freedom, the next twenty-five years of my life wanting more structure, and the last twenty-five years of my life realizing that structure is freedom."

—Winston Churchill

This guide to daily worship can be used as a general guide for helping you have a personal time of worship each day. Recite the Scripture back to the Lord, but feel free to amend and adjust it however it works best for you. The Scripture has been personalized and individualized so that it does not match any specific translation. As you read the Bible, you may find other verses that you would like to use instead of these here. You may want to use another approach for a while and later return to this.

The rule in personal worship is "Do what works." You may feel free to create other days with different Scripture passages. You may want to eliminate some things and add others. It is a guide, not a straight jacket. Some people have a greater desire for more structure than others. I have found this general approach very helpful for years, and I hope it may be helpful to you. I recite the Scripture back to the Lord each day, and follow it with my own spontaneous thoughts under each heading. I have done it so often, I have all the Scripture memorized.

Invocation

"This is the day the Lord has made. Let us rejoice and be glad in it, and may the joy of the Lord be my strength. O satisfy us in the morning with Thy lovingkindness that we may sing for joy and be glad all our days" (Ps. 118:24; 51:8; Neh. 8:10; Ps. 90:14).
(Listen to music or sing from a hymnal, etc.)

Adoration

"Whom have I in heaven but Thee? And besides Thee, I desire nothing on earth. My flesh and my heart may fail, but God is the strength of my heart and my portion forever" (Ps. 73:25-26)
(If you have other thoughts of praise, express them now.)

Confession

"Search me, O God, and know my heart; try me and know my anxious thoughts; and see if there be any hurtful way in me, and lead me in the everlasting way. If I confess my sin, You are faithful and just to forgive my sin and cleanse me from all unrighteousness" (Ps. 139:23-24; 1 John 1:8).

(Confess any specific sins the Lord makes known. Then continue.)

"Wash me thoroughly from my iniquity and cleanse me from my sin. Create in me a clean heart, O God, and renew a steadfast spirit within me" (Ps. 51:1-2, 10).

Scripture

"Thy word is a lamp unto my feet and a light unto my path. Open my eyes that I may behold wondrous things from out of Thy law"(Ps. 119:105, 18).

(Read from the Bible, perhaps along with a devotional aid.)*

Supplication/Intercession

"It is because of Your mercies that we are not consumed. Your lovingkindnesses, indeed, never cease, for Your compassions never fail. They are new every morning. Great is Your faithfulness" (Lam. 3:22-23). "May I love You with all my heart and all my soul and all my mind, and my neighbor as myself" (Matt. 22:37-39). "May I do unto others as I would have others do unto me" (Luke 6:31).

(Pray for the concerns of the day: people, activities, responsibilities, concerns, etc. You may want to keep a written record of requests and answers, and a journal, or a spiritual diary, in which you record your thoughts about your Christian life.)

Benediction

"May the words of my mouth and the meditation of my heart be acceptable in Your sight, O Lord, our rock and our redeemer" (Ps. 19:14). "Now may You make me complete in every good work to do Your will, working in me what is well pleasing in Your sight, through Jesus Christ, to whom be glory forever and ever. Amen" (Heb. 13:20-21).

* Popular Devotional Aids

Our Daily Bread is perhaps the most popular devotional aid in America. Available for free from Radio Bible Class, P.O. Box 270, Grand Rapids, MI 49501. Web site: www.rbc.net.

Unto the Hills, Billy Graham, available from a Christian bookstore.

My Utmost for His Highest, Oswald Chambers, available from a Christian bookstore.

Friends or your denomination may have other suggestions that you will find helpful.

What Is the Role of Faith in My Life?

Well Said

Faith is so important to God because it is the only thing you can do and still not do anything.

—Anonymous

Faith Is Everything

A man fell over the side of a cliff and grabbed a small tree just before plummeting many feet to his death below. As he hung there, he cried out for someone to help him, and a deep, booming voice came from everywhere.

"Do you trust me?"

The man said, "Who's that?"

The Voice said, "It's the Lord. Do you trust Me?"

The man said, "Yes, yes! Yessssss!!! I trust you! Help me!"

The Voice said, "Let go of the branch. I'll save you."

"Whaaaaaaat?!?" the man gasped.

"Let go of the branch" was the reply.

"Let go of the branch?" the man whimpered weakly.

"Yes," the Voice repeated.

The man was silent for several moments. Then he cried out, "Is there anybody else up there?"

If the man on the cliff had trusted God, he would have let go. Because he did not trust God, he was unwilling

> **Faith is everything in the Christian life.**

to let go. The same is true with our Christian life. If God tells us to let go or to hang on, we obey if we trust Him. If we doubt, we do whatever *we* think will be best for us. We always act on what we believe. Faith is everything in the Christian life.

Faith Demands Total Commitment

The executives at Coca-Cola wanted to boil down the primary loyalty, the driving motivation of their company into a single phrase they could write in a small box. They wrote "great taste" in their box and then introduced "New Coke," which taste tests told them was better tasting. In doing so, they stepped into a marketing minefield. America refused to accept the new product. So they tried again, and after hours of deliberation, replaced "great taste" with "American tradition." Pulling original Coca-Cola off the market was tampering with an American institution like apple pie, baseball, and motherhood. They put it back on the market and recovered famously.

Just as companies have to define their primary motivation, their ultimate loyalty, so must individuals. Each of us must write something in the box, and there can be only one thing in the box. One person can have only one primary loyalty. It will be either Jesus or something else.

When we write "Jesus" in our box, it is not a magical charm that ensures that the rest of our life will go smoothly. Rather, it is simply the testimony of what our driving force in life is, regardless of whether life is smooth or rough.

The apostle Paul wrote, in Romans 12:1 -2, "I urge you, brothers, in view of God's mercy, to offer your bodies as living sacrifices, holy and pleasing to God—which is your spiritual act of worship. Do not conform any longer to the pattern of this world, but be transformed by the renewing of your mind. Then you will be able to test and approve what God's will is—his good, pleasing and perfect will" (NIV).

We can be living demonstrations of the goodness of the will of God only if we have first offered ourselves as a living sacrifice to Him.

Faith Gives the Christian the Motivation to Be Obedient

We see faith having a profound effect on the Christian life in at least three areas: obedience, peace, and hope. We have already alluded to its role in obedience, and want to expand on that idea now. Here is an often-quoted statement by Pascal, a 17th-century French philosopher:

All men seek happiness. This is without exception. Whatever different means they employ, they all tend to this end. The cause of some going to war, and of others avoiding it is the same desire in both, attending with different views. They will never takes the least step but to this objective. This is the motive of every man, even of those who hang themselves.[1]

Everything God asks of us, He does so to give some good thing to us or to keep some harm from us. If it is true that all people desire their own happiness and never take the least step except to that end (even those who hang themselves), and if we deeply believe that God only asks from us that which will give us some good or keep us from some harm, then we would never willfully disobey God! When we come to the point in our lives that we deeply believe that to disobey God is to shoot ourselves in the foot, we become much less prone to disobedience and sin.

Certainly a new car or a great vacation is, for the moment, more pleasure-generating than my giving my money to a charity or socking it away in an IRA. However, stingy and selfish people are never as happy in the long run as generous and compassionate people. It shrivels the soul to live only for oneself. We were not made for that existence. And when we get to retirement time, if we do not have enough money put away, we will come to the bitter realization that the fun we had twenty years earlier was not worth the poverty we must endure now.

Sin is easier in the short run but harder in the long run, and righteousness is harder in the short run but easier in the long run.

We always obey our beliefs. The massive disobedience in the church today is rooted in massive unbelief. We do not believe that God's way is the only way to experience deep-seated, long-lasting peace, love, and joy. We go for the quick fix. We do not know—or believe—that sin is easier in the short run but harder in the long run and that righteousness is harder in the short run but easier in the long run. If we did, we would choose righteousness every time. This is how faith gives us strength to obey.

Faith Gives the Strength to Persevere

There are times when life hauls off and socks us right in the stomach, and we are often tempted to ask "Why me?" or "Where is God?" It can make us feel like giving up when God doesn't make sense. But faith steps in, like a mother settling down a rowdy group of children, and quiets the riot of questions. No, there are not always answers to our questions. But faith tells us several key things.

First, faith reminds us that God is all good and all powerful. He can be trusted, in spite of the pain.

Then faith tells us that God can use bad things for good. Romans 8:28 says, "All things work together for good to those who love God, to those who are the called according to His purpose." It does not say that all things are good, but that God will work all things together for good, giving back beauty for ashes.

> **When you look back over your life at the significant things that you have accomplished, usually they were things that were harder than you thought they were going to be as well as more rewarding than you thought they were going to be.**

Next, faith tells us that trials can make us strong, that through trials we can become more than we can become without the trials. Just as an athlete cannot excel without taking his body beyond its comfort zone, just as a musician cannot excel without taking her fingers beyond their comfort zone, just as a scholar cannot excel without taking his mind beyond its comfort zone, so a Christian will not excel without being taken beyond his spiritual comfort zone.

When pain tempts us to quit, faith tells us that God will, with the temptation, provide a way of escape so that we will be able to bear it (1 Cor. 10:13) and will use the trials to make us mature and complete (James 1:2-4). Faith tells us that our suffering will be rewarded in heaven many times over. When you look back over your life at the significant things that you have accomplished, usually they were things that were harder than you thought they were going to be as well as more rewarding than you thought they were going to be.

Suffering is often rewarded in this life, but if it is not rewarded in this life, it will be rewarded in the next. The apostle Paul said that "the sufferings of this present time are not worthy to be compared with the glory which shall be revealed in us" (Rom. 8:18).

You may be thinking, *Heaven is going to have to be pretty good to make up for what I am going through.* That is a true statement.

Therefore, heaven must be spectacular beyond our ability to envision or comprehend. Imagine someone going through the horrors of being a prisoner of war. It is unimaginable except to those have been through it. So it is with heaven.

Faith, then, in addition to giving us the motivation to be obedient, also gives us the strength to keep going in the face of suffering and trials.

Conclusion

Trials take us beyond our spiritual comfort zone. They are unpleasant. They may create confusion and uncertainty. They may even create a desire to rebel or quit.

Jesus Himself prayed that He might be spared the suffering that was prepared for Him. But trusting His heavenly father, Jesus submitted Himself to the will of God. He went through the suffering when God did not spare Him from it.

Jesus is our example. We must all go through suffering. But we must trust God when we do. If we are tempted to quit, He will with the temptation provide a way of escape so that we will be able to bear it (1 Cor. 10.13), and will use the trials to make us mature and complete (James 1:2-4).

Instant Recall

1. Faith demands total c_____.

2. Faith gives the m_____ to be obedient.

3. Faith gives the s_____ to persevere.

Think about It

If you don't understand faith . . .

- You might think that you can play around with halfhearted obedience to God and still experience the depth of spiritual life that God wants you to have and that you want to have.

- You will often not have the strength to do the hard things you ought to do, nor the strength to keep going in the face of tough times.

- Your Christian life is going to be pretty discouraging.

Action Line

Read: My book *What You Need to Know about Spiritual Growth* has much more helpful information about this subject. If you want to learn even more, read *Rediscovering Holiness* by James I. Packer.

Memorize: Romans 12:1-2.

Pray: Dear Lord, thank You that we can please You by faith. If You demanded works, none of us could qualify. Thank You that You even help us exercise the necessary faith to please You. Help me to trust You and obey You in all things. Amen.

Let Me Ask You

1. Have you ever come to a point of total commitment in your life? If not, what do you think keeps you from it? Have you made the decision to be totally committed and then realized later that you had reneged on the commitment? What do you think a person should do about it when that happens?

2. Does it seem right to you that the opposite of obedience is unbelief? Can you think of an example of disobedience in your own life (past or present) that you realize is rooted in unbelief? Explain.

What Are Some Spiritual Snares?

CHAPTER 32

Chapter at a Glance

- Intellectual intimidation is a snare.

- Materialism is a snare.

- Spiritual discouragement is a snare.

- Toying with sin is a snare.

- Spiritual exhaustion is a snare.

Well Said

There is no man so good, who, were he to submit all his thoughts and actions to the laws, would not deserve hanging ten times in his life.

—Montaigne

Look Out for the Trap!

When you go fishing, you take something the fish really like and you hide a hook in it. The fish thinks it is getting the worm, and it does. But it gets something else it didn't bargain for: the hook.

What are you tempted to go outside the will of God to get? More money? There's a hook in it! More fun? There's a hook in it! More respect? There's a hook in it! If you must go outside the will of God to get it, there is a hook in it.

Satan is a deceiver and a destroyer. He wants to defeat us in our Christian walk and will use whatever means he can to accomplish it. A head-on assault will not work with most of us, so he tries to catch us in a spiritual snare. There are five common ones.

▼▼▼▼▼▼▼▼

Satan wants to defeat us in our Christian walk and will use whatever means he can to accomplish it.

▲▲▲▲▲▲▲▲

Intellectual Intimidation Is a Snare

Some Christians silently worry about whether or not Christianity is really true. They are like me. I became a Christian because of family influence. I never considered other religions or worldviews. So, after I had been a Christian for a while, I began to doubt the validity of my decision. I was in college at the time, and I was intimidated by those who claimed that Christianity was simply wrong.

I need not have worried. After two thousand years, no one is going to ask a question that is going to bring Christianity crashing down. Truth need not fear examination.

There are three predicable questions that we must fend off as science questions the credibility of Christianity.

Question 1: How can you believe in creation in the face of all the evidence to the contrary.

Answer: There isn't "all the evidence to the contrary." There is no scientific information that disproves creation, and evolution is a theory in chaos. The more we learn and the more sophisticated our computers become, the less credible evolution is becoming. It simply isn't supported by sufficient facts.

Question 2: How can you believe the Bible when there are so many contradictions in it?

Answer: There aren't any contradictions in it. There are some variations that may appear to be contradictions, but they have all been credibly resolved. Most people who claim contradictions in the Bible are not aware of any specific ones. They have just heard that they exist, and because they don't want to believe the Bible, they latch onto the idea.

Question 3: How can you believe in miracles?

Answer: If you believe in God (and nine often American do), then why would miracles be impossible? What good is a God who can't do miracles? The very definition of God includes the fact that He is higher than and beyond humans. True, miracles aren't commonplace, or they wouldn't be miracles. But to claim that they cannot be true is to overreach our information.

But the secularist also has questions to answer. He has no answers for the fundamental questions of life: Who are we? Where did we come from? Why are we here? Where are we going? In addition, he must explain life with the formula Nothing + The Impersonal + Time + Chance = Everything We See Today. And it is impossible. How can something come from nothing? How can life come from nonlife? How can the personal come from the impersonal? Beyond all that, our increasingly sophisticated computers are telling us that it is simply not possible for evolution to account for the present complexity of the universe. When the secularist attacks Christianity, he is not doing so from a strong position. The only strength he has is that most scientists agree with him. That, however, does not make him right.

> ▼▼▼▼▼▼▼▼
>
> **If you believe in God, then why would miracles be impossible?**
>
> ▲▲▲▲▲▲▲▲

When we understand the issues, we realize that we need not be intellectually intimidated. We are on firm ground.

Materialism Is a Snare

A second spiritual snare is materialism. Someone has said that Americans spend money they don't have for things they don't need to impress people they don't like. Such is the bondage of materialism. I have seen people in America who came from very poor countries where they didn't have anything. You would think they would be forever grateful for the abundance of things in the U.S. But it took about a month for them to assess their position in the economic pecking order and begin to want more. It was no time before they were ungrateful for the things they didn't have rather than grateful for the things they did.

Regardless of the appeal of money, we will not be satisfied with what the world has to offer. Trinkets can never replace trust.

Spiritual Discouragement Is a Snare

Cervantes said, "He who loses wealth loses much; he who loses a friend loses more; but he who loses courage loses everything." It is no small thing to become discouraged. To weary of life is to walk into an emotional "badlands" where desperadoes of black emotion may ambush you at every turn.

Money Won't Make You Happy

Benjamin Franklin once said, "Money never made a man happy yet, nor will it. There is nothing in its nature to produce happiness. The more a man has, the more he wants. Instead of its filling a vacuum, it makes one. If it satisfies one want, it doubles and triples that want another way."

When you see the badlands rising on the horizon, pitch your camp, get out your compass, and review your course. There is no valor in offering your back to an assassin.

There are many causes of spiritual discouragement:

1. Biblical confusion. We feel frustrated over our failures in life, and when we go to the Bible to try to figure our what's wrong, we can't understand the important passages.

2. Unanswered prayer. We read "ask and you will receive." We ask and we don't receive. What's the use!

3. Suffering. Why does God allow my life to be in constant turmoil, to be in chronic pain? Why does He allow my loved ones to suffer?

There are no easy responses to these causes of spiritual discouragement. In chapter 28, we looked at some answers to the problem of pain:

1. We must assume there is still some information we don't have. We don't know everything yet.

2. We must understand that our ability to comprehend is limited. God's ways are beyond our ways.

*3. **We must see things from God's point of view.*** His goal is not to make us comfortable in life but to make us like Christ. Chronically comfortable people rarely become like Christ.

*4. **We must believe that our suffering matters.*** Perhaps, as in the book of Job, angels and demons are looking on as we go through a trial; and when we pass a test, all heaven breaks out in celebration at the grace of God in our lives.

*5. **In the end, all will be well.*** Our suffering will end. Joy will reign, and God's character will be vindicated to the universe.

There is more to life than we see. There is more at stake than merely our personal comfort. What we see is not all there is. We must always hope in God.

Toying with Sin Is a Snare

Many of us think we can play with fire and not get burned. So we toy with sin. That is, we do not intend to set the house on fire, but we play with matches in the living room. It may be visual lust, watching bad television or movies.

> **It is easier to deny the first illicit temptation than it is to satisfy all those that follow it.**

It may be flirting with someone at work or school. It may be padding our expense account or exaggerating our accomplishments on a résumé. It may be buying things we cannot afford. The danger is, of course, that things can get out of hand, and before know it, the house is on fire, even though that was not our intention when we started.

It is easier to deny the first illicit temptation than it is to satisfy all those that follow it. When we give in to the first temptation, we find ourselves unable or unwilling to deny those that follow. If we toy with sin, we must either quit toying or else get in deeper. We rarely stand still. Almost everyone who ends up swimming in major sin got there not by jumping in headfirst but by dangling their feet in the water. We can take steps to stop toying with sin.

1. Admit that you are toying with sin.
2. Dedicate yourself to the Lord to stop.

3. Get involved in activities that will support your decision—personal spiritual disciplines (prayer, Bible reading, etc.), church, small groups, discipleship, spiritual accountability group. If you have gone very far, you may not be able to get out alone.

4. Cleanse your environment and relationships of that which tempts you.

5. Decide ahead of time how you will respond when you are tempted.

6. If you are in so far you cannot get out without help, contact a pastor, Christian counselor, or other person who may be able to help you.

7. Understand that God deals sympathetically with weakness but harshly with rebellion. Take sin seriously. Do not fool around with it. Take extreme steps if necessary to break the bondage. While you are doing that, remember that God loves you and forgives you, even while you may be paying the price for your sin.

▼▼▼▼▼▼▼▼

Almost everyone who ends up swimming in major sin got there not by jumping in headfirst but by dangling their feet in the water.

▲▲▲▲▲▲▲▲

Spiritual Exhaustion Is a Snare

We each have an inner reservoir of spiritual and emotional energy. If that reservoir is depleted at a rate faster than it is replenished, sooner or later we will collapse. In Florida, when underwater reservoirs are drained, the earth above them collapses into the empty reservoir, causing a "sinkhole." We can have our own spiritual and emotional sinkhole.

One reason is that in some families both the husband and wife are working. Others are single-parent families. Both situations put dramatic stress on the family.

A second reason is that we are a media-saturated society, and as a result we do not get enough rest or solitude. The TV, stereo, and/or car radio are always on.

A third reason is that we try to do too many extracurricular things. On top of an overloaded schedule, we try not to miss out on the fun it seems others are having.

The symptoms of spiritual exhaustion include the following:

1. All you want to do is rest or escape. You may stop performing certain responsibilities, such as cooking, cleaning, mowing the yard, etc.

2. You stop caring about things you ought to care about: the lost, the disadvantaged, the hurting. You might even stop caring about your children's progress at school, your relationships with others, etc.

3. You may develop a short fuse with anger, depression, anxiety, or fear, being fine one moment and a mess the next.

There are things we can and must do to get control over our harried schedule.

1. Cut back on your schedule and get more physical rest. Stop watching television. Go to bed earlier.

2. Get organized. This is hard because you don't want to, but it takes less energy to be organized than disorganized.

3. If an activity replenishes you, such as reading, playing the piano, taking a walk, or listening to music, do it.

4. Get help from others. Align yourself with others who encourage and strengthen you, such as church members, fellow bird watchers, fellow workers, family members.

Think about It

If you don't realize the danger of spiritual snares . . .

- You may step into one without realizing it.

- You may keep toying with sin, thinking you can back out of it, when you really can't.

- You may feel so trapped by your life demands that you will think you can't do anything about it, until it is too late.

5. Go to church; read your Bible; reflect and meditate.

Conclusion

The solutions I've offered are hard to do, but if your need is drastic enough, the measures must be equally drastic. We think we cannot do these things, but if we collapse, spiritually and emotionally, we will do many of these things anyway, but in an uncontrolled manner rather than a controlled manner. We never read in the Bible where Jesus dropped everything and ran. If we are to be like Him, we must gain some degree of control over our schedule so that we do not become a spiritual sinkhole.

Let Me Ask You ❓

1. Are there any areas in which you still feel intimidated about your faith?

2. What areas might be serving as a cheap substitute for God in your life right now?

3. Are you spiritually exhausted, or well on the way to being so? What can you do to avert it or recover from it?

Instant Recall

There are five common spiritual snares:

1. I_____ intimidation

2. M_____

3. Spiritual d_____

4. Toying with s_____

5. Spiritual e_____

Action Line

Read: My book *30 Days to Understanding the Christian Life* has much more helpful information about this subject.

Memorize: 1 Peter 5:8.

Pray: Dear Lord, thank You that the Bible alerts us to the dangers of spiritual snares. Thank You for helping me see them, and strengthen me not to step into them. Amen.

How Do I Pray?

Well Said

We cannot all argue, but we can all pray; we cannot all be leaders, but we can all be pleaders; we cannot all be mighty in rhetoric, but we can all be prevalent in prayer. I would sooner see you eloquent with God than with men.

—Charles Haddon Spurgeon

Are We Joking?

Many of us are uneasy about prayer. To one degree or another, we feel unworthy and inadequate. We're not sure if we are qualified to pray, and we're not sure if we know how to pray. We identify with Abraham Lincoln, who told the following story on himself many times:

> Two Quaker ladies were discussing the relative merits and prospects of Abraham Lincoln and Jefferson

Davis during the War Between the States. "I think Jefferson will succeed because he is a praying man," said one. "But so is Abraham a praying man," said the other. "Yes," rejoined the first lady, "but the Lord will think that Abraham is joking."

Many of us have the nagging suspicion that when we pray, the Lord thinks we are joking.

On the other hand, we all feel pulled to pray. We instinctively thank the Lord for good things; we call on Him in times of trouble. We see the inherent virtue in prayer, and we wish that we were better at it. Most of us don't pray as much as we feel we should, not because we are unwilling but because we are uncertain how to pray and don't understand why our prayers aren't answered more consistently. We can help ourselves by looking at that which we do know and understand about prayer and that which we don't know and understand.

We Are Invited to Pray

There are four things we understand about prayer.

1. God wants us to pray. God wants us to pray not in the same way that the IRS wants us to file our income tax—with hands on hips, one eyebrow raised, and ready to box our ears if we don't. Rather, God wants us to pray in the same way that a loving parent wants to hear his or her child's requests—with an earnest desire to answer if he or she should (1 Thess. 5:17).

2. God will answer prayers. He will not answer all prayers, as we will see later, but He will answer some prayers. His invitation to us to pray is a valid one, though not without its qualifications (Matt 7:7-11).

3. Some things will interfere with our prayers. Prayer hindrances include the following:

- willingly harboring personal sin (Ps. 66:18)
- wrong motives (James 4:3)
- treating one's wife badly (1 Pet. 3:7)
- lack of trust in God (James 1:6-7)
- rejection of God's Word (Prov. 28:9)

4. We are to pray according to Jesus' instructions. In Matthew 6:5-6 Jesus said we are to pray privately, that is, not to be seen and admired by others. It isn't wrong to pray in public at a public service, but it is wrong to fabricate public opportunities to pray just so that people will hear you and think you are spiritual.

Jesus went on to say, "When you pray, do not use vain repetitions as the heathen do. For they think that they will be heard for their many words" (Matt. 6:7). This doesn't mean that it is wrong to pray for the same thing repeatedly. Jesus instructed us in Luke 18 to pray for things on an ongoing basis. But we are to do it with our mind in gear.

In Mongolia the peasants write prayers on pieces of paper and put the paper under little windmills with the belief that each time the blade of the windmill turns, it offers the prayer to God once. In a brisk wind, the same prayer could be offered fifty thousand times in a day. This isn't what God has in mind.

We Are Shown How to Pray

Jesus gave us a pattern to use as a model in our personal prayer (Matt. 6:9-13).

Worship. "Our Father in heaven, hallowed by Your name." The phrase "our Father" reminds us that we are children of God, and we can come before Him as the children of the Queen of England can come before her, their mother. The next phrase, "hallowed be Your name," reminds us that He is God and that we should revere Him and recognize that He is holy.

Yield. "Your kingdom come. Your will be done on earth as it is in heaven." It means we make Him the boss of our life: we set Him on the throne of the kingdom of our personal life. It means we yield to Him in all matters relating to our marriage, vocation, finances, family, relationships, talents, time.

Request. "Give us this day our daily bread." We recognize our dependence on God for physical provision and ask Him to provide for us according to His will.

Confess. "Forgive us our debts, as we forgive our debtors." We confess our sins, accept restoration to His fellowship, and live in a forgiving attitude toward others.

Flee. "Do not lead us into temptation, but deliver us from the evil one." We flee from temptation and flee to God for His strength and protection from temptation and the evil one.

Acknowledge. "For Yours is the kingdom and the power and the glory forever." Acknowledge that God is supreme in what He wants to do and in His ability to do it. Implicit in this acknowledgment is a thankful spirit for His blessings.

The Lord's Prayer was not intended to be an incantation or magical formula. I don't think it is wrong to use the Lord's Prayer in public or private worship. But it is not to be repeated mindlessly. Rather, we are to do each of these—worship, submit, request, confess, flee, acknowledge—in a spontaneous and personal way as we pray to Him.

We Are Guided into Enlightened Prayer

It is encouraging to read what we know about prayer. It challenges us to pray. But with a minimum of effort, prayer can become stupefyingly complex, and there are many things we do not understand about prayer.

Levels of prayer. There seem to be several levels of restriction on receiving answers to prayer. One verse says, simply, that we should ask, and we will receive (Matt. 7:7). Period. No qualifications. With this single verse taken in isolation, we would assume that there would be no request denied us.

However, there are other verses that add qualifications on our asking. For example, in James 1:5-7 we see that we must "ask in faith, with no doubting." In John 14:13 we discover that we must ask in Jesus' name. In John 15:7 the qualification is that we must abide in Him, and His word must abide in us, and *then* we can ask what we will, and it will be given to us.

Think about It

If you do not understand the ways and means of praying . . .

- You are in danger of getting frustrated and not praying at all.

- You are in danger of not praying according to Scripture and therefore not getting answers.

- You are in danger of concluding that prayer is a formula, not a facet of relationship with God, and succumbing to a "vending machine" mentality in your prayer.

In a Nutshell

Levels of Prayer

Level 1:

no qualifications

- Ask a.nd you shall receive (Matt. 7:7)

Level 2:

general qualifications

- Abide in Me/My word abide in you (John 15:7)

Level 3:

specific qualifications

- In faith, without doubting (James 1:5-7)

- Without unconfessed sin (Ps. 66:18)

- Without selfish motives (James 4:3)

Why didn't the writers of the Bible list all the possible qualifications in one place? Perhaps because we do not always need to meet all the qualifications. For example, a brand-new Christian cries out to God for an answer to prayer. He hasn't had time to abide in Christ and have Christ's word abide in him. He hardly knows what it even means to "have faith." In his "new-birth" condition, he does not know all the qualifications. But he cries out to God, out of all that he does know and understand. He simply asks. And God simply answers. "Ask and you will receive" is fulfilled. But later on in his spiritual life, God holds him accountable to know more of the Scripture and now may require some of the qualifications to be met before answering a given prayer.

The "Levels of Prayer" chart is not exhaustive, but it is perhaps representative of how the Christian might analyze his prayers before God. First, he is given the open invitation to simply ask.

If he does not receive an answer, he may check himself on level 2. Is he abiding in Christ and allowing Christ's word to abide in him? Perhaps God is delaying the answer to prayer because He wants to drive the Christian to a deeper level of walk with Him.

If he gains no insight or does not receive an answer on that level, he might look at specific qualifications. Is he asking in faith? Does he have any unconfessed sin that could be hindering the answer? Does the request conflict with anything in the Bible? Is he asking with proper motives?

If he gains no insight or receives no answer on this level, he goes to level 4, in which he simply prays, "Your will be done."

This is, of course, the prayer Jesus prayed in the Garden of Gethsemane when He asked that the Father would take this cup (being crucified) from Him. After making that request, He prayed, "Nevertheless, not as I will, but as You will."

In reality, prayer is not this compartmentalized. We ought to make a simultaneous mental check of all these things we are praying. However, having them written out this way helps us see if we have overlooked something. By going back through each of these qualifications, the Holy Spirit may help us see something which we did not see before.

Delays to prayer. Sometimes God delays His answers to our prayers:

▼▼▼▼▼▼▼

God is not a Cosmic Vending Machine that will dispense according to your will if you just learn how to ask properly.

▲▲▲▲▲▲▲

1. It may be because the timing is not right. He may answer it, but later.

2. Another reason for delay is to clarify the request. When the answer comes, God wants us to be able to recognize it. Often we don't even recognize an answer because we did not crystallize the request sufficiently in our minds.

3. A third reason why God might delay the answer is to create a sense of expectation and to call attention to the fact that it was He who answered, and it was not just good luck or natural consequences.

4. A fourth reason He might delay an answer to prayer is to give us time to repent of sin.

5. A fifth reason is to draw us into a deeper relationship with Him.

When things come easily, they are taken lightly. God does not want prayer to be taken lightly. Therefore, answers do not come easily. When we fear our prayer is not being answered and we can find no personal reason why, it may be that the answer is being delayed for one or more of these reasons.

Many people admit that when they were new Christians, their prayers were answered more directly and obviously. The longer they walk with the Lord, the fewer dramatic answers to prayer they receive. Why? Because the Lord is leading them to a more mature walk in the Word, in wisdom, and in faith.

Conclusion

God is not a Cosmic Vending Machine that will dispense according to your will if you just learn how to ask properly. Rather, God is our heavenly Father. If we envision Him as one who loves us and wants the best for us and as who answers or doesn't answer based on what His superior will is, then we can avoid a sense of failure when our prayers aren't answered.

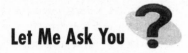

Let Me Ask You

1. Do you think God takes your prayers seriously? Why or why not?

2. Have you ever gained any insight into prayer because the answer was delayed?

3. Have you ever been guilty of a "vending machine" mentality in praying to God? If so, how would you change your approach after reading this chapter?

Action Line

Read: My book *30 Days to Understanding the Christian Life* has much more helpful information about this subject. If you want to learn even more, read *Too Busy Not to Pray* by Bill Hybels.

Memorize: John 15:7.

Pray: Father in Heaven, teach me to pray. Lift me above the level of pure selfishness, and let me commune with You. Don't let what I do not understand destroy what I do. Teach me to pray. Amen.

How Can I Know God's Will?

CHAPTER 34

Chapter at a Glance

- God's will is primarily moral,

- God's will includes making decisions.

- Pursuing God's will ends with trusting Him.

Well Said

In our quest for God's guidance we become our own worst enemies, and our mistakes attest to our nuttiness in this area.

—James I. Packer

Plow Corn!

A young farmer wanted to know God's will for his life. Each day when he went out to plow corn, he would implore God to reveal His will to him. One day the clouds near the horizon seemed to come together in an unmistakable combination of letters: "PC."

The young farmer pondered this. *What could "PC" possibly mean?* Then it hit him: Preach Christ! Finally, he knew God's will for his life. He was to become a preacher.

He rushed to his pastor's home and told the man of God the great news. Furthermore, he asked if he might have the privilege of preaching his first sermon the next Sunday. The pastor agreed, reluctantly.

After the sermon the following Sunday, the young farmer met the pastor in his study and said, "Well, what do you think?"

The pastor replied, "Son, I'm not sure if the Lord was speaking to you in the clouds the other day or not, but if He was, I think He was telling you to Plow Corn."

> **It is God's will for us that we give thanks to Him in the midst of all circumstances.**

We smile and yet deep down we identify with the young farmer. We want to know God's will, but how can we know it? Does God write His will for us in the sky? If not, how does He let us know?

God's Will Is Primarily Moral

When the Bible talks about the "will of God," it is pretty much talking about His moral will. There are only two places in the New Testament where the Bible says, "This is the will of God." The first one is 1 Thessalonians 4:3: "This is the will of God, your sanctification."

Sanctification means having been "set apart for God." Perhaps more directly, it suggests "God's possession, used for God's purposes." We are God's possession, and when we do God's purposes, we are "sanctified." That is the mindset of God's will in the New Testament.

The second passage where the phrase "the will of God" is used is 1 Thessalonians 5:18: "In every thing give thanks; for this is the will of God in Christ Jesus for you." It is God's will for us that we give thanks to Him in the midst of all circumstances. In order to do that, we must see the circumstances as God sees them. We must trust Him and believe that He is able to work in and through all circumstances to bring good out of them. We must place our hopes and dreams in the world to come, not in this world.

God lets us know what His moral will for us is, and if we follow His moral will, there is little danger of our missing His circumstantial will. God has promised repeatedly throughout the Bible to guide His sincere children and to give them wisdom. We do not have to try to "find" His circumstantial will for us, because it is not "lost." It will come to us as we remain in His moral will. It is easy for God to lead someone who has given himself to God, completely.

So when we ask, "How can I know God's will?" we realize that God's primary concern for us is that we walk in His moral will, laboring continuously to be the kind of person He wants us to be. When we live each moment with this mind-set, God can redirect us as He desires.

In a Nutshell

Five Principles

Five principles guide us when making decisions:

1. Know the Scriptures
2. Pray
3. Seek counsel
4. Develop wisdom
5. Exercise freedom

God's Will Includes Making Decisions

"Easy for you to say," you respond. "It sounds easy when you only talk about it in moral terms. However, I must decide which college to go to. I must decide whom to marry. I must decide whether to stay in this job or find a new one. I have to decide whether to spend money sending my child to an expensive college or put the money away for retirement. I must make a million decisions, and I don't know how to make them, moral will or no moral will. I don't know what the right thing to do is. How do I make decisions with any confidence that they are the decisions God wants me to make?"

Fair enough. You must make decisions. But if you are walking with the Lord, you do not have to worry about missing God's will. If you are in His moral will and making decisions the best way you know how, you can trust that God will guide you into whatever decisions He thinks are important for you to make in order to carry out His will for you.

Having accepted that, there are some biblical and common-sense principles that will help us in making decisions in life.

Principle 1: Know the Scriptures. The Bible is God's owner's manual. Just as the automakers put an owner's manual in each vehicle they manufacture, telling the owner how to operate and maintain his vehicle, so God has given us the Bible, telling us how to operate and maintain ourselves.

The Bible does not speak directly to many of the specific things we face in life, such as what color of socks to wear in the morning. But the Bible is full of commands and instructions for many of life's decisions. The more we know of God's Word, the more certain we can be of God's will.

As examples, the Bible makes it clear that we are to not murder, not commit adultery, not lie, cheat, or steal, not lust or covet. We are to forgive others, work hard, be honest, love our neighbor, give to the poor, honor our parents, help others in need, not take a fellow Christian to court, and so on. This is but a sliver of an entire giant redwood of truth found in the Bible that will give us the guidance we need for making many of life's decisions.

▼▼▼▼▼▼▼▼

Don't expect God to reveal His will for you next week until you practice it today.

▲▲▲▲▲▲▲▲▲

Scripture tends to give us principles that fit many situations, rather than to give specific circumstantial guidance. If any decisions violate the principles of Scripture, they are wrong decisions.

Principle 2: Pray. An attitude of submission and dependence is crucial when looking for guidance from the Lord. Lewis Sperry Chafer, founder of Dallas Theological Seminary, said, "His leading is only for those who are already committed to do as He may lead." Alan Redpath, the great Bible teacher of an earlier generation, said, "Don't expect God to reveal His will for you next week until you practice it today."

These are certainly true statements. God is not a genie in a bottle. Our wish is not His command. He is our God, and we are accountable to Him for doing what He shows us. As we submit to Him and pray for Him to guide us, we can rest in the confidence that He will. The Bible teaches us that we can pray to God for wisdom in making decisions: "If any of you lacks wisdom, let him ask of God, who gives to all liberally and without reproach, and it will be given to him" (James 1:5).

Paul prayed for the Colossian believers that they might be "filled with the knowledge of His will in all wisdom and spiritual understanding; that [they] may walk worthy of the Lord, fully pleasing Him, being fruitful in every good work and increasing in the knowledge of God" (Col. 1:9-10).

Principle 3: Seek counsel. Proverbs 11:14 says, "Where there is no counsel, the people fall; but in the multitude of counselors there is safety." James I. Packer once said, "Don't be a spiritual Lone Ranger; when you think you see God's will, have your perception checked. Draw on the wisdom of those who are wiser than you are. Take advice."

God has given us a capacity for wisdom, and He expects us to develop it and use it.

That is good advice. Even when you think you have not yet seen God's will, ask advice. It's the wise thing to do. Many other people will have insight that you might not have had. Use it!

Principle 4: Develop wisdom. God has given us a capacity for wisdom, and He expects us to develop it and use it. Wisdom will keep us from many bad decisions and will help us walk in God's moral as well as circumstantial will.

With wisdom we combine what has been learned through Scripture, prayer, and counsel from others and then, in the providence and leading of God, make the best decision we can.

Principle 5: Exercise freedom. Not every decision has earthshaking consequences. Whether you wear a blue shirt or a white shirt today is not likely to have any consequences. When the decision has no major consequences that you can foresee, you are free to do what you want.

For example, in 1 Corinthians 10:27, Paul wrote, "If any of those who do not believe invites you to dinner, and you desire to go, eat whatever is set before you, asking no questions for conscience' sake." The passage does not say, "If any of those who do not believe invites you to dinner, search the Scriptures, pray for days, seek the counsel of others, and make a pro and con list." It merely says, "If you desire to go . . ." So we should not strain at gnats by trying to relate all decisions to spiritual significance or sovereign importance.

Think about It

If you don't accept the principles of knowing God's will . . .

- You may be very frustrated and defeated, seeking God's will but not (in your mistaken idea) being able to find it.

- You may shoot yourself in the foot repeatedly, making wrong decisions, because you neglect the helpful principles.

- You may miss the relaxed freedom that is yours in Christ when you learn that, being in God's moral will, you cannot miss His circumstantial will.

Some decisions the Lord gives us to make based on our own inclinations. With major decisions, of course, the matter must be taken seriously. But the principle still applies. And with smaller decisions with no foreseeable consequences, we are free to act.

Pursuing God's Will Ends with Trusting Him

Martin Luther once said, "Love God and do as you please." Of course, this is the kind of statement that could easily be misunderstood or distorted. But what he meant was, if you love God, you are going to obey His commandments. The apostle John wrote, "If you love Me, keep My commandments" (John 14:15; see also 15:10). So, if you love God, you will not do anything that you understand to be wrong. But if Scripture, wisdom, and counsel do not give you an answer, you can love God and do as you please, understanding that God has overseen the process and will accept the decision.

Conclusion

In a booklet entitled *Guidance,* Philip Yancey once wrote:

I have a confession to make. For me, at least, guidance only becomes evident when I look backward, months and years later. Then, the circuitous process falls into place and the hand of God seems clear. But at the moment of decision, I feel mainly confusion and uncertainty. Indeed, almost all the guidance in my life has been subtle and indirect.

This pattern has recurred so often (and clear guidance for the future has occurred so seldom) that I am about to conclude that we have a basic direction wrong. I had always thought of guidance as forward-looking. We keep praying, hoping, counting on God to reveal what we should do next. In my own experience, at least, I have found the direction to be reversed. The focus must be on the moment before me, the present. How is my relationship to God? As circumstances change, for better or worse, will I respond with obedience and trust?

Let Me Ask You

1. Are you confident you are in God's moral will? Are you in any danger of falling into wrong circumstances because of moral drifting?

2. What danger do we open ourselves up to when we rely on intuition rather than the more objective principles?

3. What direction are you trying to ascertain from God right now? Who are some wise people you could contact for their counsel?

God does have a circumstantial will for us, but there will be times when we will not know what it is. In those times we do not have to agonize over God's failure to make His way clear to us. We may feel free to use our best judgment, following the principles of Scripture, prayer, counsel, and wisdom.

Instant Recall

1. God's will is primarily m_____.

2. God's will includes making d_____.

3. Following God's will ends with t_____ Him.

Action Line

Read: My book *30 Days to Understanding the Christian Life* has much more helpful information about this subject.

Memorize: Proverbs 3:5-6.

Pray: Dear Lord, thank You that we do not have to fear missing Your will, if we are willing to trust and obey You. Help me always walk in Your moral will and rest in the safety of Your circumstantial will. Amen.

How Do I "Give Away" My Faith?

CHAPTER
35

Chapter at a Glance

- We need to tell stories to accommodate people.

- We should tell our story of how we accepted God's story.

- We must validate our story with personal integrity.

- Evangelism must be a part of our lifestyle.

Well Said

Evangelism is not a professional job for a few trained men, but is instead the unrelenting responsibility of every person who belongs, even in the most modest way, to the company of Jesus.

—Elton Trueblood

Popcorn People

What if people who daydreamed during a church service (that is, left the church mentally) would also leave it physically, floating out a window or door? It would have a dramatic effect on preaching, I think. As a preacher, I know that if people popped in and out of church like popcorn, it would drive me to heretofore unimagined levels of commitment to be interesting and relevant.

Jesus spoke in parables, and one reason is that they are interesting. In Matthew 13:34, the apostle wrote, "All these things Jesus spoke to the multitude in parables; and without a parable He didn't speak to them." A parable is a story. If He told stories, could it be wrong for me?

The power of a story is dramatic, almost wherever it is told, and in this chapter we want to look at the value of a story in sharing the gospel with others.

▼▼▼▼▼▼▼▼▼

What if people who daydreamed during a church service (that is, who left the church mentally) would also leave it physically, floating out a window or door?

▲▲▲▲▲▲▲▲▲

We Need to Tell Stories to Accommodate People

One reason we need to tell stories is because of a shortened national attention span. That is, because of television and other influences, we do not read well, we do not concentrate well, and we have a shortened ability to keep our minds focused on things. Stories help.

A second important reason we can use storytelling with effect is because of how people perceive truth today. Many people do not believe in absolute truth. So when sharing the gospel or defending the faith, people are often not impacted by statements of objective truth. In fact, unchurched people often become suspicious and defensive when we get too dogmatic in our statements.

So, rather than give a list of objective reasons to believe in Jesus, we can tell a story of how we came to believe in Jesus. The story can incorporate the list of objective reasons. In doing so, we have told them the reasons but have done it in a way that is less intimidating to them (because they are not forced to agree or disagree with us regarding the truth of the reasons, neither of which may they want to do), and they cannot deny that those are the reasons that persuaded us. If we merely gave them the list and told them they should be persuaded by it, they could say, "No we shouldn't!" And since people's experience is respected by others, the information comes across in a much more palatable form to them.

We Should Tell Our Story of How We Accepted God's Story

God's story, in its most basic form, is simple:

1. God created humanity to live in perfect fellowship and harmony with God forever in paradise (Gen. 1—2).
2. Humanity rebelled against God in the Garden of Eden (Gen. 3).
3. Sin entered the world at that time, and humanity was separated from God, spiritually dead, lost and without hope (Eph. 2:1-13).
4. God loved us and sent His Son, Jesus, to die for our sins so that if we repent of our sin and believe in Him, God is willing to forgive our sins and credit Jesus' righteousness to us (Rom. 5:1-21; 2 Cor. 5:21).
5. When this happens, we are forgiven, spiritually born again, and destined for heaven when we die (John 3:16).
6. We will live in heaven with God in perfect righteousness and fellowship forever (Rom. 6:23).

There is much more that could be added to the story, but nothing should be taken away. When we talk to others, we should be sure to focus on the fact that God loves us and that Jesus died for our sins, that we can be forgiven and made new. We can have purpose and meaning in this life and hope for eternal life in heaven. If we focus on the story of God's love for us, we may stand a better chance of getting a hearing.

Second, we must tell our own story, which is the story of how God's life and our life intersected. We tell the story of how we came to realize that we were sinners, separated from God and without hope. We tell them how, and under what circumstances, we came to believe that we were sinners, how we believed that Jesus was the Son of God, and how we repented of our sin and gave our life to Jesus. We tell them the changes that have happened in our lives since we made the decision. We tell them the hope we have for eternal life with God when we die. We just tell them our story of salvation.

If you debate unbelievers on the reasons why we should believe the Resurrection, they can reject the reasons. But if you tell them that you believe the Resurrection for these reasons, they cannot say, "Oh, no you don't." There is nothing for them to do but listen, because you are telling it as your story. And it may give them hope that it can become their story, too.

▼▼▼▼▼▼▼

Christians ought to be the best advertisement for Christianity.

▲▲▲▲▲▲▲▲

We Must Validate Our Story with Personal Integrity

Christians ought to be the best advertisement for Christianity. People are supposed to be drawn to Jesus because of what they see of Him in us. Jesus Himself said in John 13:34-35, "A new commandment I give to you, that you love one another; as I have loved you, that you also love one another. By this all will know that you are My disciples, if you have love for one another."

The love Jesus was talking about is not the sloppy sentimentalism and hailstorm of emotions that pass as love today. Rather, this is a self-sacrificing kind of love that directs itself toward the good of another. It is described well by the apostle Paul in 1 Corinthians 13:4-7: "Love is patient, love is kind. It does not envy, it does not boast, it is not proud. It is not rude, it is not self-seeking, it is not easily angered, it keeps no record of wrongs. Love does not delight in evil, but rejoices with the truth. It always protects, always trusts, always hopes, always perseveres" (NIV).

To get a feel for the impact of this kind of love, try inserting your name where the word "love" is: "Max is patient, Max is kind. He does not envy, he does not boast, he is not proud. He is not rude, he is not self-seeking, he is not easily angered, he keeps no record of wrongs. Max does not delight in evil, but rejoices with the truth. He always protects, always trusts, always hopes, always perseveres." Try it yourself with your name in it. If doing that does not make you cringe a little, you are either a saint or callused.

That is the kind of love Jesus is calling us to. Jesus said that when Christians manifest that kind of love to one another, the world will conclude that we are authentic disciples of Christ. If we do not manifest that kind of love to another, the world will have a logical reason to conclude that we are hypocrites, a conclusion the world largely supports.

They may be wrong, of course. We may be true disciples of Christ. But our common character has given the world a legitimate reason to conclude the opposite.

In another passage Jesus again mentioned the profound power of love. In John 17:20-21, He said in a prayer to God the Father, "[I pray] that they all [My followers] may be one, as You, Father, are in Me, and I in You; that they also may be one in Us, that the world may believe that You sent me."

Snapshot

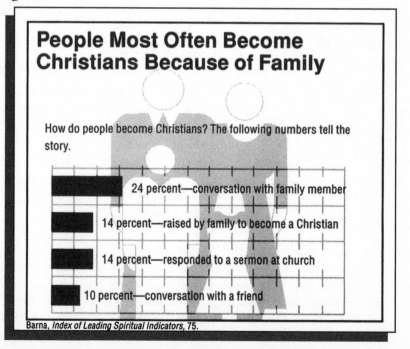

People Most Often Become Christians Because of Family

How do people become Christians? The following numbers tell the story.

- 24 percent—conversation with family member
- 14 percent—raised by family to become a Christian
- 14 percent—responded to a sermon at church
- 10 percent—conversation with a friend

Barna, *Index of Leading Spiritual Indicators*, 75.

Think about It

If you don't believe in the importance of stories . . .

- You may miss many opportunities to make an impact on others for the cause of Christ.

- You may fail in your responsibility to be able to defend your faith (1 Pet. 3:15).

From this passage we learn another startling truth. The unity that Jesus prayed for can only be produced by mutual love, such as we saw in the 1 Corinthians 13 passage. If we love one another with that kind of love, it produces unity, and the unity persuades the watching world that Jesus has been sent by God. If the world does not see that kind of unity produced by love, then they have a legitimate reason to conclude that Jesus was not sent by God. They would be wrong, but they would have a legitimate reason for that conclusion. Francis Schaeffer developed this point very clearly in his marvelous little book *The Mark of the Christian*.

When we fail to love one another, the world has a valid reason to conclude that we are not true disciples (we are hypocrites) and that Jesus was not sent from God (He was just a man). By and large, these are two of the most formidable conclusions the world has come to.

When we tell our story without backing it up with authentic Christlike character, the story is diluted, washed out, and anemic. It has a fraction of the impact it should. But when we tell our story with a backdrop of authentic Christlike character, the story is augmented, strengthened, and powerful.

Evangelism Must Be a Part of Our Lifestyle

Many people are turned off by "program" evangelism. But evangelism that flows naturally out of our lifestyle is very effective. There are four principles in evangelizing others with our lifestyle.

1. Sowing and reaping. We must not become preoccupied with reaping, that is, actually leading others to Christ. If we sow faithfully—meaning if we share our faith in Christ with others—then we may reap where others have sown and we may sow where others will reap. We must be occupied with being faithful in telling others about Jesus, and let Him determine our results. Otherwise, we may become discouraged and quit altogether.

2. Preparation. We must know and understand the gospel ourselves, and learn how to share it with others. We begin by mastering God's story (page 285). Then we work out in our own minds how and why we came to Christ. Next, we simply tell others when we have the chance. If we are asked questions we don't know the answer to, we can find out and answer them later.

3. Life impact. As we do our best to live out our spiritual convictions, people will see the difference in our lives, and it will create opportunities to share our faith. There are people out there who want to become a Christian, but they don't know how. No one is reaching out to them. Their lives may be falling apart, and they are longing for someone to help them find truth. You will not be forcing yourself on anyone. Rather, you will be offering water to a thirsty soul.

4. Reliance. We trust God for the results. We must relax in God's sovereignty. He doesn't demand results. He only asks faithfulness to a lifestyle of evangelism.

Conclusion

The newer generation of people whom we are commissioned by God to reach for Christ must often be reached in ways different than past generations. Many don't believe in absolute truth, so presenting verifiable, logical information, which has worked well in the past, does not always work with them. The new generation appreciates it when we keep our language plain and simple, and if we want to make a point, we must not overload them with dry content.

We don't have to change the ultimate goal of Christlikeness. Mature disciples of Jesus know the Bible well. We don't have to lower the top of the ladder. But we may need to add some rungs to the bottom to help others get the foothold they need. We can wish it weren't necessary. We can lament the loss of absolute truth and mental concentration. Or we can accept that that's the way it is, and we can find a way to reach them. Telling truth with stories, as Jesus did, can be a helpful way to reach people for Christ.

Instant Recall

1. We need to tell s_____ to accommodate people.

2. We should tell our story of how we a_____ God's story.

3. We must validate our story with personal i_____.

4. Evangelism must be a part of our l_____.

Let Me Ask You

1. Are you part of the newer generation, or part of the older? How can you use your place in history to best further the kingdom of God?

2. Have you studied God's story enough so that you could tell it briefly from memory? Would you be willing to if you have not? Study the summary in this chapter to help you.

3. Have you ever thought through your own story to the point that you could share it with someone? If not, would you be willing to?

Action Line

Read: My book *What You Need to Know about Defending Your Faith* has much more helpful information about this subject.

Memorize: 1 Peter 3:15.

Pray: Dear Lord, help me to take Your story deep into my heart, and help me to share it authentically with others. Give me the great privilege of leading others to Christ. Amen.

What Are the Spiritual Disciplines?

CHAPTER 36

Chapter at a Glance

- Discipline is necessary for freedom.
- Meditation renews and illumines our mind.
- Prayer links us with God.
- Fasting heightens our spiritual sensitivity.
- Simplicity frees us from worldly bondages.
- Solitude frees us from the distraction of the world.

Well Said

*No horse gets anywhere
until he is harnessed.
No steam or gas ever drives anything until
it is confined. No Niagara is ever turned
into light and power until it is tunneled.
No life ever grows great until it is focused,
dedicated, disciplined.*

—Henry Emerson Fosdick

"Read Not *The Times*"

Henry David Thoreau, the Boston Transcendentalist of the 1800s, got many things wrong. But he understood better than most of us that our inner lives wither from inattention and that our outer life is not what it should be without sufficient attention to the inner life. We fill our minds with news, weather, and sports rather than nurture an inner life of joy and satisfaction." We live lives, Thoreau said, of "quiet desperation." "Read not *The Times,*" he concluded, "read the Eternities."

We face the same problem today. Without an inner life, we use television, music, computers, and cell phones to fill the dead space. But it's just as wrong today. It leaves us shallow and unsatisfied. We must discipline our inner life and simplify our outer life if we are to escape the quiet desperation.

Discipline Is Necessary for Freedom

Winston Churchill once said, "I spent the first twenty-five years of my life wanting more freedom, and next twenty-five years of

Snapshot

Americans Need to Get a Grip!

- 34 percent read the Bible during the week
- 78 percent pray during a typical week
- 24 percent meditate during a typical month
- 8 percent fast during a typical month

Barna, *Index of Leading Spiritual Indicators*, 61–63.

my life wanting more structure, and the last twenty-five years of my life realizing that structure is freedom."

In the military there are disciplines and training that must be completed or one does not make a good soldier, and a bad soldier is one who is likely to get killed in action and get other people killed. The same is true with athletics. It is nothing for an Olympic athlete to practice eight to twelve hours a day for four to six years or more just to be able to do one fairly simple thing a little better than anyone else in the world. The same is true with constructing a building. Skyscrapers must be constructed with scrupulous attention to detail and the laws of physics or the whole thing will come down in a heap.

Just as the military, athletics, and building must be characterized by great discipline, so the Christian life must be lived with great discipline if it is to be satisfying. To be free to sail the seven seas, the proverb goes, one must be a slave to the compass. You may elect to be free from the compass, but then you are no longer free to sail the seven seas. To turn from righteousness is to choose a life of heavy burdens, darkened understanding, and shallow relationships.

Meditation Renews and Illumines Our Mind

To break free of quiet desperation, we must know the Bible so well that we think of its truths as we go throughout our days, and apply them in life's situations. We must constantly be reviewing the Bible in our minds, practicing a key spiritual discipline: meditation. Meditation is thinking deeply on the words and truths in Scripture for the purposes of understanding, application, and prayer.

Joshua 1:8 includes a powerful promise of prosperity and success when we have become so familiar with the Scripture through meditation that we are careful to *do* all that Scripture says.

Prayer Links Us with God

Prayer is conversation with God. It builds our relationship with Him, and links us to Him as no other activity. There are several reasons why we should pray:

1. Because the Bible instructs us to (Matt. 6:5-15; Luke 11:25-26; Col. 4:2; 1 Thess. 5:17)
2. Because God wants us to (Luke 18:1-8)
3. To deepen our walk with God (Ps. 63:1-5)
4. Because God answers prayer (Matt. 7:7-11)

Prayer is often frustrating and confusing. We often don't get what we pray for, and we often don't even know how to pray. But in all the mystery about prayer, we know that Jesus prayed, and men and women of God through all ages have always prayed. If we would be godly, we must pray.

Any possession or activity that furthers His kingdom in and through our lives is legitimate, no matter how elaborate. Any that does not is illegitimate, no matter how simple.

Fasting Heightens Our Spiritual Sensitivity

Fasting demonstrates an earnestness and commitment that God honors. It is hard to go without food, so we would do it only for a significant reason, and by fasting, we can demonstrate to God the intensity of our spiritual longing.

In addition, as Thomas à Kempis once wrote, "Restrain from gluttony and thou shalt the more easily restrain all the inclinations of the flesh." When we bring on ourselves the suffering of the fast, we conquer ourselves and increase our ability to allow Christ to conquer us too.

Simplicity Frees Us from Worldly Bondages

Simplicity is a virtue. It is a blessing. It is a centering force in our lives that orients us toward a right perspective on things and activities in life. It puts Jesus at the center of life, and puts everything else in proper perspective and proportion around Him.

Unless we have adopted the discipline of simplicity, we either fall prey to materialism (in which we must have "things" to be happy) or we fall prey to legalism (in which we consider "things" bad). Both are wrong.

We must simplify not only our possessions but also our activities. Most possessions and activities are not wrong in and of themselves. But we must ask ourselves if they are important to God. Do we move purposefully through life, focusing on biblical priorities, rejecting incidentals? Or are we caught up in the tyranny of the urgent, running helplessly from one activity to the next in the pursuit of things that are not biblical priorities? Any possession or activity that furthers His purposes in and through our lives is legitimate, no matter how elaborate. Any that does not is illegitimate, no matter how simple.

▼▼▼▼▼▼▼▼

Most possessions and activities are not wrong in and of themselves. But we must ask ourselves if they are important to God.

▲▲▲▲▲▲▲▲

Solitude Frees Us from the Distraction of the World

If we are going to live lives of purpose, meaning, and satisfaction, we must learn to be quiet. We must learn to be alone. We must learn to draw inner strength, personal strength, divine strength from being alone and being quiet. Thinking. Listening to see if God is going to plant a seed in our heart or mind that we would miss if we didn't stop to be quiet. Theologian and philosopher Kierkegaard once said, "If I were a doctor and were asked for my advice, I should reply, 'Create silence.'"

Get alone. Get quiet. Listen. Thoughts, ideas, values, desires will come to you that, like timid rabbits, do not come out when surrounded by hustle and bustle but will hop out into the open and sit there to be seen and heard when all gets quiet.

Submission Generates Trust in the Sovereignty of God

Martin Luther once said, "A Christian is a perfectly free lord of all, subject to none. A Christian is a perfectly dutiful servant of all, subject to everyone." And so it is. The Christian is free but uses his freedom to serve others.

Almost all family quarrels, almost all work-related conflict, almost all church fights and splits occur because people do not have the freedom to give up their rights (perceived or real) to others. They are in bondage to selfish interests. Only when we have learned the discipline of submission can we come to the place where a selfish spirit no longer controls us. Only a spirit of submission can free us to distinguish between genuine issues and stubborn self-will.

Repentance and Confession Restore Moral Integrity

Confession is the admission that something one has done, said, or thought is wrong. It is very difficult for some people to admit that they are wrong and face the consequences. It is hard to admit to themselves they are wrong. It is harder to admit to God they are wrong. It is virtually impossible to admit to others they are wrong.

The first step is private confession. We must admit to ourselves that we have sinned, and we must confess that sin to God (1 John 1:8-9). But often our confession must go further than only admitting to ourselves and to God that we have sinned. There are times when we must confess our sins to others. A good rule of thumb is to confess the sin to whoever was involved. That is, if you sin against one person privately, there is only need to confess it to that one person. But if the sin is against many people and very public, then the confession may need to be a public one.

Worship Deepens Our Relationship with God

On the personal level, it is difficult to schedule the time for personal worship or to make it meaningful.

On a corporate level, worship can be equally difficult. The church service you attend may not readily encourage your worship. Nevertheless, we are admonished in Scripture to worship God.

The most important avenue to meaningful worship is the focus of the inner life on God. We are to live a life centered inward on the indwelling God, so that He is the source of our words, thoughts, and actions. If we are accustomed to carrying out the business of our lives in human strength and wisdom, we will usually do the same in worship.

Generosity Detaches Us from This World

If God has our hearts, He will also have our money. If He doesn't have our money, it is because He does not yet have our hearts completely. Jesus said our hearts will be where our treasures are (Luke 12:34).

There are at least six major reasons why we ought to exercise the spiritual discipline of generosity.

1. Scripture commands it (2 Cor. 9:7).
2. We are citizens not of this world but of the next (Matt. 6:19-21).
3. Giving is an act of worship (Phil. 4:18).
4. It reflects our trust in God (Mark 12:41-44).
5. We demonstrate to God that we can be trusted (Luke 16:10-13).
6. We become eligible for God's blessing (2 Cor. 9:6-8).

Conclusion

The whole point of the disciplines is freedom. They are not intended to limit us or restrict us or hamper us. They are intended to give us the strength and insight to do the things we want to do.

Think about It

- If you don't agree with the need for meditation, you condemn yourself to a mediocre walk with God.

- If you don't agree with the need for simplicity, solitude, and silence, you may get eaten alive by a frazzled lifestyle.

- If you don't believe you need to keep "confessed up" with God and others, your relationships will deteriorate dramatically.

- If you don't get emancipated from bondage to money, you will never know the great joy of giving to others and to the Lord.

Just as the athlete's physical regimen is not intended to limit him but to give him freedom to excel in his chosen field, so the Christian's spiritual regimen is intended to give him freedom to excel in his walk with God.

Instant Recall

1. D_____ is necessary for freedom.

2. M_____ renews and illumines our mind.

3. P_____ links us with God.

4. F_____ heightens our spiritual sensitivity.

5. S_____ frees us from worldly bondages.

6. S_____ frees us from distractions of the world.

7. S_____ generates trust in the sovereignty of God.

8. R_____ and confession restore moral integrity.

9. W_____ deepens our relationship with God.

10. G_____ detaches us from this world.

Let Me Ask You

1. What is your greatest struggle in praying? What do you think you could do to help yourself?

2. How would you describe the discipline of simplicity in your own words?

3. What do you think the greatest stumbling block is for people regarding the discipline of submission?

4. Is it hard for you to give a percentage of your income to the Lord? If so, why? If not, how did you come to the point of freedom in this area?

Action Line

Read: My book *What You Need to Know about Spiritual Growth* has much more helpful information about this subject. If you want to learn even more, read *The Spirit of the Disciplines* by Dallas Willard, *Celebration* *of Discipline* by Richard Foster, or *Spiritual Disciplines for the Christian Life* by Donald Whitney.

Memorize: 1 Corinthians 9:24-27.

Pray: Dear Lord, thank You that freedom comes through structure and that freedom in Christ rests on obedience to Him. Help me to be strong in Your strength to walk in Your good ways. Amen.

Notes

Chapter 1—Who Is God?

1. Deidre Sullivan, *What Do We Mean When We Say God?* (New York: Doubleday, 1990), 8.
2. Ibid., 117.
3. James I. Packer, *Concise Theology* (Wheaton, Ill.: Tyndale, 1993), 26.

Chapter 3—What Has God Done?

1. R. C. Sproul, *Essential Truths of the Christian Faith* (Wheaton, Ill.: Tyndale, 1992), 62.

Chapter 5—What Did Jesus Teach?

1. Adapted from Jack Canfield and Mark Victor Hansen, *Chicken Soup for the Soul* (Deerfield Beach, Fla.: Health, 1993), 284-85.
2. Green, *Who Is This Jesus?* 36.

Chapter 7—Who Is the Holy Spirit?

1. Packer, *Concise Theology,* 41.

Chapter 10—What Is the Story of the Bible?

1. James I. Packer, *God Has Spoken* (Downers Grove, Ill.: InterVarsity, 1979), 50.

Chapter 12—How Can We Understand the Bible?

1. H. L. Bussell, *Unholy Devotions* (Grand Rapids, Mich.: Zondervan, 1983), 119.

Chapter 15—What Happens When I Am Saved?

1. Packer, *Concise Theology.*

Chapter 16—What Is the Spiritual War?

1. Billy Graham, *Angels: God's Secret Agents* (Garden City, N.Y.: Doubleday, 1975), 3.

Chapter 26—Why Believe Jesus Is God?

1. Josh McDowell, *Evidence That Demands a Verdict* (Nashville: Thomas Nelson, 1993), 167.

Chapter 27—Why Believe the Bible?

1. McDowell, *Evidence That Demands a Verdict,* 65.

Chapter 28—How Can I Believe in Spite of the Pain?

1. D. James Kennedy, *What If Jesus Had Never Been Born?* (Nashville: Thomas Nelson, 1994), 234-37.

Chapter 29—How Do I Make the 'Great Wager'?

1. Huxley, *Ends and Means, 273.*

2. Alister McGrath, *Intellectuals Don't Need God & Other Myths* (Grand Rapids, Mich.: Zondervan, 1993), 64-66.

Chapter 31—What Is the Role of Faith in My Life?

1. Blaise Pascal, quoted by John Piper, *Desiring God* (Sisters, Ore.: Multnomah, 1996), 15.